The Spirit of Biblical Law

The Spirit of the Laws

Alan Watson, General Editor

The *Spirit of the Laws* series illuminates the nature of legal systems throughout the world. Titles in the series are concerned less with the rules of the law and more with the relationships of the laws in each system with religion and moral perspectives; the degree of complexity and abstraction; classifications; attitudes to possible sources of law; authority; and values enshrined in law. Topics covered in the series include Roman law, Chinese law, biblical law, Talmudic law, canon law, common law, Hindu law, customary law, Japanese law, and international law.

THE SPIRIT OF
BIBLICAL LAW

Calum Carmichael

The University of Georgia Press
Athens & London

BS1199
.L3
C37
1996

© 1996 by the University of Georgia Press
Athens, Georgia 30602
All rights reserved
Designed by Walton Harris
Set in 9.5/14 Trump by Books International, Inc.
Printed and bound by Braun-Brumfield, Inc.
The paper in this book meets the guidelines for
permanence and durability of the Committee on
Production Guidelines for Book Longevity of the
Council on Library Resources.

Printed in the United States of America
00 99 98 97 96 C 5 4 3 2 1

Library of Congress Cataloging in Publication Data

Carmichael, Calum M.
    The spirit of biblical law / Calum Carmichael.
       p.   cm. — (Spirit of the laws)
    Includes bibliographical references and index.
    ISBN 0-8203-1845-0 (alk. paper)
       1. Law (Theology)—Biblical teaching.   2. Jewish law.   3. Bible.
O.T.—Criticism, interpretation, etc.   I. Title.   II. Series:
Spirit of the laws (Athens, Georgia)
BS1199.L3C37   1996
241'.2—dc20   96-21568

British Library Cataloging in Publication Data available

To Gregory, Gwen, Iain, Juliana, Nicolas, and Tara

CONTENTS

PREFACE

No body of rules relating to law and morality is so well known as that found in the Bible. Perhaps the best known are the Ten Commandments—a misnomer, in fact—long thought to constitute the foundation of so much other law. Why rules from quite different spheres of life come together as they do in the Decalogue, why these rules and not others were selected, and why they are uttered—in Hebrew they are called the Ten Words—in circumstances reminiscent of the creation of the world are tantalizing questions. Then there is the ethical rule to love one's neighbor as oneself, clarification of which cannot be divorced from the significance of the preceding part of the rule, namely, neither to seek vengeance nor to bear grudges against "the sons of thy people."

Such ethical and legal material in the Bible has received unreserved positive assessment from later readers. Rather different is the perception of what the famous formula—found only in the Bible—"life for life, eye for eye, and tooth for tooth" signifies. In the popular imagination the formula has been taken literally. The scholarly world, on the other hand, always showing a tendency toward adopting more liberal positions, does not necessarily concur. Far from expressing a primitive, barbaric system of literal retaliation, the formula means something quite different to scholars. In fact, for them it betokens a progressive development. The formula signifies an advance in moving from a system of self-help, in which there is potentially uncontrolled vengeance, to one in which the public authorities intervene and commendably place limits on the punishments that can be exacted. Neither interpretation of the formula is on the mark, although the popular reading that sees a literal tearing apart of a body comes much closer to what "life for life, eye for eye, and tooth for tooth" means than does the scholarly progressive view.

Despite the great interest in the famous aspects of the subject, a scholarly explanation of biblical law might nonetheless seem to be a rather narrow and specialized inquiry. The aim of this volume is to show that, on the contrary, the study of biblical law opens up a broad range of vistas. Most compelling is the realization that a thorough knowledge of some of the most renowned stories of the Bible is necessary to understand biblical laws. Just as proverbs the world over have an interesting and colorful character that is often the product of an idiosyncratic occurrence, so biblical laws have a fascinating relationship to the strange twists and turns found in many a biblical story. If anything captures the spirit of biblical law, it is the spirit of biblical stories themselves.

In the opening two chapters I introduce views about the nature of biblical law and explain how my approach differs from the mainstream. I then proceed (in the next three chapters) to examine material that has been at the center of my research for the past two years, namely, the legal material in the Book of Leviticus. The thesis that I have developed for many years about the integral relationship between the laws in the Books of Exodus and Deuteronomy and the narratives of the Bible (*Law and Narrative in the Bible* [1985], *The Origins of Biblical Law* [1992]) works for this Priestly material too. I then turn (in the following three chapters) to material—the Decalogue; the formula "life for life, eye for eye, and tooth for tooth"; and the theme of life and death—that I have reworked in new directions from previous publications. Finally, in the last two chapters I explore some well-known biblical narratives— for example, King David's adultery and Saul's suicide—and note again the interplay between law and narrative, but this time from a different angle.

In writing a book on the spirit of biblical law I cannot fail to record how enlivening over the past thirty years has been my association with that great master of the law and literature of so many cultures, David Daube. Through correspondence and very regular meetings in Berkeley and Oxford, we have had the closest contact, sharing each other's work and endlessly finding one delight after another in the study of biblical law. My wish is that some of that pleasure may be communicated in the following pages.

I am indebted to the Robbins Collection and its director, Professor Laurent Mayali, The School of Law, University of California, Berkeley, for the award of a research fellowship during 1994–95. I also owe much to Alan Watson, John Sawyer, and Takamitsu Muraoka for their encouragement and critical comments, and to my wife, Debbie, for her invaluable assistance with the writing of the manuscript.

In quoting biblical texts I have relied upon the King James Authorized Version of 1611, but I made changes where these were called for. I used the AV because it is almost always a more literal rendering of the Hebrew original than any other translation. It also has the merit of reminding the reader of something I consider to be very important, namely, that biblical literature is a product of the past and hence of a quite different culture from our own.

ABBREVIATIONS

AB   Anchor Bible

ABD   *Anchor Bible Dictionary*, ed. D. N. Freedman (New
            York, 1992)

AJCL   *American Journal of Comparative Law*

AnBib   Analecta Biblica

ANET   *Ancient Near Eastern Texts Relating to the Old
            Testament*, 3d ed., ed. J. B. Pritchard
            (Princeton, 1969)

AOAT   *Alter Orient und Altes Testament*

ASTI   *Annual of the Swedish Theological Institute*

AV   Authorized Version

BAR   *Biblical Archaeology Review*

BBB   Bonner Biblische Beiträge

BCOT   Biblical Commentary on the Old Testament

BDB   F. Brown, S. R. Driver, and C. A. Briggs, *A Hebrew and
            English Lexicon of the Old Testament* (Oxford, 1906)

Bib   *Biblica*

BSC   Bible Student's Commentary

BWANT   Beiträge zur Wissenschaft vom Alten und
            Neuen Testament

CB   Century Bible

CBC   Cambridge Bible Commentary

CBQ   *Catholic Biblical Quarterly*

CBSC   Cambridge Bible for Schools and Colleges

CH	Code of Hammurabi
CLR	*California Law Review*
D	The Deuteronomic literary strand in the Pentateuch
EPC	Expositor's Bible Commentary
ET	English Translation
FRLANT	Forschungen zur Religion und Literatur des Alten und Neuen Testaments
H	The Holiness Code
HAR	*Hebrew Annual Review*
HAT	Handbuch zum Alten Testament
HTR	*Harvard Theological Review*
IB	Interpreter's Bible
ICC	International Critical Commentary
IDB	*Interpreter's Dictionary of the Bible,* ed. G. A. Buttrick (New York, 1962)
JAAR	*Journal of the American Academy of Religion*
JAF	*Journal of American Folklore*
JBL	*Journal of Biblical Literature*
JBQ	*Jewish Bible Quarterly*
JE	The Y(J)ahwistic and Elohistic literary strand in the Pentateuch
JITE	*Journal of Institutional and Theoretical Economics*
JJS	*Journal of Jewish Studies*
JLR	*Journal of Law and Religion*
JLS	*Journal of Legal Studies*

JNES	*Journal of Near Eastern Studies*
JPS	Jewish Publication Society
JPSC	Jewish Publication Society Torah Commentary
JQR	*Jewish Quarterly Review*
JR	*Juridical Review*
JRS	*Journal of Roman Studies*
JSNT	*Journal for the Study of the New Testament*
JSOT	*Journal for the Study of the Old Testament*
JSS	*Journal of Semitic Studies*
LCL	Loeb Classical Library
LE	Laws of Eshnunna
LXX	The Septuagint
MAL	Middle Assyrian Laws
Mekhilta	A second-century c.e. Rabbinic commentary on the Book of Exodus
MT	The Masoretic Text
NCBC	New Century Bible Commentary
NEB	New English Bible
NICOT	New International Commentary on the Old Testament
NTS	*New Testament Studies*
OTL	Old Testament Library
P	The Priestly literary strand in the Pentateuch
RB	*Revue Biblique*
RJ	*Rechtshistorisches Journal*

RSV   Revised Standard Version

SBS   Stuttgarter Bibelstudien

SBT   Studies in Biblical Theology

SLR   *Stanford Law Review*

SVT   *Supplement to Vetus Testamentum*

TDOT   *Theological Dictionary of the Old Testament*, ed. G. J. Botterweck and H. Ringgren (Grand Rapids, 1980)

TOTC   Tyndale Old Testament Commentaries

VT   *Vetus Testamentum*

WBC   Word Bible Commentary

WC   Westminster Commentary

WMANT   Wissenschaftliche Monographien zum Alten und Neuen Testament

ZAW   *Zeitschrift für die alttestamentliche Wissenschaft*

ZSS   *Zeitschrift der Savigny-Stiftung für Rechtsgeschichte*

The Spirit of Biblical Law

Introduction

The long-prevailing view of biblical law among scholars is that a body of law and ethical rules grew in piecemeal fashion over many centuries. To explain the many repetitions and sequences of rules that are haphazardly presented in the Bible, modern scholars postulate that laws were compiled and edited (the term generally used is *redacted*) at three distinct periods of time. Most of the laws are thought to have existed before the attempt to collect them; some are thought to have been newly drafted.

First in time and placement in the biblical record is the Book of the Covenant (Exod 21:2–23:19). It is dated very roughly around 1000 B.C.E. because, in showing no indication of kingship in ancient Israel, it must, it is thought, predate that institution. Second, there is the code of laws in Deuteronomy 12–26 that is associated with the reform of King Josiah in the year 621 B.C.E. and is written about in 2 Kings 22, 23. Third, there is the material largely but not exclusively concerned with the cult and Priestly interests that extends throughout such books of the Pentateuch as Exodus, Leviticus, and Numbers. This material is commonly dated to the exilic period (post 587 B.C.E.).

Scholars take for granted that a literary and sociohistorical approach to this material can separate out strands that relate to different times and places in the history of Israelite society. Thus, where one finds similar rules—about slaves, for example—in different codes, their differences must reflect changes in social conditions over time. This method of reading the texts seems the obvious way to proceed, but it is, I contend, spectacularly wrong, the result of a miscreation that has become a tradition in scholarly circles. It seems the correct way to proceed because the biblical compilers themselves present their material so as to convey a picture of the historical life of ancient Israel. In what is a very effective device for making the reader think that the law is as real as the history and the history as real as the law, the compilers even go so far as to embed the codes of law in their historical narratives. But this presentation is a façade.[1] Behind it is a process of enormous sophistication on the part of the biblical authors.

It is not just that modern inquirers have failed to see through the sophisticated artifice of the biblical authors and have consequently been duped into pursuing their literary and sociohistorical method with total confidence in its efficacy. The method itself is plagued with problems. There is the major problem that what counts as history to modern inquirers is of a quite different order from what counted for it to ancient writers. It is problematic, to say the least, for modern interpreters to bring their method of historiography to bear on a presentation of history informed by a quite different conception of what constitutes historical knowledge. Interpreters fail to recognize the problem because they pay no attention to the fact that modern historiography is a product of sixteenth-century legal humanists working primarily on Roman law. Suffice it to say, without going into the reasons why these humanists began to proceed as they did,[2] that they were the ones who began to study the past for its own sake. Modern methods of historiography depend on their pioneering efforts. Since these humanists were themselves interested in applying the law to their own societal conditions in the sixteenth century—they found the prevailing Roman law alien to their needs—they assumed that Roman law must reflect the realities of ancient Roman society. It is this fundamental assumption that laws must necessarily relate to a society's practical problems that I take issue with in regard to the understanding of biblical law.[3] The recent awareness that the Near Eastern codes constitute a "schools" tradition, and did not necessarily apply to the problems of the communities that produced them, should have cast doubt on the long-standing approach to biblical law.

Although from my early schooldays I was instructed in the source division (JE, D, and P) of the Pentateuch—and still think there is something in such a division—I have come to read the Pentateuch, not for any religious reason, on its own terms. That is, I take with the utmost seriousness the attribution of the laws to the lawgiver Moses.

That this attribution is an invention on the part of ancient writers is, for me, the key to comprehending the substance, sequence, and overall presentation of the legal material in the Pentateuch. The result is that I too am interested in a literary and historical exercise, but it is less the one devised by modern inquirers than it is, I believe, the one used by the biblical writers themselves. My method of studying biblical law is both similar to the standard one and also radically different from it.

I view those who present the laws in the various compilations in Exodus, Leviticus, and Deuteronomy as engaged in historical reconstruction, not for its own sake along the lines of the sixteenth-century legal humanists and their successors, but in order to suit their own quite different needs. As is typical for ancient recorders of events, they likewise conflate past, present, and future.[4] They take the figure of a legendary lawgiver, Moses, and have him—that is, themselves, in effect, many centuries after he is recorded as having lived—pass judgment on matters that occurred in the lives of his ancestors (Abraham, Isaac, Jacob, etc.), in his own time, and also in centuries yet to come (for example, in the time when the temple in Jerusalem stood and kings reigned). Their sources for carrying out this exercise are the ones in the biblical records, namely, the traditions in Genesis through 2 Kings. All the issues and problems that Moses takes up in his laws come from these narrative sources—that is, from the history or, better, the legends, sagas, and etiological myths found in them.[5]

Here is an example of how I differ from the standard approach in interpreting biblical rules. Menachem Haran and Jacob Milgrom think that the rule in Leviticus 20:6 against mediums and wizards (those who deal with the dead) should be read as a negative response to activities that occurred in the reign of King Manasseh in the eighth century B.C.E. A rule was set down, they believe, in response to a societal problem. The title of Haran's article reveals his approach: "Behind the Scenes of History: Determining the Date of the Priestly Source." No such easy correlation between institutions in the law codes and what may have happened in the history of ancient Israel is, I claim, possible.[6] This rule, I argue, takes up these particular practices because the lawgiver sees their beginnings in Judah's relationship to the Canaanite cult prostitute Tamar; specifically, in the means she employs to act on behalf of her dead husband (Genesis 38). A widow without a child to continue her husband's name and inheritance, Tamar dresses as a sacred prostitute and seduces Judah without revealing her identity. Her secret aim is to act on behalf of her dead husband to obtain seed for him. The resultant rule speaks of an Israelite's prostituting himself in his involvement with those who have dealings with the dead.[7]

Typical of biblical rules is that the lawgiver looks at the first occurrence of a problem in Israelite history and then, surveying similar developments in succeeding generations, targets a full-blown, concrete example of the problem at a later time. This is why the rule about mediums and wizards singles out the development in the reign of Manasseh. He went in for the actual practices cited in the Levitical rule (2 Kings 21:6). Running parallel to what the lawgiver does is the way the narratives in the Book of Genesis recount problems among the patriarchs that foreshadow problems that will arise in later Israelite history. Genesis 38, for example, about Judah's involvement with Canaanites, is read as foreshadowing the much later territorial expansion of the tribe of Judah and the consequent intermarriage with Canaanites.

History in retrospect, not history in the making, informs both the rules and the narratives. I cannot tell whether there ever was in fact a comparable rule in effect during the reign of Manasseh. There may have been, but I know of no way to ascertain such information. For me, the dating of the rule in Leviticus 20:6 is also unobtainable, but I tend to think that all biblical law was produced around the time of the exile in 587 B.C.E.; that it comes from an attempt, so common in the history of so many cultures, to salvage in the form of invented traditions what was being lost because of the collapse, actual or imminent, of the culture in question.[8] All the biblical rules have been filtered through the historical imagination of the Deuteronomic and Priestly lawgivers,[9] who linked the laws to the history known to them. I know of no way by which modern inquirers might undo this link and pursue the kind of historical reconstruction they favor.

Here is a second illustration of how I think the laws should be read in contrast to how other scholars read them. Consider the two slave laws in Exodus 21:2–11 and Deuteronomy 15:12–18. The first incident involving a slavelike situation experienced by an ancestor of the Is-raelites concerns Jacob (Israel) himself. Jacob goes as a Hebrew to the land of Aram to his mother's brother, Laban, who ends up treating him both as a hired servant and as a slave (Genesis 29). Laban cheats Jacob into taking his two daughters as wives—Rachel, whom Jacob wants, and Leah, whom he does not want—in return for fourteen years of ser-vice. Jacob then serves Laban for another six years before, it is said, God has him seek release from his oppressed situation (Gen 31:3, 41). The lawgivers, I claim, here imagine themselves in the position of Moses, who knows how his ancestor was ill-treated. In the rules of Exodus 21:2–11 about the manumission of slaves and the sale of daugh-ters as concubines, Moses looks at Jacob's situation. He pronounces his judgment on how a Hebrew slave should be treated (not as Laban treated Jacob) and on how daughters sold as concubines should be treated (neither like Laban treats them when he negotiates the sale of his daughters to Jacob, nor like Jacob's subsequent ill-treatment of Leah).[10] The Genesis tradition accounts for the formulation of the first law about slaves in Exodus 21:2–11.

At a later time, as recounted in the Book of Exodus, all Israelites—males and females—become Hebrew slaves in Egypt. They are given their release from their master, Pharaoh, at the hand of God, and, most curiously, on departing they receive valuables: "jewels of silver, and jewels of gold, and raiment" (Exod 12:35; cp. 3:21, 22, 11:3). Moses lives through that experience of slavery and, in another code of laws, pronounces another judgment on how Hebrew slaves, male and fe-male, should be treated (Deut 15:12–18), including such details as how they too must receive benefits on their release and how the recipients of the rule should remember the experience of their forebears enslaved in Egypt.[11] The curious provision of jewelry to the departing slaves in Exodus 12:35 influences the language the lawgiver uses when he re-quires an Israelite to give provisions to a freed slave. Thus he uses the unusual verb *'anaq* in the figurative sense of "making a necklace" of agricultural provisions to the manumitted slaves.[12]

I speculate, then, that the lawgivers take on the mantle of Moses and proceed to do what they fictionally claim he did. What ideas about the institution of slavery went into their judgments I do not know, other than what they picked up from the traditions they studied. It is at this point that my understanding of the rules differs from that of other scholars. They see the two rules in Exodus and Deuteronomy as related to each other in that the one in Exodus applied at some stage in Israel's history, and the one in Deuteronomy modified it in order to meet the needs and perceptions of a later time in that history.[13] These scholars will have nothing to do with Mosaic authorship of the rules other than to suggest that, yes, they are attributed to Moses along the lines of a common convention in antiquity, and/or the historical Moses probably did lay down rules about slavery—namely, the ones in Exodus and Deuteronomy, which despite continuous updating do contain some kernel that goes back to him.

Even here my view runs parallel to theirs, yet it is still very different. When the lawgiver in Deuteronomy 15 writes out his law, he still incorporates features—the issues of the slave's permanent attachment to the master's household and the cost of a slave relative to a hired servant—picked up from the experience of the first ancestor, Jacob/Israel.[14] The incorporation of parallel experiences of succeeding generations of Israelites shows up in this rule too. The Deuteronomic rule is an update of the Exodus rule in some sense, but not in the sense that the latter was a rule actually in effect in the society and then later modified. Other scholars see two rules that belong to two different periods of time, which, at different junctures (when they are written down) are attributed to Moses. Theirs is a claim about the historical reality of the institution of slavery in ancient Israel. I do not reject this position outright. I am just not willing to make any claims about the societal history because I do not see how it is possible to do so based on the way the rules have come to be formulated.

I can put forward a thesis based on certain assumptions—which, to be sure, may be erroneous—that permit me to present detailed evidence in support of it. By contrast, those who hold to the regnant hypothesis are by and large neither aware of the nature of the assumptions (obvious to them) they make in their historical reconstruction nor, because of their commitment to their method, able to produce any direct evidence in support of it.

The reason for the lack of direct evidence to support the historical research of most biblical scholars is clear. Apart from some indirect illumination from archaeology and comparative studies, the Old Testament is the only source of information about Israelite society. Consequently, there can be no means of corroborating the kind of historical reconstruction that biblical scholars carry out.[15] Little wonder that there exists a plethora of such reconstructions. Fundamentally, they are speculative exercises.[16] No doubt, if we had certain social and economic data available to us, the views propounded might well have something to them. Unfortunately, the texts of the Old Testament provide this kind of sociological insight only in a very indirect and difficult to understand way.

Another aspect of the standard approach to the study of biblical law is the issue of how the biblical codes line up with the ancient Near Eastern law codes: Ur-Nammu, Lipit-Ishtar, Eshnunna, Hammurabi, the Assyrian laws, the Hittite laws, and the Neo-Babylonian laws. To see biblical law as somehow related to similar legal material in surrounding cultures is again an idea that seems obvious. But, as highlighted in the work of Raymond Westbrook, for example, the ancient Near Eastern material sometimes becomes the primary perspective for the study of biblical law. When a rule in the Bible proves difficult to interpret, a somewhat similar rule in the Near Eastern source is brought in for illumination, often with the highly unsatisfactory consequence that the reading of the Masoretic text of the Hebrew Bible is rejected.[17] There is something strange about this sense of priority.

An exemplary illustration of a scholar first seeking illumination from Near Eastern sources in the study of the Bible is the attempt to make sense of the name of Hamor (Ass), the head of the Canaanite group, the Hivites. In a widely accepted proposal, W. F. Albright argues that one finds "sons of Hamor" designating the Hivites (Gen 33:19; Josh 24:32) because according to the Mari documents (eighteenth century B.C.E. Mesopotamia) the slaying of an ass was part of the ratification of a treaty.[18] Yet the biblical record gives a straightforward explanation for the derogatory use of the name Ass for a Canaanite; namely, that the Israelites thought Canaanites should be their servants (Gen 9:25–27; cp. 49:14, 15). The name Ass—the proverbial beast of burden—is therefore applied to the head of this group of Canaanites in the same way that some characteristic feature of a person may give rise to his name; for example, when the child in Rebekah's womb takes his twin brother, Esau, by the heel ('aqab; Gen 25:26) and becomes known as Jacob (ya'aqob, one who follows at the heel; that is, who overreaches). Jacob's name contains a play on the word for "heel" because the aim is to bring out the later fact that Jacob usurped Esau's position in the family.[19] The refusal to look first and foremost at the biblical record to see how its compilers understood the name Hamor is what is odd.

A number of intangible factors explains the elevation of the Near Eastern sources as primary for understanding biblical material. First, there is the excitement and novelty of their discovery and the recognition that in some striking ways they deal with issues and themes similar to those found in the Bible. Second, many of those who seek to interpret the Bible against its historical background do so for religious reasons. They hold the text of the Bible to be sacred and seize on any argument that testifies to its historical truth as a product of a certain kind of religious society living at a certain period in history—a society that this type of interpreter constantly seeks to affirm as unique. Third, contrary to those who adopt a religious stance are those who are opposed to such a stance. They wish to be fiercely "scientific" and objective in their scrutiny of the Bible as a product of a certain time and place. They downplay the uniqueness and idiosyncrasies of the biblical material and resolutely set it in the broader context of Near Eastern culture. The result is again that the biblical texts are not given the close scrutiny necessary to appreciate their sophistication. It is, in fact, enormously difficult to establish direct links between Near Eastern and biblical legal material because the gaps in time, in culture, and in modes of composition are so considerable.

Although I see the narratives of Genesis through 2 Kings as crucial sources for understanding how biblical laws came to be formulated, I do not pursue the question of what function these narratives may have served prior to their use by the lawgivers. If the narratives were used to elicit laws, as I claim, then is it possible that the narratives have been used for comparably specific purposes? Geoffrey Miller thinks that they were. Using methods of analysis derived from the contemporary study of law and economics, he views the narratives as more than mere stories or national epics. Instead he sees them as themselves having a degree of legal force before they were codified, along the lines I indicate, in the explicitly legal material.[20] From my perspective, he therefore raises a very interesting question: Why were these narratives used as the basis for the subsequent elaboration of the law? When and under what conditions in ancient Israel were the narratives reworked? What political environment made it desirable to produce rules from them? Was the work done by an individual, a school of scholars or antiquarians, or a scribal guild? To what use might these legal materials have been put?

At the present state of my inquiries I can give but passing attention to these important but very difficult questions. However compelling our desire to pursue historical inquiry, the evidence is largely beyond our reach. It is not just that there are huge obstacles in transcending the gap between the available sources and the reality of the past—a problem for anyone engaged in historical research—but that the biblical sources do not lend themselves to the kind of historical inquiry so favored by biblical scholars. I would have readers try to break the spell of looking for historical and sociological knowledge from biblical literature. It is not that I wish to exclude such interests, but I want readers to appreciate the marvelous sophistication of ancient minds working and thinking in ways different from ours.

1 Narrative Inspired Law

It is almost exactly two thousand years ago that we come upon, between the school of Shammai and the school of Hillel (*mishnah Gittin* 9:10), a division of opinion about the meaning of the only rule in the Hebrew bible that has "legislation" respecting divorce. Similar divisions of opinion continue to this day. To those whose nightly reading does not extend to such disputes, their unending nature must seem bewildering. The poet T. S. Eliot once got into a London taxi and, rather pleased to be recognized by the driver, asked him how he knew who he was. "Oh," said the taxi driver, "I have an eye for famous faces. Just last week I picked up Bertrand Russell and I said to him, 'Well, Lord Russell, and what's it all about?' And do you know, he couldn't tell me!" Perhaps scholarly disputes continue because those engaged in them really do not know enough to determine, for example, the subtleties of a rule whose origin is more than twenty-five hundred years old. Still, some of us are driven by the conviction that it is possible to know a thing or two about the historical aspects of Jewish law. No doubt such convictions, and our delusions too, will continue to perpetuate the tradition of inquiry that has gone on for such a remarkable length of time.

I turn to the rule that King Henry the Eighth paid some attention to but Richard Burton and Elizabeth Taylor ignored altogether. A man divorces his wife; she becomes the wife of another man, who in turn divorces her or dies. The first husband cannot take her again as his wife. The rule is unique in world legal literature:

If a man takes a wife, and marries her, and it come to pass that she find no favour in his eyes, because he hath found the nakedness of a thing in her: and he writes her a bill of divorcement, and gives it in her hand, and sends her out of his house, and she departs out of his house, and she goes and becomes another man's wife. And the latter husband hates her, and writes her a bill of divorcement, and gives it in her hand, and sends her out of his house; or the latter husband dies, which took her to be his wife; her former husband, which sent her away, cannot take her again to be his wife, after that she is defiled; for that is abomination before Yahweh: and thou shalt not cause the land to sin, which Yahweh thy God giveth thee for an inheritance. (Deut 24:1–4)

Reuven Yaron, whose view has met with recent approval, holds that the rule is designed to protect the second marriage.[1] This supposition is perhaps based on a likely occurrence: In a small community, somewhere in a rural area in ancient Israel, I suppose, a husband divorced his wife, she married another man, and the first husband began to have second thoughts.[2] He wanted her back. She in turn responded to his regrets. The strain on the second marriage was intolerable, and the authorities devised the rule in Deuteronomy 24 to protect the second marriage. The first husband and his ex-wife may have soft feelings for each other, but that is just too bad. It is too late. She has contracted a second marriage and can never return to him. Not even—how overwhelmingly austere is the position of the authorities—if her second husband should divorce her so that she is free to marry again. Not even if he dies and she is a free woman on that account. She might contract a third marriage, and a fourth, but never can she return to the first husband. To do so would constitute a defilement of her, but on what basis it is impossible to say.

It is strange that the law should pay attention to the sensitive feelings of the parties in question and devise a rule to render them forlorn. If the second marriage is under strain, for whatever reason, surely that is a concern to be resolved by the second husband and the wife, especially bearing in mind the reluctance of early—and not so early—law to become involved in family matters.

The attempt by modern scholars to sketch the historical circumstances that prompted a rule is often really a form of storytelling. The fictional art that goes into such reconstruction of the past is disguised by the invention and addition of as many realistic details as possible.[3]

Modern authors, not admitting that they engage in the same kind of fiction making that was common in biblical antiquity itself, sincerely believe that they are in touch with the past. No doubt they are encouraged in this belief because sometimes historical reconstruction is possible, even though the imaginative, fictional element is still a feature. The point I wish to make is that modern scholars are in good company. While much of what they do might be new, a good deal of it is not.

I refer to the universal phenomenon whereby ideas, opinions, beliefs, and explanations are sometimes relayed as if their historical origin were known. Biblical literature is replete with examples of this, from the account of the origin of shame in the Adam and Eve story, through Moses' farewell speech to the children of Israel on the plains of Moab as they are about to enter conquered territory, to the extreme literary artifice of the Johannine material in which religious ideas determine the historical reporting.[4] Inventing the past has many benefits. Communication is simplified, for example, and wisdom and authority are enhanced by suggesting that some event or train of circumstances actually took place.

But let us return to the explanation of the rule about the return of the divorcée. The magic of storytelling is very much the crux of the matter, but not along the lines of made-up historical background. Consider, first of all, the much-cited Talmudic tale about how Moses, some fifteen hundred years after his death, turned up at a legal discussion in Rabbi Akiba's academy (*babylonian Menahoth* 29b). He did not understand a word but left after he was assured that all the rules under discussion went back to him. The story is sophisticated. The enormous role of reinterpretation—or better, misinterpretation—in the development of the law is recognized. One can probably also detect in the tale the influence of Pharisaic views about resurrection: Moses is not *imagined* as turning up, he turns up.

The story is important to my discussion because of the use of the person of Moses. It is not the first time that he is conjured up to confer status on someone else's lawmaking. Already in the biblical epoch, when he is about five hundred years old, he surveys the national life over the past five centuries, recalling, for example, the lives of the kings, his own eventful life, and its antecedents in the lives of the ancestors Abraham, Isaac, Jacob, Judah, and Joseph. The result is the strange, apparently haphazard compendium of judgments found in one of the most influential books of the bible, Deuteronomy. We shall never know the real author of Deuteronomy. He chose—and it is a common phenomenon in antiquity—to submerge his identity by giving it over to a legendary figure from the past. No doubt secure in their own individual worth, these anonymous authors could exercise boldness of imagination in pursuing their fictional aims. The phenomenon demands exploration because it is so much more extensive than we realize. We have to wonder why King Herod can claim Jesus is John the Baptist back from the dead, why Jesus can make John the Baptist Elijah, and why the Rabbis can make Balaam into Laban.

The Moses who speaks just before dying in the book of Deuteronomy is intent on leaving his mark for the future, or rather that is how he is presented. The entire sweep of significant events in the history of his nation lies before him, and, oddly, these events include those yet to be; for example, the later institution of monarchy and the temple cult in Jerusalem. Moses is, however, depicted as the supreme prophet. Event after event, past, present, and future, are singled out, and he judges matters that arise from them. This grand scheme of judgment, which surely influenced later religious conceptions of the last judgment as one involving prior significant events in Israelite history,[5] is not a cosmetic gloss, as scholars who pay some, but not very much, attention to the feature have tended to think. Every law is primarily shaped by this process of Moses' judgment on issues in Israel's history. Only when the outline of this process is deciphered for each law can we ask the questions legal historians might wish to put to these laws.

Consider how three laws, including the one about the return of the divorcée, came to be formulated. First is a rather strange rule, although at first sight it might not appear so. If you are walking through someone's vineyard or field of grain, you may pluck with your hand to obtain some nourishment, but you may not use any piece of equipment: "When thou comest into thy neighbour's vineyard, then thou mayest eat grapes thy fill at thine own pleasure; but thou shalt not put any in thy vessel. When thou comest into the standing corn of thy neighbour, then thou mayest pluck the ears with thine hand; but thou shalt not move a sickle unto thy neighbour's standing corn" (Deut 23:24, 25). The oddness of the rule resides in the lawgiver's need to state that while one may help oneself as a passer-by to some hand-picked crops, no implement should be used. The issue is not permission to take another's possessions but a limitation on how much can be taken. Yet it seems inconceivable that custom would not have already established such a limitation and that it ever needed to be spelled out. Any unauthorized use of implements in another's ground would be known by all to be theft. There is no indication in the rule, however, that theft is in any way the lawgiver's concern. There is no mention, for example, of sanctions for those who, for reasons far from clear in the ordinary course of events, might use implements in the belief that it is in order to do so.

It is possible to argue that somehow the issue actually arose in everyday life, despite the force of custom I have pointed to, and that the rule in question was formulated as a response. If such an occasion in ordinary life is its origin, then we can find the rule of value only for its antiquarian aspect. This background hardly seems a sufficient reason for its being set down as an important rule of the great lawgiver Moses.

I suggest another approach to the origin of the rule. In his time Moses confronts the following problem. As the leader of the Israelites at a place near Kadesh, he meets with a negative response to his request that his people be allowed to pass through the territory of Edom (Num 20:14–21). He appeals to Edom as a brother on account of their ancestors, the brothers Jacob (Israel) and Esau (Edom). He assures the Edomites that in passing through their territory the Israelites will keep to the king's highway and will not stop at any well to drink water, nor will they enter any Edomite field or vineyard and take of the crops. Edom's response is open and direct: should they even try to pass through, they will be put to the sword. The Israelites continue their appeal and this time mention that should they take water from any well they will pay for it. They do not bring up the possibility of eating and paying for Edomite grain or grapes. The Edomites' response this time is by action. They set upon the Israelites.

In this history, with its own focus and aims, Moses does not bring out the real underlying issue between Israel and Edom. Hundreds of years later, however, he, in the person of the Deuteronomist, has had time to think about it and address it in the context of relations between fellow Israelites. In the original situation a claim to traverse someone's territory is made on the basis that the two groups share a common ancestry. Nothing comes of that claim because the Edomites know that to pass through on foot is one thing, but to stop and assuage thirst and hunger is quite another. This problem emerges from a reading of the text. There is first Israel's assurance that no water, grain, or grapes will be taken. When Edom still refuses passage, Moses then communicates that any water taken would be paid for, although he still says that the Israelites will just pass through on foot, nothing more. Either the Edomites do not believe a word of it or they see that they have much more to lose than to gain from this group, which is not passing by casually but is equipped with instruments. I am reminded of the joke about the contrary situation in the city of Aberdeen, where the people with great hospitality invite you in for afternoon tea, and there is indeed a splendid array of scones and cakes and the like. It is only when you sit down that you are told that everything is reasonably priced.

The issue in the original, extraordinary situation between Israel and Edom is much more realistic than the issue found in the Deuteronomic law. The incident shows up well the tension between one's obligation to grant a favor in certain circumstances to fellow human beings when some common bond is asserted and one's concern about how far they will go in response.[6] Moses, in judging how his fellow Israelites should deal with the issue, looks beyond the conflict that prevented some arrangement being made between the Edomites and the Israelites. He judges that passage through someone's fields and vineyards is in order, and he can even permit some picking of crops, but not on such a scale that implements can be used. His experience of the real fear of the Edomites is the basis for a distinction that in ordinary circumstances is unnecessary.

My claim is that the formulation of this food law, if not its origin—it will have its roots in customary behavior[7]—owes its existence to someone long after Moses' time making explicit an issue that is largely implicit in the history but readily calls for deeper reflection. The issue arises at that time in Moses' life when he has been denied the prospect of entering the new land. This denial is itself related to the problem of the journeying Israelites, who complain that they lack, among other provisions, grain and grapes (Num 20:5). How appropriate that Moses at the end of his life makes a farewell speech to his people before they enter the promised land, and presents as one of his directions a ruling about what is proper when they go on a journey and have need of food.

Is it possible to fathom why the rule about the return of a divorcée should follow the food law? Conventional theory would postulate haphazard legal draftsmanship. Consider, however, Moses' all-encompassing eye when he views the history of his people—past, present, and future—and observes similar developments. After all, we are to believe that Moses delivers these rules not when he is 500 years old, as critical scholarship would rightly claim, but when he is 120 years old, his eye still undimmed, his natural force unabated (Deut 34: 7). Moreover, because he is taking leave of life, it is a time of special vision. Time is telescoped, and if the Rabbinic principle that there is no before and after in Scripture should not be read back into the period of Deuteronomy,[8] we can nonetheless claim that whoever brought Moses back from the dead, so to speak, moved readily between one period of time and another. Moses' line of reasoning is that Israel's situation at Kadesh is reminiscent of the ancestor Abraham's situation near the same place ("between Kadesh and Shur"; Gen 20:1). Recall that Abraham, traveling in unfamiliar territory and accompanied by his wife, Sarah, has her agree to pass herself off as his sister so that the males of the place will be well disposed to them.

The two situations have interesting parallels. Both occur in the same geographical area, and both Moses and Abraham need to be welcomed by another group but have reason to fear a hostile response. There is another, equally remarkable link. In order to appeal to what in effect is a foreign group, each exploits a kinship tie. Moses brings up the tie between Israel and Edom—their ancestors were brothers. Abraham has in mind a prospective tie between his people and those of the kingdom of Gerar.[9] He means to present his wife as his sister so that she will be free to forge for each of them a new family tie with a member of the Gerar community: Sarah as the man's wife, Abraham as the brother-in-law. When his scheme is eventually uncovered, Abraham even justifies his strategy by telling Abimelech, the king of Gerar, that he and Sarah are indeed brother and sister because they have the same father.

Whoever wrote about Abraham's use of his wife to benefit himself was already alarmed by the morality of the arrangement. The introduction of the deity into the account in Genesis 20 reveals this dimension. The deity characterizes Abraham's transfer of his wife to Abimelech as adultery on the part of the king, pronounces a capital sentence for the offense, and shows his displeasure by afflicting the women of Gerar with sterility. Abimelech rightly protests the deity's judgment because he has been deceived about Sarah's true status. The deity relents; acknowledging Abimelech as a fundamentally decent type, he interferes just in time, by means of a dream, to prevent Abimelech from actually taking Sarah.[10] The deity's action is prompted by his refusal to accept the idea that Sarah's status as a wife has changed. From his point of view the condition for Sarah to be restored as Abraham's wife is that she remain untouched by another male. Presumably, union with Abimelech would have constituted a defilement of Sarah and consequently a bar to her restoration as Abraham's wife.[11]

Whatever the identity of the ancient moralizer who revealed his views by inventing a role for the deity, he concentrated on the results of Abraham's deception. The deity makes no comment on the initial situation, in which a husband feels constrained to give up his wife because of her attractiveness to another, more powerful male. A story, after all, is directed toward an ending, and one can hardly stop just as it has begun.[12] A lawgiver, however, can choose to be more focused and can pay attention to initial developments. This is precisely what Moses does. By observing the process in question, moreover, modern readers obtain insight into how the biblical lawgivers thought of their laws as having divine authority.

Whenever theological language is introduced into a story, it is usually an indication that there are spheres of influence and modes of action recognized to be beyond earthly, human capability. At best, its insertion inculcates proper values and reveals that while human action is desirable, it is limited in what it can do. By and large, a law-giver cannot translate the deity's response to an unacceptable situation into a rule that will achieve the same result. He can, however, try to reflect the same values within the limits imposed by human institutions. It is in this sense that certain biblical rules are put forward as partaking of divine authority. Indeed, much of the lawgiver's motivation for constructing such rules is his aim to convert supposed supernatural intervention in human affairs into rules that, if they do not necessarily approximate the intervention, at least embody its spirit.

From the Genesis narrative Moses takes up the matter of a wife's release from her marital bond because it is to the benefit of the husband that another male seek to have her.[13] Moses proceeds to handle this issue not along the lines by which the deity handled it with Abimelech, but in line with later Israelite life and institutions. The problem that might present itself among later Israelites is that a man may divorce a wife not because he dislikes her—the usual reason for a divorce—but because he finds a vulnerability in her (namely, her attractiveness to another male) that he chooses not to oppose. Even though the rule was not drafted to cover the facts of Abraham's situation, its language nonetheless reflects it closely. When Abraham anticipates that the exposure of Sarah to other male eyes will be a problem for him, the result for her is that *as his wife* she now finds no favor in his eyes.[14] The language of the rule accurately conveys the situation in the Genesis narrative: "And she find no favour in his eyes, because he hath found the nakedness of a thing in her." What Abraham has just discovered about Sarah is not that she is desirable to look at, but that her looks on display to foreign males render both of them defenseless in the face of these males' likely reaction to her.[15] The Hebrew word 'ervah (nakedness) well conveys this notion of defense-lessness.[16]

When we turn to the descriptions of the two divorces in the law—the woman loses favor with the first husband and experiences hatred from the second—we see that their negative aspect has misled interpreters to read into the phrase "the nakedness of a thing" something negative about the woman herself. The surprising mildness of the language about losing favor in the first husband's eyes should have made them more cautious. The term *'ervah* almost inevitably pulls in the notion of shame, but it is crucial to note that this secondary sense emerges only when the situation in question is public and not private, when the focus is on the woman's role in public, not on any private deficiency.

Shame, by its very nature, comes into being only when the switch from the private to the public realm is made. The situation of Noah, lying naked in his tent in a drunken stupor, becomes shameful only when his son looks upon him and tells his two brothers what he has seen (Gen 9:22). Human excrement is not shameful, but it would become so if the deity, going the rounds of the Israelite army encampment, should see it within that area of ground.[17] In that situation the expression *'ervat-dabar* (the nakedness of a thing), used only one other time in the Bible, in the law in Deuteronomy 23:15, takes on a negative connotation. Egyptian territory is open for all to see. Nothing untoward about that, but if spies are taking stock of it, as the disguised Joseph claims his brothers are (Gen 42:9), then "the nakedness of the land" (*'ervat-ha'areṣ*) points to something negative. Just as Joseph cannot protect the land against the prying eyes of foreign visitors, so Abraham cannot protect his wife against the prying eyes of foreign males. In each instance the problem is neither the land itself nor the woman herself. The problem lies in wrongful looking on the part of others, as in the example of Noah's son looking upon his father's nakedness. On account of their alleged ulterior motives, Joseph's brothers should not have been viewing the land, nor should the foreigners of Gerar have been viewing Sarah.

Consistent with the use of *'ervah* in other contexts, in regard to the woman in the rule it refers to an aspect of nature; namely, how she looks. There is consequently no need to seek to apply it to her conduct, as translators and commentators usually do. No wonder they have difficulty in specifying her offense: they make it fall short of adultery, rightly so because of the rule in Deuteronomy 22:22, but still insist on some kind of sexual offense. We cannot tell from a reading of the law itself what is going on. We have to assume that the law was composed with the narrative about Abraham and Sarah specifically under review.

The expression 'ervat-dabar as applied to the divorcée refers, then, to a public situation, in particular to how she is viewed by someone outside her marriage. Here it is crucial to note that when she leaves the first marriage she enters upon a second. The language of the law, contrary to what the RSV makes of it, is not conditional in character. The language is not "And *if* she goes and becomes," but "And she goes and becomes." It is the one clue in the law that a second marriage is anticipated for her. We can consequently speculate from a reading of the law itself that the first marriage is dissolved because another male is being encouraged to acquire her. If this speculation has merit, we can easily understand why there is a prohibition against the first husband taking her back should the second husband divorce her, or even should he die. What is being condemned out of hand is the release of the woman from a marriage because, for whatever reason, the husband anticipates a favor by letting her go to another man.[18]

The law goes on to say that the woman would be defiled should she return to the first husband. The verb used here, *tame'*, "to defile," refers to sexual defilement. She can be so regarded precisely because her first husband had encouraged her to seek a relationship with another man. No doubt, should she become free again, he would presumably be as willing to have her back as he was opportunistic in releasing her. While the outward conduct is in order because of the use of the machinery of divorce, its motivation is base.[19] In ancient Rome, under the *lex Iulia de adulteriis* of Augustus (18 B.C.E.), a husband who did not divorce a wife caught in the act of adultery was guilty of *lenocinium*, pandering (*Digest* 48.5.30[29]).[20] The biblical lawgiver views the husband as a panderer too, even though he uses the institution of divorce as a cover for his pandering.[21]

A further puzzling feature of the law is worth commenting on. Much of its language is unnecessary. The drafting of laws at this stage of legal development is typically to the point and not inclined to spell out what can be taken for granted. There is consequently no need to set out the reasons for the two divorces or to mention how a written document of divorce is handed to the departing spouse. Only if such a written document constituted an innovation might we expect a reference to it, but nothing indicates that this is the case. Why such unnecessary description? To contrast, one might suggest, the situation of Abraham and Sarah, which cannot be legislated for, with one in later Israelite life that can be. The issue of a formal divorce does not arise when Abraham and Abimelech each in turn release Sarah from her ties to them. Only the deity could control the developments that arose with them. The law, on the other hand, can have access to a comparable situation only if the development occurred among the Israelites themselves, and if it involved the legal machinery of divorce. The formulation of the law reflects this attempt by a human lawgiver to transform the unmanageable circumstances described in the Genesis tale into manageable ones. Even with this transformation we can still observe the powerful influence of the story on the law.

There is, as I have already indicated, the transfer of the notion of Sarah's exposure into the expression 'ervat-dabar, and this can explain a crucial aspect of the interpretation that I am suggesting for the law. Why, if this really is a case of a husband encouraging his wife to seek another liaison, does the rule not refer to a transaction between the first husband and the second? Realistically, we would expect collusion between the two. Such an indication would have put the interpretation of the rule beyond doubt. The influence of the story on the rule must again be reckoned with. Abraham knows only that some male will be attracted to his wife. He decides on his scheme before he knows the identity of the second husband. The law proceeds from a description of the first husband's release of his wife to a simple statement that she goes and becomes another man's wife. The statement leaves us wondering whether the second husband knows the woman while she is still married to the first husband or only after she is divorced. The story has prompted the lawgiver to keep the matter open, hence the omission of any reference to collusion between the two men.

Even the double description of the woman's release from her second marriage—the husband divorces her because he hates her, the husband dies—may owe much to Abimelech's position with Sarah after he realizes what her deception has done to him and his kingdom. He rightly protests to the deity that she claims she is Abraham's sister, not his wife. He now has occasion to change his attitude toward her, from attraction to aversion. After all, a plague of sterility has struck the women of Gerar because of his association with her. Worse, Abimelech has been sentenced to death because of her presence in his house. The law contemplates two possibilities by which the woman may be released from her second marriage: the husband dislikes her, or he dies. These two possibilities can be read as the equivalent of the idiosyncratic ones cited in the story, namely, Abimelech's aversion to Sarah and the death sentence hanging over him.

The law has the odd reference that sin is caused to the land because of the woman's relationships with the two men.[22] Abimelech protests that sin has been brought upon his kingdom because of Sarah's relationship with Abraham and then with him. The law also states that should the divorcée return to her first husband after her marriage to the second, such a move would constitute an abomination to the deity. This characterization is in line with the depiction of the deity's response in the Genesis tale.

When historical speculation has to be relied on to make sense of rules,[23] it is virtually impossible to suggest the circumstances that might explain why one particular rule follows another. Why, for example, does a rule exempting a man from military duty, or any other type of duty, for one year after marriage follow the rule about the divorcée? While historical reconstruction has not been possible here, the inclination has been to observe the role of "catchwords" in the linking of rules and to pursue the problem of historical background in another way. The rules, so the reasoning goes, belong to different times and places and are linked together in this loose way. Underlying such an approach is the resolute belief that a real-life situation once prompted the rule. The attempt to identify such a reality seems to reflect a desire to render the material "living" and to enhance its relatedness to our times, to re-create life in the ancient biblical society with a view to appropriating its values.

If we adopt the biblical writer's viewpoint that Moses is delivering these rules at the end of his life, there is no need to adhere to this usual approach. The setting is that Moses' death is approaching and life in the new land for his fellow Israelites is beckoning. Situations in which death is imminent, like the one confronting Moses, engage the lawgiver's attention. In the situations he scrutinizes, moreover, there is also a threat to the promise, so prominent elsewhere in Deuteronomy, of the blessing of fruitfulness and increase of numbers. At Kadesh, Israel on its way to the new land meets with a life-threatening response from the Edomites, as does Abraham near Kadesh when he and Sarah, having previously received the promise of acquiring the land (Gen 17:8), approach the males of Gerar. The threat to Abraham, which prompts his plan to let Sarah be acquired by one of these males, is also the background for the rule about the newlyweds: "When a man hath taken a new wife, he shall not go out to war, neither shall he be charged with any business: but he shall be free at home one year, and shall give joy to his wife which he hath taken" (Deut 24:5).

At Gerar, Abraham and Sarah have not yet produced a child, even though they have been married a long time. The deity has promised them one (Gen 18:10), but Sarah has yet to conceive. The supernatural assistance to overcome Sarah's age barrier to pregnancy and the removal of the threat to Abraham's life are parts of the history known to Moses.

Marriage and the birth of a child are very much bound together, especially in this society, where contraception was rarely practiced. Marriage followed by childbirth within a year would have been a common development, and thus the problem of any barrier to conception would have come up very soon. A great many biblical rules came to be formulated when the lawgiver picked up a problem from a highly unusual situation in the history of his ancestors and then turned to a comparable problem in more normal circumstances. In this instance, the move is from the example of an aged couple who, exceptionally, are going to have a child but the husband faces a threat to his life, to newlyweds who are likely to have a child but are prevented from doing so by some circumstance.

Moses' task, precisely because his special relationship to the deity is unique, is to issue rules that reflect the deity's interests. The rule about the newly married couple incorporates the concern with the threat to Abraham's life, but it does so in the more conventional instance, drawn from later Israelite life, of death on the battlefield. Aside from exemption from military duty, the rule also permits a man to stay at home and be free of any other duty or business for a year. In the story, Abraham is engaged away from home in an unspecified business transaction in Gerar when he runs into danger (Gen 20:1). (In the comparable story in Genesis 12:10, he is away from home in order to purchase food in Egypt.)[24]

The rule primarily incorporates the concern with Abraham's childlessness. This focus on children in the rule can be inferred from both the man's exemption for one year and the language about him giving joy to his wife. The association between joy and the birth of a child is a standard one in biblical antiquity (Isa 66:10; Jer 20:15; John 3:29, 30, 15:11, 16:21, 17:13). Typical of the formulation of a rule is that its language echoes the tradition that inspired it. The surprising emphasis in the rule about giving pleasure to the woman derives from Sarah's speaking this way when she hears that she will be made pregnant: "After I am waxed old shall I have pleasure, my lord being old also" (Gen 18:12).[25]

2 Laws of Leviticus 19

No body of biblical laws is regarded as so representative of its spirit as the rules in Leviticus 19, one of which is the rule to love one's neighbor as oneself (Lev 19:18). Johannes Hempel refers to these rules as the "fundamental social ethical law of Yahwism."[1] More explicitly than other interpreters, Arie Noordtzij states the standard view:

> To the Western mind, the content of this chapter [Leviticus 19] seems rather heterogeneous and gives the impression of being a more or less arbitrary assemblage of commandments that deal partly with religious, partly with moral, and partly with civic life. We are disposed to regard life as composed of various realms that, to our way of thinking, have little or no connection with one another. The perspective of the ancient Near Eastern world was more unified, however, for not only were the cultic and moral spheres considered to be two sides of the same concern . . . but civic and political life were also controlled by a religious outlook. The whole of life was thus religious in character.[2]

The fundamental assumption underlying the standard view is that the material in Leviticus 19 reflects the living reality of ancient Israelite society. Jacob Milgrom in his recent commentary has no doubt about this relationship between law and life. The material came into existence in response to real-life issues, and its content can consequently communicate the operating principles at work in the society. Thus, if the moral and ritual rules are bound together, this is because the society in question did not distinguish between them in the way modern communities do.[3] Baruch Levine expresses similar sentiments: "Holiness, an essentially cultic concept, could not be achieved through purity and worship alone; it had an important place in the realm of societal experience. Like the Ten Commandments and other major statements on the duties of man toward God, this chapter [Leviticus 19] exemplifies the heightened ethical concern characteristic of ancient Israel."[4]

The view shared by these scholars is based on a misunderstanding of the nature of the material they are interpreting. My starting point is the same as theirs: namely, the perplexing arrangement of the laws in Leviticus 19, which invariably invites comment. On the one hand, scholars use the miscellaneous character of the laws as evidence that they have different sources, that they belonged to different times and places before they found a common location in Leviticus 19.[5] At the same time, however, scholars see the miscellany of the laws as evidence of the undifferentiated nature of all aspects of human affairs in ancient Israel. They infer that the sequence of the rules must have made ready sense to their recipients, and that these ancient Israelites would not have found it jarring to hear sequentially a rule about a sacrificial offering, a rule about leaving behind grain and olives for the poor at harvest time, and a rule about stealing.

METHOD IN THE STUDY OF BIBLICAL LAW

The kind of thinking that delineates source after source for the rules in Leviticus 19 rests on a misunderstanding of how biblical laws came to be formulated. A different picture emerges once one takes stock of a process of legal formulation so deeply implanted in every part of the Pentateuch that it accounts for the unique integration of law and narrative that is the Pentateuch. Moreover, once one understands why the lawgiver moves from one topic to the next, one also understands the sequence of the material. Real-life needs that were readily communicable in sequential fashion to the ancient recipients do not come into the reckoning. The assumption that the ancients did not differentiate between cultic and ethical matters, for example, is unwarranted. The lawgiver is first and foremost engaged in a literary exercise whose mechanics structure the material in a way different from that imagined by modern interpreters. The laws represent judgments on literary traditions. The legal material in the Pentateuch turns out to constitute the major redactional strand in the composition of biblical literature. In conventional scholarly terms, Deuteronomy (D) and Priestly (P) writing critically edit other literary strands in the Bible, for example, the Jahwistic Elohistic (JE) strand of the Pentateuch. Their authors' editorial work contains much more of substance than has hitherto been realized.

The lawgivers of the Pentateuch formulated biblical laws in relation to biblical narratives. They went through the historical traditions of Israel and set down rules in response to events or issues that arose in these traditions, rather than in response to problems in their own time.[6] Viewing the material in this light can explain the archaizing presentation of biblical laws; namely, their attribution to the legendary figure of Moses, who judges matters past, present, and future. The primary impetus in the composition of the laws was to create for the nation of Israel its own ancient legal tradition, with the laws explicating the epics of the past. The process that accounts for the presentation of the narratives is the same process that accounts for the presentation of the laws. The narratives do two major things: they reflect the compilers' interest in universal and Israelite origins (from the origin of the world in the Book of Genesis to the origin of kingship in the Book of Samuel), and they record matters that recur throughout succeeding generations (from the problems of the first family in the Book of Genesis through the problems of the kings in the historical books). The compilers of the laws did likewise. They took up problems that first presented themselves in the biblical narrative history and addressed comparable problems that recur in succeeding generations of that history.

The Deuteronomic and Priestly writers compiled all the laws in the Pentateuch, and, as I shall observe, they proceeded in identical fashion.[7] Their rules reflect a special mode of ancient law teaching that to date has gone unnoticed. For example, frequently a narrative tradition that recounts a dispute in which the deity plays a decisive role is taken up in a law, and a legal rather than a divine judgment arbitrates some equivalent dispute.[8] Similarly, the deity's judgment in a narrative tradition often translates into a rule that applies to an approximately corresponding situation in the world of experience.[9] Meir Malul stresses that the Near Eastern codes represent a literary tradition that was not necessarily used to inform the practice of law in the real world.[10] I wish to emphasize that the links between the laws and narratives in the Pentateuch represent Israelite literary activity equivalent to that found in the broader Near Eastern culture. I do not exclude the possibility that the Israelite lawgivers gave the Mosaic equivalent of laws from the Near Eastern codes by asking themselves what, in light of Israelite and patriarchal history, Moses' judgments would have been in the same situation.

The lawgiver did not set down a rule that corresponded exactly to some obvious offense committed in the narrative. Presumably there was no need for him to do so because the narrative communicated the wrongdoing well enough. Rather, the lawgiver came up with a problem related to the one that dominates the story. A parallel to this procedure appears in the hypothetical cases that the prophets sometimes constructed in response to actual offenses. For example, King Ahab fails to kill King Ben-hadad of Syria when he ought to have done so after defeating him in battle (1 Kings 20:26–43). Instead Ben-hadad, hiding in the city of Aphek, sends messengers to Ahab to see if he will spare his life. Ahab responds positively and receives Ben-hadad well, especially after Ben-hadad promises to restore some cities that his father captured from Ahab's father and authorizes the Israelites to set up bazaars in Damascus. A member of a prophetic guild goes in disguise to Ahab and presents him with a fictitious case that concerns an offense analogous to Ahab's: "Your servant [the disguised prophet] went out into the thick of the battle; then a soldier turned and brought a man to me, and said, 'Guard this man; if he is missing, your life shall be given for his life, or else you shall pay a talent of silver.' While your servant was busy here and there, he was gone" (1 Kings 20:39, 40).[11]

Ben-hadad was not given over to Ahab with an instruction to guard him, whereas in the fictitious case someone gives the soldier an enemy to guard. The soldier is under no obligation to kill his ward, but is simply warned not to lose him. Ahab, on the other hand, is, it is understood, under an obligation to kill Ben-hadad. When the king hears the case about the soldier he judges that the soldier has been derelict in his duty. In so judging, Ahab condemns himself for his analogous offense, as the prophet, revealing himself, spells out: "Thus says Yahweh, 'Because you have let the man go whom I had devoted to destruction, therefore your life shall be for his life, and your people for his people'" (1 Kings 20:42).

There is no question, then, that the made-up offense derives from Ahab's situation. The offense that the prophet invents is comparable to Ahab's offense but not the same, presumably because it is crucial that the prophet not address Ahab too directly lest he be struck down on the spot. The way that biblical lawgivers constructed legal formulations from narrative accounts of ancestral offenses is very similar to the prophet's procedure. Indeed, the lawgivers probably identified themselves with these prophetic guilds, not only adopting their method of constructing judgments but also, when judging Israel's ancestors, taking the same religious, moral, and legal perspective. The lawgivers' motivation in judging their ancestors is in one way strikingly similar to these prophets when they judge monarchs: the lawgivers only indirectly attack ancestral conduct.

Martin Noth's view has been highly influential in the study of biblical law and literature.[12] Noth distinguishes between an earlier composition, Deuteronomy, and a later one, Joshua through 2 Kings, which consisted of annals that a Deuteronomistic writer redacted by incorporating the ideas and judgments of Deuteronomy. Noth calls this redaction the Deuteronomistic history. I do not accept Noth's view that Deuteronomy existed first, at least in the historical sense that he assumes, and was followed by a Deuteronomistic redaction of the historical material in Joshua through 2 Kings. I find Noth's understanding of the relationship between Deuteronomy and the Deuteronomistic history (Joshua through 2 Kings) to be more an assumption on Noth's part than a thesis. I agree with him that annals existed, but I am inclined to think that the "person" who redacted them also formulated the rules, although of course I cannot be sure. I also agree with Noth that most of the laws found in Deuteronomy would have had a prehistory, some going back to Moses and some preceding him. I know of no way to reconstruct this prehistory, whereas Noth claims that it can be reconstructed from Deuteronomy, a version of which, he believes, turned up during the reign of King Josiah. I think that the account of this discovery in 2 Kings 22:3–13 is more fiction than fact, and thus as historically problematic as the law code itself.

A striking feature of Noth's work on the Deuteronomistic redaction of Joshua through 2 Kings is how few rules in Deuteronomy, a mere seven, he cites.[13] My view of the laws would add considerably to Noth's understanding of Joshua through 2 Kings because the links I draw between many of the Deuteronomic laws and the narratives in Joshua through 2 Kings support the extensive character of the Deuteronomistic redaction of the annals. We differ in our views of how to read the material historically. For example, Noth says that the last instance before Josiah's reign when we hear of a Deuteronomic law is in 2 Kings 14:6.[14] Amaziah, the king of Judah, "slew his servants which had slain the king his father. But the children of the murderers he slew not: according unto that which is written in the book of the law of Moses [Deut 24:16]. . . . The fathers shall not be put to death for the children, nor the children be put to death for the fathers; but every man shall be put to death for his own sin." Noth takes this account as historically factual and argues that Amaziah conformed to the law in Deuteronomy 24:16.

I assume otherwise. The lawgiver formulated this Deuteronomic law in response to the first incident in Israel's history when a father suffered death because of his son's offense (Shechem's seduction of Jacob's daughter Dinah and its aftermath; Genesis 34). I speculate that the Deuteronomistic redactor of the annals of the kings noted how the annalists recorded that Amaziah killed the fathers, but not the sons, and approved of this focus on the offenders; he therefore recorded that Amaziah observed the law of Moses. In effect, the legendary lawgiver Moses approves of such a focus because it conforms to a Mosaic rule that the redactor—that is, "Moses"—has been able to formulate from his ethical and legal scrutiny of all the history available to him from Genesis through 2 Kings. The Deuteronomic lawgiver formulated the first part of the rule in reaction to the incident in Genesis 34 of a father being killed for the offense of a son, the only incident of its kind in biblical literature. The second part the lawgiver formulated for the much more usual situation, such as the one Amaziah avoided, when sons die because of the father's offense.[15]

Assessing my position in relation to Noth's, Bernard Levinson characterizes my understanding of the Deuteronomic laws as conferring upon them esoteric meaning.[16] One has to understand them in light of their relationship with the narratives in order to appreciate their full meaning. That is indeed my position. I do not, however, hold that the rules were meaningless except in light of the narrative background. I do not know how to study their reception, which the biblical record (2 Kings 22:8) attributes to a discovery in the reign of King Josiah around 621 B.C.E. The retelling of what happened in his reign was ideologically motivated, and is therefore historically suspect, and we are told only about a very few of the rules; we are left in the dark about most of them.

The view that my reading of the rules is esoteric points to a problem faced by all scholars attempting to understand an ancient text. Every scholar must devise a technique, a theory, or a system to solve the puzzles the text presents. Surely one can characterize the process whereby students of biblical literature master the principles of modern critical scholarship as an initiation into scholarly mysteries. According to today's most widely accepted theory—one with which I do not agree—we cannot read many laws in the Bible without appreciating the fact that they contain layers of historical background. In other words, the rule had an original formulation that over the centuries needed modification in light of changing historical circumstances. Scholars describe these circumstances, and only then can the readers truly interpret the law.[17] If my model for understanding the laws is esoteric, then so too are all other models. In order to understand Scripture, which is a product of the past, a twentieth-century reader must have a key.

Aside from the difficulty of reading an ancient text through the prism of modern scholarship, there is also an esoteric aspect of biblical law that is both original to it and one of its most tantalizing features. I refer to the pseudepigraphical character of the material with its fictional attribution to a past figure of great authority, namely, Moses. My studies constitute an attempt to uncover the character of this fiction of construction; I concentrate exclusively on the fiction. Noth and other scholars, in contrast, attempt to uncover the supposed historical circumstances that explain the laws. They do appear to recognize the fictional device that underlies the material. For them, however, the fiction is an invitation to uncover the unrecorded history that lies behind the laws. I do not believe that the biblical text provides sufficient evidence to support historical reconstructions. I raise questions, rather, about why the lawgiver threw a cloak of fictionality over the presentation of his laws. These questions are legitimate and point to the topic of concealment.

My thesis can formulate and address such questions as the following. While Moses' laws concern matters that occurred both before and after his lifetime, why does the Deuteronomic lawgiver explicitly cite historical incidents only from Moses' lifetime, and not incidents from the lives of the patriarchs (for example, Jacob's conferral of the birthright upon Joseph, his son by his loved wife, Rachel [Gen 48, 49:22–26], and not upon Reuben or any other son by the hated wife, Leah, which inspired the rule about the inheritance rights of the hated wife's firstborn son in Deuteronomy 21:15–17) or from future Israelite history (for example, Solomon's multiplication of horses, wives, silver, and gold [1 Kings 10:14–25, 27, 11:3–8], which inspired the law of the king in Deuteronomy 17:14–20)? Citing events solely from Moses' lifetime, I argue, aided the creation of the fiction. Levinson rightly notes that I refrain from sketching the historical development of Israelite law.[18] I clash with those scholars who focus on such development because I view the historical material in Genesis through 2 Kings as built into the fiction.

To date, no other interpreter has seen what I claim to see in regard to the systematic nature of the links between the laws and the narratives. I relate linguistic links between law and narrative to my hypothesis about the fundamental connection between the laws and the narratives; this has nothing to do with noting common language in two different biblical passages and thereby claiming they must perforce be related. These linguistic links are only one kind of evidence that I use to support my hypothesis, but they are far from being the primary evidence. I rely more on the parallelism and identical sequence of topics between the narratives and the laws in building my argument, with the linguistic links sometimes offering fine supporting evidence.

In the previous chapter, and in previously published books and papers, I have spelled out in detail how the Deuteronomist worked with narratives when formulating his laws. In this chapter I present evidence that the Priestly author of the rules in Leviticus not only knew how the Deuteronomist worked, but formulated his rules in a similar fashion by taking up issues presented in the narratives. As soon as one considers the arrangement of the topics in Leviticus 19—such as fear of mother and father, sabbaths, idols, peace offerings, harvesting crops, stealing, and lying—one wonders about the logic of the sequence and asks why one topic follows another.

The link between the topic of one rule and the topic of the next often seems impossible to discern. For example, a prohibition against the complete harvesting of crops comes after a prohibition against eating a sacrifice two days after it has been offered. How does one explain this lack of logical connection between the subject matter of one rule and that of the next? What we should not do, I submit, is what scholars typically do. They look at the two rules together and try to puzzle out a link, despite the gulf in substance between them. This approach has proved a fertile breeding ground for observations that wrongly attribute to the ancients concepts and beliefs that these modern scholars think are peculiar to the ancient Near Eastern world; for example, that no distinction was made between moral and ritual rules. The error in this approach is comparable to the error of a modern reader who turns to an index of topics in a scholarly treatise and relates one entry, say, "carnivore," to the one that comes before it, say, "carnival." This would result in the strangest of notions about carnivals. In fact, of course, one relates each index entry to the appropriate place in the body of the book. So too in puzzling out why one biblical law follows another. We should not read them in their immediate context. Instead we should relate each rule back to the issue the lawgiver picked up from the body of biblical literature he was working with. The lawgiver was interested in matters that turned up again in succeeding generations of his ancestors. Often, while tracing a theme from one generation to the next he found other problems unrelated to the problem for which he first formulated a rule. This kind of move explains why the topic of one law frequently bears no resemblance to the topic of the law that comes before or after it. The question about the sequence of the rules is the impetus for my thesis. I shall comment on laws in the order in which they appear.

LEVITICUS 19:3

Ye shall fear every man his mother, and his father, and keep my Sabbaths: I am Yahweh your God.

The focus here is on Joseph.[19] One may expect a survey of Israel's experience in Egypt that starts with Joseph's experiences within his family because of the notice in Leviticus 18:3 about the problems of Egyptian (and Canaanite) influence on the Israelites: "After the doings of the land of Egypt, wherein ye dwelt, shall ye not do." In Genesis 37, Joseph interprets his dream about the sun, moon, and stars bowing down to him and acknowledging him to be superior to themselves as meaning that his parents should bow down and worship him. Rather than teaching respect for one's parents the dream communicates the opposite. Joseph's father rebukes him. For the Priestly lawgiver, the proper perspective, as set out in the Decalogue (Exod 20:12) and taken up again by him here, is that a son acknowledge his parents as his begetters. Since the act of procreation is the one human activity in which human beings participate in God's creation (compare the notice in Genesis 4:1, where Eve conceived and gave birth to Cain with God's aid), proper reverence is necessary. The rule cites the mother first because the Priestly writer's focus is on procreation. The mother gives birth to the child.[20]

The acknowledgment of God's creation is the focus of the rule about keeping the Sabbaths, as the Priestly version of the Decalogue (Exod 20:8–11) and the Priestly material in Exodus 31:12–17 spell out. Joseph's dream that he was superior in status to the sun, moon, and stars requires a reminder that God is the creator of such entities and that Joseph should not compete for that honor. As in the Decalogue, in Leviticus 19:3 the Sabbath rule is juxtaposed with the rule about parents because procreation is linked to the original creation. Philo expresses the link thus: "Parents, in my opinion, are to their children what God is to the world, since just as he achieved existence for the nonexistent, so they in imitation of his power, as far as they are capable, immortalize the race" (*De Specialibus Legibus* 2.225; cp. *Quod Deterius Potiori insidiari solet* 54; *De Vita Mosis* 2.209).

Moshe Weinfeld thinks the rules about parents, Sabbaths, and idols in Leviticus 19:2–4 are based on the Decalogue.[21] He mistakes analogy for influence. He speaks first of how all the laws in Leviticus 19 resemble the Decalogue, but then of their dependence on it. The fact that two sets of rules share similar topics is no argument for one set's dependence on the other, especially when the rules in question deal with topics that recur frequently throughout biblical material. If the shared topics were of an arcane nature and were only found in these two places, there might be cause for considering a link other than resemblance. Weinfeld explains away the difference between the formulation of the rule about fearing parents in Leviticus 19:3 and the formulation about honoring them in the Decalogue by arguing that in Leviticus 19:3 one fears out of respect, and hence the verb meaning "to fear" (*yr'*) parallels the verb meaning "to honor" (*kbd*), because each rule fundamentally insists on respect.[22] I account for the difference in formulation by arguing that the rule in the Decalogue is a response to Cain's act of dishonoring his parents by killing their son Abel,[23] whereas the rule in Leviticus 19:3 concerns the issue of Joseph's arrogance. It is not a question of one lawgiver taking up an issue from another, but rather that the same method of formulating rules from different narrative sources applies in each instance.

Weinfeld's attempt to show that other rules in Leviticus 19 depend on the Decalogue reveals how strained his position is. He thinks that the rule about adultery in the Decalogue inspired what he thinks are similar rules in Leviticus 19:19–25, namely, laws about mixing kinds, intercourse with a slave girl, and even a law about uncircumcised fruit. He further claims that the rules about idols, the Sabbath, and parents in the Decalogue inspire the three rules in Leviticus 19:30–32 about Sabbaths, appealing to ghosts and soothsayers, and respect for an old man. (He puts "elderly" to suggest that both sexes are included, as in the rule about parents.) He speaks of the topics in the Decalogue recurring "with slight variation,"[24] but consultation with those expert in dealing with the dead is hardly a "slightly different" topic from the worship of idols.

LEVITICUS 19:4

Turn ye not unto idols nor make to yourselves molten gods: I am Yahweh your God.

With the topic of creation in focus, the lawgiver goes on to oppose the reliance on man-made gods. For him, the making of idols would be an affirmation of human beings as supreme creators, in opposition to God as creator. Joseph's dream necessitates this objection to the exaltation of humankind. Viewed from a religious perspective, the dreams are problematic because they exalt Joseph to godlike status (cp. Gen 44:18, 45:8).[25] In the story, *'alumim* ("sheaves," from *'alam; Piel*, "to bind"; *Niphal*, "to be dumb") bow down to another sheaf. In the rule, the Israelite is not to bow down to *'elilim* ("idols"; the etymology is uncertain but probably from *'al*, "nothingness"), possibly with the sense that they are dumb idols.[26] Aside from the possibility of wordplay, where *'alumim* influences the choice of the term *'elilim*,[27] in the first dream the sheaves behave like human beings, the sons of Israel, but they do not speak; nor does the sheaf that is the object of veneration. The dream conveys the idea of the veneration of a dumb object.

Although the molten gods in the rule recall Aaron's golden calf (Exodus 32), they especially recall Jeroboam's golden calves because of the plural designation. Jeroboam is a descendant of Joseph (1 Kings 11:26; *Genesis Rabba* on 37:6, 7). Aaron's molten calf is the earliest example of Israelite idolatry in the Pentateuch, and Jeroboam's activity represents the recurrence of the problem in a later generation. This recurrent feature explains the lawgiver's focus. The reason he turns to Aaron's and Jeroboam's activity, however, is that Joseph's other dream, in which the sun, moon, and stars bow down to him, similarly raises the issue of idolatry. Deuteronomy 4:15–19 prohibits the worship of the calf along with the worship of the sun, moon, and stars.[28] In his rule, then, the lawgiver takes into account successive developments in different generations regarding the topic of idolatry.

This kind of survey is a prime characteristic of his procedure. It is again detectable in the next rule, about peace offerings.

LEVITICUS 19:5–10

And if ye offer a sacrifice of peace offerings unto Yahweh, ye shall offer it for your acceptance. It shall be eaten the same day ye offer it, and on the morrow: and if any remain until the third day, it shall be burnt in the fire. And if it be eaten at all on the third day, it is abominable; it shall not be accepted. Therefore everyone that eateth it shall bear his iniquity, because he hath profaned the hallowed thing of Yahweh: and that soul shall be cut off from among his people.

And when ye reap the harvest of your land, thou shalt not wholly reap the corners of thy field, neither shalt thou gather the gleanings of thy harvest. And thou shalt not glean thy vineyard, neither shalt thou gather every grape of thy vineyard; thou shalt leave them for the poor and the sojourner: I am Yahweh your God.

What is the lawgiver doing? On the one hand, he finds that Joseph's dreams raise troublesome issues; on the other hand, he still views them as divinely inspired. The next two rules reveal this ambivalence. First, he will continue to focus on the issue of worship that a negative reading of the dreams raised; second, he will turn to the positive reading and focus on the harvest.

The lawgiver's interest in wrongful worship begins with the intimation of idolatry in Joseph's dreams and leads him to the earliest actual example of idolatry: when Aaron makes the golden calf. In particular, the lawgiver scans the history of worship involving Aaron and his family. The rule is about peace offerings, and it is notable that Aaron wrongfully offers them to the molten calf, whom he identifies as Yahweh (Exod 32:5). The tradition records two further problems to do with the wrongful worship of Yahweh in Aaron's family.

First, Aaron's sons Nadab and Abihu make a wrong offering ("strange fire") to Yahweh, and fire consumes them for the offense (Lev 10:1–3). And there is a subsequent, related incident when Moses complains about the failure of Aaron's other sons, Eleazar and Ithamar, to eat their proper due from the sin offering (Lev 10:16–20). No punishment follows for this offense. We might note in passing how the rules in Leviticus 10 are intimately tied into the narration of certain historical events.

The rules in Leviticus 19 are addressed to all the Israelites, to sons of Israel like Joseph and his brothers. Consequently, the lawgiver focuses on a cultic offense that involves not the priestly family of Aaron as such, but all Israelites who worship Yahweh. He therefore takes up, I suggest, an offense comparable to the failure of Aaron's two sons to treat sacred food in an appropriate manner. He does so in relation to the consumption of the peace offering because it is the only sacrifice involving both priests and laypersons.[29] Aaron's sons fail to consume sacred food in a sacred area, food only they can consume, and burn it instead. In the rule, the comparable offense is that the people consume sacred food at a time (on the third day after the sacrifice was offered) when it should be burned instead. Although the two brothers suffer no consequences when they offend, the rule lays down the penalty that those who eat the sacred food on the third day will be cut off from the community of Israel.

A humanitarian rule about leftovers from the annual harvest follows the cultic rule. Why should this be so? The reason is that both the cultic rule about the peace offering and the following rule about harvesting and gleaning stem from Joseph's dream about himself as a sheaf.[30] Immediately after Joseph's dream, his brothers, the other sheaves in the dream, do not bow down reverently to him. Quite the contrary, they humiliate him and he is sold into slavery in Egypt.[31] They slaughter an animal on the occasion, true, but they do so not to honor him but rather to cover up their getting rid of him. The narrative describes an unholy act of slaughter in relation to Joseph, who is the object of worship in the dream. As a consequence, Joseph is exiled. As I have just argued, the Priestly lawgiver, surveying related developments in Aaron's time, turns to proper slaughter in an act of worship. He then focuses on an unholy aspect of the worship, eating the sacrifice on the third day, which results in the worshipper being exiled from the community.

The harvest rule is also about food, but in this instance it is about providing for the poor and needy; therefore, apparently, the matter involves no sacred overtones. The rule, however, focuses on the consequence of the brothers' unholy act against Joseph. Joseph is cut off from his family (Jacob/Israel's family), but the agricultural policy he, inspired by Yahweh, puts into effect in Egypt brings relief from starvation to the needy (Gen 41:33–57). Just as the role of food in the Exodus story came to be commemorated in the sacred regulations of the Passover ceremony (Exodus 12), so this rule about provision of food for the needy looks back on Joseph's time in Egypt on behalf of both the Egyptian needy and those of his own family in need.

Joseph's dream about himself as the dominant sheaf of grain alludes to what is to come after he is sold abroad. His accurate prediction of successful harvests followed by failed ones leads to his appointment as overseer of food in Egypt.[32] When his brothers come to Egypt seeking grain, they acknowledge Joseph's dominance, just as his dream foretold (Gen 42:6, 43:26, 44:14). His elevation to power, however, comes only after he is forgotten in prison by the butler whose dream he interprets and who is asked to remember Joseph when he is released (Gen 40:23). Joseph is remembered only when Pharaoh's dreams need interpretation (Gen 41:9–14). He is like the forgotten sheaf in the Deuteronomic law: if the harvester remembers the sheaf, he gives it to the sojourner, the widow, and the orphan (Deut 24:19–22). The Deuteronomic rule commemorates Joseph's experience, sees how his harvest dream bridges the entire historical episode, and explicates its significance.[33]

The Priestly lawgiver takes over the Deuteronomic rule and similarly turns to its background in Joseph's life. The Priestly rule's reference to the poor is a typical attempt to categorize the two types cited in the Deuteronomic rule: the widow and the orphan. The Priestly lawgiver does not create the rule directly in relation to Joseph's story—that was the Deuteronomist's doing—and hence he removes its eccentric, impractical feature about the forgotten sheaf.

The Deuteronomic rule is impractical because the poor will obtain something from the harvest only if the owner of the field should happen to forget that he has left a sheaf standing in his field. This would probably not be a frequent, or even likely, occurrence. The Priestly rule, on the other hand, guarantees that the poor will receive food each year. If one is to assume that one lawgiver was aware of the other's rule, it seems obvious that the Priestly rule is the later formulation.

Yet Moshe Weinfeld claims that the Deuteronomic formulation is the more pragmatic one and came after the Priestly rule. His reasoning is difficult to fathom. As evidence of the more pragmatic character of the Deuteronomic rule, he states that Deuteronomy presents it "in a more tangible manner and, characteristically, adds a religious-moral justification."[34] Whatever this statement means, it is not an argument about pragmatism. Weinfeld further postulates that ancient magical beliefs explain why the Deuteronomic rule avoids giving a command about not cutting the corner of one's field (*pe'ah*). Supposedly (no evidence is cited), Deuteronomy reacted against the Priestly formulation because corners of fields were left uncut to appease the spirits of the fields and demons. The weakness of the arguments arises from Weinfeld's commitment to the theory that Deuteronomy came after the Priestly material.

LEVITICUS 19:11–12

Ye shall not steal, neither deal falsely, neither lie one to another. And ye shall not swear by my name falsely, neither shalt thou profane the name of thy God: I am Yahweh.

The preceding rules place the initial focus on how Joseph came to be cut off from his people. His brothers stole him (Gen 40:15). The next series of laws explores aspects of their theft, and also aspects of theft in the history of Jacob/Israel.

Like the Deuteronomic lawgiver, the Priestly lawgiver, dealing with the origin and history of the nation of Israel, seeks out the earliest example of a problem. The issue of theft involving brothers also arises in the generation previous to Joseph's when the original Israel (Jacob) steals the paternal blessing from his brother, Esau (Genesis 27). Esau's loss of the right of the firstborn son compares to Joseph's loss of sonship, particularly since Joseph's dreams portray him as the favorite son.

In order to carry out his theft, Jacob deals falsely with his father; he deceives blind Isaac with the clothes he wears when he brings him meat to eat. Jacob also lies about his identity when he claims to be Esau. There is a religious dimension to these two rules that the next rule brings out. In the commission of his theft, Jacob claims that Yahweh his God—both names are used—has granted him success because he quickly obtains meat to give to his father (Gen 27:20). This is a falsehood, the use of God's name to cover up a duplicitous action. The Priestly lawgiver thus produces the cluster of rules in Leviticus 19:11–12 in reaction to Jacob cheating Esau out of his birthright.[35]

LEVITICUS 19:13

Thou shalt not defraud thy neighbour, neither rob him: the wages of him that is hired shall not abide with thee all night until the morning.

Aspects of theft continue to dominate the lawgiver's interest. Two links with the previous focus on Jacob's theft of Esau's birthright are noteworthy. First, the preceding rule about false swearing focuses on Jacob profaning God's name in the commission of a theft. In the story on which the rule about defrauding a neighbor is based, Laban accuses Jacob of stealing his household gods (Gen 31:30). Depending on his point of departure, the lawgiver is proceeding forward (from Jacob with Esau to Laban with Jacob) or backward (from Joseph back to Jacob) through the history of the generations. In light of this strategy, the order of the rules does not depend on the order of the narratives.

Second, the story about the theft of the gods is part of a much wider issue. There is a claim and counterclaim about one party defrauding the other; Jacob claims that Laban defrauded him (Gen 29:25, 31:7, 41).[36] An important aspect of the story brings out the link to the preceding rules (stealing and the false use of Yahweh's name) and their background: Jacob's cheating his blind father meets with its own mirroring retribution when he in turn is cheated by his father-in-law, Laban. Instead of giving Jacob the younger daughter, Rachel, as his wife, Laban fraudulently substitutes the elder daughter, Leah, on the wedding night, when Jacob doubtless cannot see properly.[37] This act very closely mirrors Jacob's cheating his elder brother Esau out of the blessing of the firstborn son.[38]

Laban, Jacob claims, would have robbed (*gazal*, as in the rule) him of his wives, Rachel and Leah (Gen 31:31). In the preceding rule about stealing (Lev 19:11), the theft of a person is also the issue because the brothers' theft of Joseph was under review.

Jacob also accuses Laban of arbitrarily changing his wages many times (Gen 31:7, 41), which readily explains why a rule about the wages of a hireling follows—most oddly, it would appear—a rule about robbery.

LEVITICUS 19:14

Thou shalt not curse the deaf, nor put a stumbling block before the blind, but shalt fear thy God: I am Yahweh.

From a story in which a daughter treats her father with contempt by stealing his household gods (Gen 31:34–35), the lawgiver returns to an earlier instance of similarly contemptuous conduct—namely, a son's (Jacob's) treatment of his blind father (Isaac). Both actions concern the rights of children. The verb *qalal* in both Exodus 21:17 and Leviticus 20:9 has the same sense of treating someone with contempt, and in each rule the focus is abuse of a parent.[39] In Leviticus 19:14 the lawgiver uses the verb *qalal*, and again the issue is the abuse of a parent.

The lawgiver has picked up a topic from the narrative in focus, in this instance the contemptuous treatment of a parent. The choice is not arbitrary, however, because in his law about dealing falsely and lying (Lev 19:11) he had already come upon the topic of a son's contemptuous treatment of a father (Genesis 27). That similar conduct turns up in Rachel's treatment of her father impels the lawgiver to return to the earlier example and formulate a rule on the subject.

Why does the law address offenses against the deaf? Probably the lawgiver wanted to offer a parallel to the offense against the disability found in the story, blindness. Deafness and blindness are parallel disabilities in Exodus 4:11 and Isaiah 29:18, 35:5, 42:18, 19, and 43:8. The offense against Isaac involves both hearing and sight. For example, Isaac is the victim of his wife's eavesdropping. Jacob's theft of the right of the firstborn begins when Rebekah, overhearing her husband's plan to bless Esau, instructs Jacob on how to get Isaac's blessing instead. Hearing, therefore, plays a crucial role in the story: "Now Rebekah was listening when Isaac spoke to Esau his son. . . . Indeed I [Rebekah] heard your [Jacob] father speak to Esau your brother" (Gen 27:5, 6).

The lawgiver, however, probably focused on a specific subsequent aspect of Jacob's shocking treatment of his father. When Jacob appears before Isaac to receive the blessing from him, Isaac asks him who he is. Jacob replies that he is Esau, a lie that the preceding rule in Leviticus 19:11 prohibits. Isaac has to rely on his sense of touch to determine that it is Esau and not Jacob who stands before him. Isaac's hearing does function, since he thinks that the voice is Jacob's. Looking for an offense parallel to Jacob's manifest deception of his blind father, however, the lawgiver could find in Jacob's lie an example of someone abusing another's sense of hearing. The implication would be that Jacob thinks he can use his own undisguised voice with Isaac and still not be found out. Or, alternatively, one can infer that although Isaac hears sounds that he thinks he recognizes, he nonetheless has to try other, more dependable faculties such as touch and smell (Gen 27:27) to determine the reality. Whatever the lawgiver's assessment, this particular aspect of the narrative illustrates how a son contemptuously treats a father in both matters of hearing and sight.

The admonition in the rule, "Thou shalt fear thy God: I am Yahweh," is readily understood because, as with the rule in Leviticus 19:12, Jacob's treatment of his father involves the use of God's name to conceal cheating.

Jacob uses Esau's clothes and puts on animal skins in order to mislead his blind father. Jacob in turn will be deceived by Joseph's garment stained with animal blood (Gen 37:33).[40] The narratives themselves show an interest in the nature of justice, especially the variety now called poetic justice. Fraudulent conduct is thus the central issue behind the presentation of this rule about the deaf and the blind and the next rule.

LEVITICUS 19:15

Ye shall do no unrighteousness in judgment: thou shalt not respect
the person of the weak, nor honour the person of the mighty: but in
righteousness shalt thou judge thy neighbour.

Jacob's cheating causes his father to give the wrong judgment, to give
the right of the firstborn to him instead of to Esau. The Priestly lawgiver next pursues a particular feature made explicit in the narrative:
the contrast between the inferior, hairy hunter Esau and the superior,
smooth tent-dweller Jacob, and the father's partiality to the former and
the mother's to the latter. In other words, the topics of partiality and
the unequal standing of two parties show up in this tradition, just as
these topics are the joint concern of the law about unrighteousness
in judgment. A noteworthy issue in the struggle between Jacob and
Esau, aside from Jacob's chicanery, is whether or not Esau deserves
Isaac's bestowal of the birthright. Esau offends his parents by marrying
Canaanite women (Gen 26:34–35), unions that particularly distress his
mother (Gen 27:46). Although Isaac does admonish Jacob to avoid such
marriages (Gen 28:1), he presumably would still have given Esau the
birthright because his partiality for the game dishes Esau brings him
would have prevailed over all other considerations.

In the next generation, similar problems of unrighteousness in judgment recur with Jacob's sons. Just as Jacob the son manipulates his
father's judgment and causes him great anguish, so Jacob's own sons
settle their dispute with their brother Joseph in an outrageously unfair
way, bringing terrible anguish on their father. The brothers take it on
themselves to avenge the wrong Joseph did to them in reporting their
actions to Jacob (Gen 37:2). Their solution amounts to the theft of
Joseph, the topic that dominates so many of the lawgiver's preceding
laws. Joseph's dreams about his superior position as the top son further compound the brothers' dispute with him. As the head of the
family, Jacob should arbitrate disputes between his sons, but he is
biased in favor of Joseph.[41]

The brothers, with the exception of the elder son, Reuben, who is
responsible for Joseph's well-being in the absence of the father, heed

Judah's fundamentally unjust solution to their problem with Joseph. Judah proposes that they sell Joseph and thus avoid slaying their own flesh and blood (Gen 37:26–27). The appeal of the money, especially to sons not independent of their father, and the false kindness suggested by sparing Joseph's life, determine their support for Judah's solution.

Joseph presents himself to his brothers as someone who is high and mighty, but the lawgiver does not consider Joseph's superior standing, as revealed in his dreams, a reason to overlook his possible wrongdoing regarding the report about his brothers that he gave to his father. The fact that Jacob favors Joseph over his brothers indicates that Jacob might have overlooked Joseph's talebearing—the topic of the next law—had he moved to settle the dispute. The lawgiver draws out the wider issues that emerge in the history of the two generations: in matters of judgment, neither sympathy for someone's inferior standing nor the inclination to honor (hadar) the mighty should color one's judgment.[42]

The term hadar used in the sense of paying honor to a person is found in only three places: here; in Leviticus 19:32, where Judah is the focus of the lawgiver's concern; and in Exodus 23:3, where Judah and his brothers are the focus.[43] The noun hadar, "honor," is used by Moses in Deuteronomy 33:17 when he affirms Joseph's elevated status by referring to Joseph's firstborn son as a noble bull.

LEVITICUS 19:16

Thou shalt not go up and down as a talebearer among thy people:
neither shalt thou stand against the blood of thy neighbour:
I am Yahweh.

The issue under scrutiny is again Joseph's report about his brothers. Since only his side of the story is presented to Jacob, Joseph's report could be regarded as rumormongering.[44] The brothers respond to his report by conspiring to slay him (Gen 37:18).[45] In fact, they too decide to concoct a story: that a wild beast has devoured Joseph (Gen 37:20).

In other words, the brothers themselves are guilty of talebearing, including the false notion about Joseph's blood being shed by the beast. The curious language in the rule about standing against the blood of someone may refer to this aspect of Joseph's alleged fate. His brothers' attitude certainly reveals that they were "standing against the blood" of Joseph.

The lawgiver may also have considered the parallel development that occurs later, when Joseph attempts to get even with his brothers by putting out false stories about them, namely, that they are spies and thieves. These alleged offenses could cost them their lives (Gen 42:9–22, 44:1–17).

LEVITICUS 19:17

Thou shalt not hate thy brother in thine heart: thou shalt in any wise rebuke thy neighbour, and not carry sin concerning him.

The brothers hate Joseph (Gen 37:4). Instead of conspiring against him, however, they should have communicated their complaints to him, as their father did when he was offended by the arrogance of Joseph's dreams (Gen 37:10). Wise counsel calls for the reproof of a companion (Prov 9:8: "Rebuke a wise man, and he will love thee"; cp. Prov 19:25, 25:12, 28:23). The lawgiver judges that if such communication had taken place, Joseph's brothers might have avoided their subsequent offenses against him. Likewise, Joseph might not have resorted to falsely accusing them of being spies and thieves (Gen 42:9, 44:4–8). The difficult statement "Thou shalt not carry sin concerning him" may well express the problem of consequent wrongdoing, since the original issues that divided the brothers and Joseph are not taken up.[46]

The switch from the term *brother* to the term *neighbor* in the rule represents a common phenomenon in legal drafting, namely, a move from the particular to the more inclusive. The interesting aspect is that the particular focus on the brother in the rule comes from the spotlight on Joseph in the story.

LEVITICUS 19:18

Thou shalt not avenge, nor bear any grudge against the sons of thy
people, but thou shalt love thy neighbour as thyself: I am Yahweh.

The topic of retribution is central in the Joseph narrative under scrutiny. In this rule the lawgiver turns to Joseph's vengeance against the injustice done to him.[47] Joseph's motives are complex. While he certainly pursues vengeance against his brothers, visiting upon them precise retribution for their actions, he also shows deep affection for them (Gen 42:24, 43:30–31, 45:1–15). Inextricably tied in with Joseph's hounding of his brothers is his kind treatment of them. He is one of their own. In this narrative about hatred of a brother, he is portrayed as wanting nothing more than to be part of the family again. Emotions are very much on display. So the narrative is about vengeance and affection—the same odd combination in the law. It is not realistic in most situations to oppose vengeance and love at the same time. More realistic is Proverbs 27:6: "The kisses of an enemy are perfidious." The situation within Joseph's family, however, presents a coming together of the two emotions of vengeance and affection.

Why does the rule not follow the condemnation of vengeance and grudges with a simple "But thou shalt love thy neighbour"? Why add "as thyself," or, more accurately, "who is like thyself"?[48] The statement is not about self-love. It is about how Joseph as an Egyptian nevertheless treats the Hebrew visitors from the neighboring country of Canaan as kin, because he is indeed one of them. The lawgiver extrapolates from this historical episode the rule about loving one's neighbor who is like oneself: a son of Israel should deal with another son in the wider community of Israel as if he were a brother. In the wider community, one Israelite is a neighbor to the other. The language of the rule first prohibits avenging "the sons of Israel" and then talks of loving "thy neighbor." The exceptional situation of one Israelite's overlaid Egyptian identity brings out the fact that his relationship to these visiting Israelites is that of brother to brother. We have a prime example of how an odd, idiosyncratic development in a story prompts a rule.

My interpretation of the rules in Leviticus 19:2–18 (about twenty of them in sequence) coincides with my method of explaining the presentation of other legal material in the Pentateuch. If my method has merit, some aspects of the Pentateuch require more emphasis than they ordinarily receive. First, one must consider that the laws in the Pentateuch are embodied in a narrative history.[49] This integration of law and narrative is unique—comparative legal history provides no parallel—and it explains the singular formulation of the biblical legal material that I have outlined. Second, before imposing methods of historical inquiry on the Pentateuchal literature, scholars should consider the "historical" methods of the biblical authors. Both those who recounted the narrative histories and those who set down the laws exercised their historical imagination in creating their material. They usurped the authority of the figure of Moses, for example, and they had an intense interest in origins and recurring patterns of conduct throughout the generations. Third, the study of biblical law is the study of law before it took on the institutionalized character so familiar in the contemporary world; this observation also applies to other ancient bodies of law. The modern features so familiar to us were lacking in the ancient world. There was no formal lawmaking body, no professional jurists, no professional judges or prosecutors, no police force, no forensic science. Scholars should not be surprised if the characteristics of ancient law and the creation of law differ markedly from those of their modern counterparts. Ancient laws are more likely to partake of broader cultural features than our own legal culture does. The use of national epics in the creation of a body of law, as I am suggesting is the origin of the biblical law codes, is not so strange in light of the nonformal nature of law in biblical times.

3 Laws as Miniature Narratives

Proverbs are often condensed stories. The proverbial expression "Don't eat sour grapes" distills the essence of Aesop's "The Fox and the Grapes." Some biblical rules are not only inspired by developments in biblical narratives, they constitute proverblike encapsulations of the developments themselves. In a sense the injunctions are miniature narratives. I refer in particular to certain rules about forbidden mixtures that have long been a source of puzzlement—and indeed, almost in keeping with their contents, a source of much confusion (on my own part, for example). The rules are the following:

Deuteronomy 22:9–11: Thou shalt not sow thy vineyard with two kinds of seed: lest the whole yield be rendered taboo: the seed which thou hast sown and the produce of the vineyard. Thou shalt not plough with an ox and an ass together. Thou shalt not put on *shatnez*, wool and linen together.

Leviticus 19:19: Ye shall keep my statutes. Thy cattle thou shalt not breed with two kinds. Thy field thou shalt not sow with two kinds of seed. And a garment of two kinds, *shatnez* shall not come upon thee.

In an article entitled "Forbidden Mixtures," I argued that the Deuteronomic rules about forbidden mixtures (Deut 22:9–11) were not meant to be understood literally but were to be read as commentary, involving figurative language, on sexual matters in the Book of Genesis.[1] In that article I claimed that the Priestly writer (P) no longer understood the Deuteronomic (D) rules and was the first interpreter in the long history of Jewish law to make literal sense of them. I was mistaken. P understood the Deuteronomic rules very well.

I assumed what critical scholarship in general has assumed, that one should compare the Deuteronomic and Priestly rules as if D came first and P later, or vice versa; and that P adapted D's rules (or D adapted P's) to meet the changing circumstances of Israelite society.[2] This is too narrow an approach to the relationship between the two sets of rules. It is an approach, moreover, that is tied to a literal reading of the rules.

The difficulty with giving literal meaning to the rules about mixtures is illustrated by the continuing attempts of modern commentators to do so. They are not bothered by the fact that the ancient Israelites *did* crossbreed their animals, *did* sow mixed seeds in their fields, and *did* wear a mixture of cloths. Jacob's experiment with Laban's cattle presupposes the practice of crossbreeding animals (Gen 30:25–43). Mules existed (2 Sam 13:29, 18:9; 1 Kings 1:33, 18:5), so even different species were sometimes mated.[3] Different seeds were planted in the same field (Isa 28:25, cp. Cant 1:14). The Israelite priests wore wool and linen together.[4]

Among the views of modern interpreters we find, for example, the claims that the land would be impoverished more quickly if different kinds of seed were sown in the same piece of ground rather than rotating the crops; and that garments made from two different types of material produce static electricity in tropical climates and are consequently uncomfortable to wear.[5] Or that different threads in warp and woof would cause the different parts of the garment to shrink differently.[6] Arie Noordtzij states that the prohibition against plowing with the ox and the ass together was meant to prevent excessive strain on the weaker donkey.[7] If any of these factors applied, why would the rules, taken in a literal sense, even be necessary? Practical experience would largely take care of such matters. Moreover, why would the rules be part of the Deuteronomic or Priestly codes, which concern themselves with far weightier matters than agricultural and domestic practicalities?

Another widely accepted view of the rules concerning mixtures is that they offend against the ordering of nature as laid out in the creation story in Genesis 1.[8] "Creatures or things of one nature are not to be mixed with those having another."[9] Thus, wool from an animal should not be mixed with linen from vegetable fiber, and different species of animals should not be mated or used together to perform tasks. There are problems with this view as well. It is not clear, for example, how the sowing of different crops fits into it. Planting different kinds of seeds together on the same plot of land does not usually result in hybrid plants. There is a major problem about mating different species of animals, revealed by Martin Noth's comments. The idea that underlies the rule in Leviticus 19:19 about cattle (*behemah*) is, he claims, that union between heterogeneous stock is against the divine ordinance: "Concretely, the veto is directed against the pairing of different species of animal."[10] Does he really mean that implausible matings such as that of an ox with an ass or a cow with a sheep were the subject of legislation? The fact that Noth, like other commentators, then brings into his discussion the existence of mules in ancient Israel indicates that he does indeed believe that the lawgiver intends to interdict such bizarre pairings as ox with ass and cow with sheep. Why would the lawgiver bother to do so? Michael Fishbane similarly gets caught up in this kind of confusion. He sees that the mixed plowing in the Deuteronomic rule may (although he does not spell out the implications) refer to sexual activity and wonders whether the rule confines itself to oxen and asses or whether it includes all mixed plowing.[11]

The source of the confusion is the wrong assumptions that (1) these rules have to be read literally, (2) the Deuteronomic rules are extensions of the Priestly ones and help to explain them, and (3) the term *kil'ayim* used with regard to animals refers to two animal species rather than two varieties of the same species. If there was such remarkable sensitivity to differences in the natural world, and if combinations of categories were unacceptable, as most commentators imagine, we would then expect that vegetables could not be eaten with meat, and even that two kinds of vegetables could not be eaten together. We would also have to wonder why some combinations are ruled out and others receive no mention.

The true cause for puzzlement here is that commentators have been so ready to interpret these rules literally. If they were to come upon a rule in their own culture that one should not lie on a bed of nails, or a statement that a rolling stone gathers no moss, or, to come closer to the language of the biblical injunctions, that a criminal sentenced to hang must ride a horse foaled by an acorn, would they seek a literal meaning for the rule and accept the statement at face value? Their attempts to give meaning to the biblical material testify to the difficulty of understanding how a different culture chooses to express itself. If he gave up a literal reading of the rules, Gordon Wenham would not need to discuss the view that we go "from the sublime to the ridiculous" in switching from the rule about love of neighbor in Leviticus 19:18 to the rules about mixtures in Leviticus 19:19.[12]

In contrast with this literal approach, I believe that the rules about forbidden mixtures are like proverbs and represent clever, cryptic judgments on specific aspects of patriarchal history. I have already argued for this view in regard to the Deuteronomic rules. Thus Judah's attempts to increase the vine of (Jacob) Israel by using mixed seed—that is, by uniting his half-Canaanite–half-Israelite sons with the Canaanite Tamar (Genesis 38)—is under review in the Deuteronomic proverb-type rule against sowing two different kinds of seed in a vineyard. Judah's marriage with a Canaanite wife is under review in the Deuteronomic rule against plowing with an ox and an ass. This rule's formulation reflects a typical procedure of the biblical lawgivers. Like the narrators of the traditions, they consider similar developments over succeeding generations, past or future depending on their point of departure. In this instance, D goes back to the first occasion when the issue of a marriage between a Canaanite and a member of Jacob/Israel's family seriously arises, namely, when the Canaanite Shechem seduces Dinah and seeks to marry her (Genesis 34).[13] Shechem is the son of the Ass, Hamor, and he seduces (sexually plows, in the colloquial of the time) Dinah, the daughter of the Ox, Jacob/Israel (Gen 49:6).[14] The rule against putting on *shatnez*, wool and linen together, is a negative judgment on Judah, who on his way for his yearly supply of wool becomes involved with Tamar, who has disguised herself as a prostitute and wears the typical garb of that profession, which contained linen. In sum, the prospect of an Israelite daughter marrying a Canaanite, Judah's actual marriage to a Canaanite, his attempt to perpetuate his family line by sowing with different seeds and incorporating Canaanite blood, and his intercourse with a Canaanite cult prostitute are all reviewed in Deuteronomy.[15]

What sets the scene for the Priestly rules about prohibited mixtures are issues that arise not in the Judah story but in the Joseph story. The

Egyptians have rules against mixing with the Hebrews, and these trigger a comparable Israelite concern on the part of the Priestly writers. Thus both Deuteronomic and Priestly lawgivers give expression in their rules to the direction cited in Leviticus 18:3: the Israelites are to take stock of Canaanite and Egyptian influences and counter them. Both the Deuteronomic and the Priestly rules about forbidden mixtures serve to remind the Israelites of how their past experiences with Canaanites and Egyptians threatened their national identity. The narrative under review by Deuteronomy is Judah in Canaan (Genesis 38); the Priestly lawgiver is reviewing the narrative about Joseph in Canaan and Egypt (Genesis 37, 39–48)—the narrative into which Judah's history has been incorporated.[16]

In their review of this epic material both D and P did what we have always attributed to them, but to an extent not before realized. It has long been recognized that as literary editors they followed through on the doings of their ancestors' generations, laying out the successive histories, inventing some of them, seeking out parallel developments, and conveying, either by arrangement of the material or by comments integrated into the histories, moral and religious judgments. What has not been recognized is that their laws are an extension of this process. Their evaluative work with the narrative epics is both continued and extended, with the result that their law codes are separate compilations of legal and moral judgments. A striking aspect of their mode of working is that they did not revise narratives to bring them into line with their own judgments. By and large they allowed problems to stand and expressed, much more extensively than in their redactional activity, opposition or criticism in the laws. It is this fundamental link between the laws and the narratives of the Bible that accounts for the unique integration of law and narrative that is the Pentateuch, and also for the unique nature of biblical law. I know of nothing comparable in world legal literature to the compilation of the biblical law codes.[17]

P's rules about forbidden mixtures take up from the story of Joseph. Joseph becomes an Egyptian after being forcibly excluded from his own family. At the climax to his story, when he is about to reunite with his family, his Egyptian standing is such that he cannot, as a host normally would, eat with the visiting Hebrews, his brothers, because the Egyptian food laws prohibit it: "The Egyptians might not eat bread with the Hebrews; for that is an abomination unto the Egyptians" (Gen 43:32). The law in Leviticus 19:18 that precedes the Priestly rules on mixtures is about not avenging or bearing a grudge against the sons of one's people, about loving one's neighbor as (an Israelite like) oneself. The lawgiver has focused on Joseph and his brothers coming together in love and harmony after the hostility between them, and on the welcome disappearance of the distinction between the Egyptian Joseph and the Joseph who is the son of Israel.[18]

The Priestly lawgiver has the concern with Joseph's identity in mind when he takes up the Deuteronomic rules about contacts with a foreign group (the Canaanites) and forges parallel rules that have similar symbolic force, only this time in relation to Israel's experience in Joseph's Egypt. At the point in the narrative when Joseph and his brothers are sitting down to eat, whatever other factors are at play, Joseph presents the example of a Hebrew who has so lost his identity that he is unable to eat with fellow Hebrews. The scene is one among others that prompted P to compose certain proverb-type injunctions about incompatible mixtures that would bring to the attention of later Israelites the problem of retaining their national identity.

We can observe with some precision how, as regards both their substance and their sequence, the lawgiver worked with the Genesis narrative in setting down his rules. All critics agree that a major Priestly insertion into the Joseph story occurs in Genesis 46. The climax to the Joseph story comes in Genesis 45, when Joseph, reconciled with his brothers, requests that they bring his father down to Egypt. In Genesis 46 a broader perspective shows up. Israel's (Jacob's) role in relation to the larger patriarchal history and future history in Egypt comes into prominence. Jacob's deity, the God of his father, Isaac, communicates with him about the future of his people in Egypt (vv. 1–5). This divine communication may be pertinent to the fact that, unlike the surrounding rules in Leviticus 19, the Priestly lawgiver expressly indicates here that his three rules about mixtures are divine ordinances ("Ye shall keep my statutes"). As we shall shortly observe, these rules take up specific issues in the narrative material that immediately follows Genesis 46:1–5.

In Genesis 46:6–27 comes the Priestly contribution: how the family of Israel take their cattle and the possessions they acquired in Canaan and come to Egypt, "Jacob and all his seed" (vv. 6, 7). The term *seed* (*zera'*), as is common, refers to Jacob's offspring. The Priestly rule employs the verb *zara'*, "to sow seed." The Priestly narrator gives precise details as to who these offspring are, and in verse 26 refers to sixty-six bodily descendants of Jacob ("who came from his loins") who come down to Egypt. Since Joseph and his sons, Manasseh and Ephraim, by his Egyptian wife Asenath (v. 20) are already in Egypt, P provides a separate notice about them. Including Jacob himself, the total number of the house of Jacob "which came into Egypt was seventy."[19]

Cattle Breeding

After this Priestly insertion in Genesis 46:6–27, the narrative resumes the description of the brothers' occupation as cattlemen in Egypt, telling how "every shepherd is an abomination unto the Egyptians" (Gen 46:34). Then, when Jacob and his family eventually meet Pharaoh, the latter requests—curiously because of Egyptians' dislike for shepherds—that some of them oversee his own cattle (Gen 47:6).

P's rule against breeding two different kinds of cattle—it corresponds to the Deuteronomic rule against plowing, in the sexual sense, with an ox and an ass—is in this case not a sexual metaphor at all. It takes up the issue of the Israelite cattlemen in their dealings with the Egyptians. Occupation is a potent indicator of identity, and these sons of Jacob are specifically identified as "men of cattle" (Gen 46:32, 34). Since the Hebrew brothers have cattle of their own, Pharaoh's request that they oversee the Egyptian cattle means that a mixing of breeds is to be expected. The interbreeding of the Israelite and Egyptian cattle represents the merging of the newcomers into the host nation. The example of this potential development in Egypt prompted the Priestly lawgiver to set down an injunction against interbreeding two kinds of cattle.[20] Exactly how the rule was to be understood will be considered shortly. Its aim was to reinforce Israelite resistance to foreign influences. The attitude is doubtless in the spirit of the one expressed in Leviticus 18:3: "After the doings of the land of Egypt, wherein ye dwelt, shall ye not do . . . neither shall ye walk in their ordinances."[21]

Many exegetes, as Claus Westermann points out, think that the Egyptians' distaste for shepherds must refer to non-Egyptian nomads.[22] If this is correct, then Pharaoh's invitation to Joseph's brothers to have them settle on the land and supervise his animals is an invitation for them to overcome the stigma and become Egyptian. The Genesis narrative itself would thus indicate an important change of identity undergone by Joseph's brothers.

Mixed Seed

The Genesis narrative (Gen 47:13–26) next focuses on Joseph's own occupation. In order to feed the Egyptians, he exchanges corn for, first of all, the people's money, then for their animals, and then for themselves and their land. After this, Joseph arranges to give them seed to sow the land so that in the future they will have food, and Pharaoh will have a portion of what they sow and harvest. P has noted this description of Joseph's occupation and has taken stock of the fact that, just as his brothers face the prospect of merging into Egyptian society, Joseph has already done so. He married an Egyptian woman and produced seed by her in the sense of progeny (Gen 48:4, 19).

Most noteworthy is that the narrative itself goes from the topic of Joseph's dispensing agricultural seed to the topic of his own "seed" by Asenath. Thus Genesis 47:27–48:22 describes how Jacob at the end of his life incorporates Asenath's two children into his own family on an equal standing with his own sons. Their names, Manasseh and Ephraim, actually bring out the concerns that P expresses in his rule. The name Manasseh means "For God hath made me forget all my toil, and all my father's house" (Gen 41:51). This name brings out Joseph's loss of connection with his previous identity as a member of Jacob's family. The name Ephraim means "For God hath caused me to be fruitful in the land of my affliction" (Gen 41:52) and brings out the fact that Joseph has put down roots—sown a field, in the language of the Priestly law—in a new cultural setting.

P sets down his rule about mixed seed in response to this development in Joseph's family life: among the seventy bodily descendants of

Jacob are some of mixed seed. The rule is consequently figurative and very similar to the Deuteronomic rule about the vineyard, which refers to Judah's sons by his Canaanite unions. These sons are actually cited in Genesis 46:12 (cp. v. 10). The "field," like the "vineyard," stands for the fruit-bearing capacity of the house of Jacob/Israel.[23] Like the vineyard and the garden, the field is, for example, a figure "for the female reproductive apparatus."[24] From the lawgiver's perspective, Jacob's field consists of Jacob with his wives, and his sons with their wives in their seed-producing capacity. In Genesis 46:15, 18, 22, and 25 it is noteworthy that P lists the offspring according to the matriarch with whom they are associated in his genealogical list.[25] With Joseph's contribution from Asenath, foreign seed is mixed in with the other seed. From P's later perspective, some such negative assessment of the Genesis narrative lies behind the formulation of his rule about mixed seed.[26]

Mixed Garment

The next rule, about the garment of two kinds, takes us to a facet of Joseph's integration into Egyptian society that is bound up with his marriage to Asenath. The result is that P presents a rule parallel to D's rule about *shatnez*. D's rule pinpoints how Judah, on his way to collect his yearly supply of wool, lies with Tamar, who has disguised her identity by changing out of her widow's clothes into those of a prostitute—indeed, those of a Canaanite cult prostitute. Prostitutes typically attracted their clients by donning a linen costume. The proverb-type rule expresses Judah's encounter with Tamar. He puts her on sexually, as one puts on a garment.[27] It is a mixing of wool and linen. P in turn looks at Joseph's sexual life—he has just done so in formulating his rule about mixed seed—and how it brings out the issue of his, and hence Israelite, identity. Remarkably, in the Joseph story wool and linen again prove to be key elements in the issue of identity.

The lawgiver works with the Genesis narrative in the following way. Joseph's stewardship of the Egyptian agricultural resources concludes with his decree that the Egyptians have to give Pharaoh a fifth part of the produce of the seed that Joseph has given to them (Gen 47:26). The narrative then describes how Joseph's sons are incorporated into the family of Israel, which brings the lawgiver to set down his prohibition of mixed seed. Joseph's decree about the tax on the land has its precedent in the tax that he established to cope with the earlier problem of the famine (Gen 41:34). The lawgiver typically returns to such precedents and notes that it is because Pharaoh approves of Joseph's initial tax policy that Joseph is received into Egyptian high society. Since this reception involves Pharaoh giving Joseph a wife, and since the lawgiver has just been concerned with Joseph's children by her, he turns back from the issue of the incorporation of Joseph's mixed seed into the family of Israel to the issue of the incorporation of Joseph into Egyptian society.

Joseph's wife, Asenath, is the daughter of an Egyptian priest. Her link to a foreign temple recalls the text in Genesis 38:21, 22, which describes Tamar as a cult prostitute. Joseph's union with Asenath is an important part of his Egyptian identity. The text relates how Pharaoh first changes Joseph's name to an Egyptian one and then gives him a wife (Gen 41:45).[28] Immediately before this development Pharaoh "arrayed him in fine linen" (Gen 41:42). Joseph's coat played a major role in the acquisition and loss of an elevated status within his family. His new linen garb betokens that his status is again an elevated one, but this time as an Egyptian.[29]

The Priestly equivalent of the Deuteronomic rule again drops the sexual metaphor, as did P's rule about cattle in relation to D's rule about the ox and the ass. The Joseph narrative determines P's formulation. A key element is a tantalizing notice in Genesis 46:34. That text raises the possibility that, just as in the Deuteronomic law, so in the Priestly law, not just foreign linen (in the form of Joseph's attire as Pharaoh's top official) but wool too played a role in P's thinking. Commentators puzzle over the reference that "every shepherd is an abomination unto the Egyptians" (Gen 46:34). It is Joseph who communicates this information to his father's household, and he is referring to his brother Israelites' trade. Note how, as in the rule about crossbreeding cattle, the focus is on the occupation of the brothers, just as Joseph's linen garment indicates his official occupation.

The Egyptian abhorrence of shepherds would not have extended to the products of sheep—for example, wool—because the Egyptians had their own flocks and herds (Gen 47:17; Exod 9:3). Their abhorrence, it appears, extended only to non-Egyptian nomadic shepherds. It follows that the opposition in the Joseph story is between linen as an indicator of Egyptian societal status and wool as an indicator of Israelite societal status. This contrast brings out the clash between Joseph's Egyptian identity, symbolized by his linen dress, and the brothers' Hebrew one, symbolized by their dealing in wool. What is also brought out—in fact, it will be the primary contrast—is the clash between Joseph's previous identity as a member of Jacob's shepherding family, when he was favored with a special garment, and his new identity as a member of the Egyptian ruling class in his distinctive linen garment.

P's alertness to such a conflict of identity is what underlies his injunction about a garment of two kinds. For P, the type of clothing an Israelite wears proclaims his identity, and with Joseph's Egyptian garb particularly in mind, he prohibits the mixing of foreign attire with native in order symbolically to maintain Israelite identity uncompromised.[30] The prophet Zephaniah predicts dire punishment for those in Judah of high status who dress in foreign attire (Zeph 1:8): "The garments they [the upper class] wear reveal the nature of their ideal. They do not hesitate to surrender their distinctive national characteristics in their desire to make themselves and the nation one with the neighbouring peoples."[31]

The foreign term *shatnez* in the Deuteronomic law probably designates a prostitute, because the linen clothing she uses to attract clients identifies her ("A sweet disorder in the dress/Kindles in clothes a wantonness").[32] It is common for a distinctive item of clothing to convey a person's identity; for example, *sans-culotte,* Brown Shirt, high hat, hard hat. Even a general term such as *skirt* can designate a woman (Deut 23:1; Ruth 3:9; Ezek 16:8).[33] In the Deuteronomic law we should read: "Thou [the Israelite] shalt not put on [sexually] *shatnez* [the linen-bedecked prostitute], wool [emblematic of the Israelite] and linen [emblematic of the prostitute] together." In the Priestly law the term *shatnez* refers to the foreign linen garment that is put on Joseph and conveys the notion of undesirable foreignness. We should read the second half of the Priestly law as unfolding the meaning of the first half: "A garment of two kinds—*shatnez* [foreign linen dress] shall not come upon thee [whatever the Israelite is wearing]."[34] The *shatnez* worn by an Israelite like Joseph betokens an unacceptable dual identity.[35] By relating the Deuteronomic and Priestly rules about *shatnez* to respective issues in the narratives, we can do what no interpreter has accomplished before, namely, we can account for the significant differences in the formulation of each rule.

It is important to stress the proverbial nature of the rule. Like many a proverb, its abbreviated language is for the purpose of putting the hearer into a reflective mode, and the second half of the sentence is intended to illumine the first half. The rule's odd content is also an integral feature of its makeup. Presumably, in ordinary life there was nothing untoward about mixing materials in clothing. The idea that there was something wrong about it would occasion surprise. Hence, a prohibition on mixing two materials is intended to puzzle. What enlightens the hearer is the use of the foreign word *shatnez*. In the Deuteronomic law the word conveys the use of linen to elevate a foreign woman to the peak of sexual attraction for an Israelite, while in the Priestly law the word conveys the use of linen to elevate an Israelite to high standing in a foreign land. The lawgiver uses the foreign word to indicate that he is raising the issue of national identity. Had a standard Hebrew word been used instead, the meaning would not have been conveyed and the result would have been puzzlement.[36]

How are we to understand the rules about prohibited mixtures? All three prohibitions are, in fact, arresting in nature. Not to appreciate this feature is to lose the significance of what they communicate. If the rules had prohibited animals (of the same species) from crossbreeding, a field from being sown with different seeds, and clothing from comprising different materials, they would have prohibited ordinary, sensible usage. Their appearance of denying standard practice is what makes them arresting. The rules' intended meaning lies in the language used. Thus the special term *kil'ayim*—only two, not three or more—plus the foreign word *shatnez* would make the hearer realize that the lawgiver is evoking a particular set of circumstances, in this instance the experience of an Israelite in Egypt.[37] In light of that past situation, the Israelite hearer would see that involvement in foreign ways could compromise his cultural and ethnic identity.

How are we to understand the reception of these rules about prohibited mixtures? Critical scholarship rightly distinguishes between two audiences when reading the texts in question. First there is the fictional audience about to enter a new land to which Moses addresses these rules. This audience of Israelites was close in time to the previous situation in Egypt and probably still remembered what had happened there. Consequently, they should have been able to understand the rules in the soon to be acquired land of Canaan.

These rules, however, are not in fact from Moses, but from some later lawgiver, and they are addressed to an audience unknown to us. This lawgiver's Israelite audience was centuries removed from the first-time entry into Canaan, and the rules would consequently strike the hearers as odd. But it is precisely the effect of startling the hearer that the lawgiver aims for. This actual audience had to identify itself with the fictional audience addressed by Moses and consequently become familiar with its situation and history. The rules elicited reflection and made the hearer perceive that they encode historical messages, in this instance, about problems of Israelite identity in the past. The Israelites who were now long settled in the former land of Canaan were therefore to pay regard to threats to their national identity in their current lives. Or alternatively, and more likely, if the historical setting of this audience was in fact the one in exile in Babylon, then all the more appropriate to remind it of past problems of Israelite identity in a host foreign nation.

4 Incest in the Bible

The topic of incest occasions surprise in unexpected ways. It is not much matter for comment to find the topic turning up with increasing frequency in films and fiction. It is, however, surprising to find, if James Twitchell of the University of Texas at Austin is correct, that there are undertones of father-daughter incest in advertisements by such well-known companies as Pepsico and the Metropolitan Insurance Company.[1]

The Bible contains its own surprises when it comes to the topic of incest. In a very real sense, a central tradition in the Old Testament and a major, arguably the major, religious doctrine in the New Testament condone incest. Consider the case cited by Paul in 1 Corinthians 5.[2] A man is living with his stepmother, his father's wife. Probably the father died or divorced her. Paul condemns the union in question, but it has to be pointed out that in doing so he counters a fundamental Christian doctrine, re-creation. His condemnation should not conceal the underlying religious belief that prompted the couple's relationship. Two features of the situation occasion surprise.[3] First, Paul says that not even the pagan world permits marriage to a stepmother; second, and most remarkable, the Corinthians he is writing to are very proud of this couple's union. They are "puffed up" about it. Why should that be?

Certain Christians tried in Lyons and Vienne in the second century were charged with "Oedipodean intercourse."[4] Church historians dismiss the accounts as malicious slander against the Christians. They are wrong. The same profound religious doctrine underlies these incestuous unions and the one between the son and stepmother in Corinth.[5] The doctrine in question states that a person who becomes a Christian undergoes a passage from death to life. He or she is a new creation, newborn in such a real sense that no longer is he or she the same person. All the person's old relationships are dissolved. So, for example, if a brother and his sister convert, they are no longer brother and sister and are free to marry.

The belief in rebirth is one that Paul took from the Judaism of his time. In his day, a person who converted to Judaism was considered newly born. The new birth was taken so seriously that the law of inheritance, for example,[6] was affected. In regard to marriage, however, the Rabbis introduced a restriction that disallowed unions contrary to Gentile law and morality, and several incestuous unions were banned as a result. The Rabbis' reasoning was that the outside world might not appreciate the miracle of new birth, for so they regarded it, and would judge Jews to be lax in sexual matters if unions prohibited by the surrounding culture took place. The Jewish leadership did not want that kind of response from Gentiles.

When Paul says that not even the Gentiles permit the union that the couple in the Corinthian church has contracted, he is applying the same restriction. The Pauline position is that the church has to put up with second best: the couple having become newborn, and therefore no longer stepmother and son, must nonetheless avoid marriage. Fundamentally, they are free to marry, but consideration for the milieu in which they find themselves, the dictates of public policy and public relations, rule it out. The Corinthian community's failure to understand the limitations on their newfound freedom was as damnable as gross incestuous intercourse under the old law. Paul excommunicated the offending couple.[7]

There are traditions in the Old Testament that might well have been viewed at some point as, potentially at least, offering a license for incestuous unions. I refer to the remarkable number of liaisons between close kin in the early narratives of the Bible. For example, in the Books of Genesis and Exodus the daughters of Lot produce sons by their father; Abraham marries his half-sister Sarah; Jacob marries two sisters who are his first cousins; Nahor marries his niece (that is, his brother's daughter); Judah's daughter-in-law, Tamar, seeks a remedy for her childless state by having intercourse with her father-in-law; Moses' father marries his aunt (that is, his father's sister). In 2 Samuel 13,

David's daughter, Tamar, tells her half-brother, Amnon, who is sexually harassing her, that he should go to their father so that King David can find a proper way by which the two siblings can marry.

Abraham, Jacob, Judah, Moses, and David were outstanding figures in Israelite tradition. It surely mattered that the issue of incest arose with them. My contention is that it mattered very much. The patriarchs' incestuous involvements are the key to the case I will make for a new way of understanding how the incest rules of Leviticus 18 and 20 came to be formulated. Let us note right away that these rules treat the relationship that Abraham has with Sarah, the union of brother and half-sister, as incest, hence too the relationship that Tamar discusses with Amnon. A relationship with a daughter-in-law is ruled out. So too is marriage to two sisters while both are alive. These Levitical rules also prohibit the union that Moses' own parents contracted, namely, between a man and his aunt. On the other hand, the lists do not prohibit a union between first cousins or a union between a man and his niece.

A pressing question is this: How do we relate the rules about incest in the legal parts of the Bible to what occurred among the founding fathers of the nation? The biblical lawgiver justifies the rules by saying that the Israelites must not imitate the practices of the Egyptians and the Canaanites. All later commentators have readily accepted these reasons. One must wonder, however, were the compilers of the rules not aware of the conduct of some of their ancestors? I shall return to this question.

But first I raise a general question: Why are there rules barring incest at all? Alas, there are no ready answers. Today we know that incest can lead to defective offspring, but no ancient source has much to say about that. If the ancients had known of a causal connection between incest and defective children, surely they would have used it in support of their rules. They did not, so I think we can rule out any awareness of genetics as relevant to the origin of incest rules.[8]

The Bible does provide an indication as to why some incest laws might exist. Consider again the story of Amnon's violation of his half-sister Tamar (2 Samuel 13). His deed so enrages Tamar's full brother, Absalom, that Absalom has Amnon slain. What motivates Absalom to take such extreme revenge for his brother's misdeed? After all, it appears that Amnon could have married his sister if he had gone about it in the proper way—namely, by speaking to their father, King David.

One major reason to prohibit incest is to ensure that family life is as sexually unimpassioned as possible. Otherwise, violence of the kind that Absalom inflicted on Amnon is the likely outcome. The potential for violence is well brought out by an incident in the Book of Genesis. Jacob's oldest son, Reuben, lies with one of his father's wives. This situation draws to our attention the peculiar problems that may come up when polygamy is practiced. In a polygamous setup, when a father takes a new wife, a son by a previous wife may be about the same age as the new wife (though this consideration does not apply with Reuben). In ancient Mediterranean society there was little social mixing of the sexes, and it cannot surprise that a son might have conceived a desire for his father's new wife. To permit the two men to compete for her sexual favors is a recipe for violence. We can be fairly sure that the prevention of such conflicts constitutes one powerful reason for some incest rules.[9]

But let us return to the question of incest and the fathers of the nation Israel. How do we square the incest rules in the Bible with some of the relationships that existed among these revered ancestors? The view generally adhered to is that we have to reckon with historical development. A relationship that was acceptable in one period was not acceptable at a later time.

My view is different. I see a direct link between patriarchal sexual conduct and the existence of the incest rules in Leviticus 18 and 20. The reason for the link is that the Priestly lawgivers disapproved of what they found in some of their nation's traditions on the grounds that these traditions condoned incestuous relationships. I do not hold that biblical laws reflect the social history of the times when they were formulated, the standard assumption among scholars who interpret biblical laws.[10] Instead, I believe that the laws take up issues that appear in the stories and legends in, for example, the Book of Genesis. My assumption is that the biblical lawgivers set out to tackle the ethical and legal problems they encountered in their reading of these tales. Biblical laws consequently constitute commentary on matters arising in the national folklore. I shall come back to the notable fact that the lawgivers lash out at the Egyptians and the Canaanites for incestuous practices but not at their own ancestors who did the same things.

I first turn to the lists of incest rules in Leviticus 18 and 20 in order to draw attention to some of their peculiar features. It is puzzling, for example, to find that a prohibition—the first in the list—against a son's violation of his father or his intercourse with his mother should be set down at all. By and large, lawgivers addressing societal problems are not motivated to set down in writing what no one questions, just as no university has rules stating that those giving lectures should not come dressed in spacesuits.[11] Everyone takes for granted that relationships such as a son with his father or a son with his mother are forbidden. They are so taboo that they do not even come to consciousness, except, for effect, to modern filmmakers. Yet we find this peculiar formulation at the head of a list of incest prohibitions.

The list contains no express prohibition against intercourse with a full sister. Nor is there a prohibition against intercourse with a son or a daughter—that is, where the father, not the child, is the target of the prohibition. We must take this seriously and ask why the initial rule is addressed to the child of a family as though he, or she, would be the instigator of an incestuous liaison.[12] After all, the sexual abuse of a son or daughter by a parent (or a sister by a brother) is much more likely in the world of experience at any time.[13] No one, so far as I am aware, has bothered to ask why the child and not the parent is the target of this particular rule. The concern with a child who initiates an incestuous liaison and the lack of any rule about more commonly occurring liaisons within a family suggest that the usual attempt to read these rules against the social practice of ancient Israel is the wrong approach to understanding them.

Yet another problem in studying the biblical incest rules is that mixed in with them are rules that have nothing to do with incest; for example, rules about a marriage to two sisters while each is alive, sex with a menstruating woman, adultery, child sacrifice, homosexuality, and bestiality.

Another puzzle is the arrangement of topics in the series of rules. We have to ask whether it really is the case that additions over time can account for the seemingly disorganized arrangement of the rules in Leviticus 18, although it is easy to understand why this view has become so embedded in scholarly approaches. Two rules about intercourse with a half-sister, one rule more general than the other, are separated by a rule prohibiting intercourse with a granddaughter. A rule about the worship of Molech seems out of place in a series of rules involving sexual offenses.[14] And how do we explain the sequence menstruation, adultery, and then Molech worship?[15] Can we solve these problems without resorting to the assumption that biblical scribes went in for redactions of existing lists of rules unaware that their insertions and additions were so badly done? I believe we can, if we bear in mind the process of legal formulation that I have described in accounting for the unique integration of law and narrative that is the Pentateuch.

Once we recognize the link between the rules in Leviticus 18 and certain narratives in the Book of Genesis the puzzling structure and formulations of the rules are not puzzling at all. The reason why the prohibition about sexual relations with parents is the first in the series in Leviticus 18, and why it was formulated at all, is because legends in the Book of Genesis determined the lawgiver's concerns. Moreover, because the Levitical rules were formulated as a reaction to what went on in these legends, and not to what went on in ordinary life, it becomes understandable why many of the rules strike us as implausible. There is, for example, in Leviticus 18:17 a quite extraordinary rule against a man's having a relationship with three different generations of women: a woman, her daughter, and her granddaughter.

Interpreters do draw attention to the fact that patriarchal history provides examples of unions that are prohibited by the incest laws of Leviticus 18 and 20,[16] but they do not go far enough in their observations. If, as is universally agreed, the Priestly (P/H) writer not only knew but worked with the ancient traditions of his people that are contained in the Pentateuch, it can occasion no surprise that much, to him, objectionable behavior became the focus of his concern. It is precisely this kind of analytical and critical response to his sources—largely Genesis, but also Exodus—that accounts for both his setting down the rules in Leviticus 18 and the order in which he arranged them. After all, many of the relationships cited in Genesis and Exodus involve kinship ties.

After presenting my analysis of some rules in Leviticus 18, I shall address a few of the other puzzling features about them. H—the designation commonly used for Leviticus 17–26 (the Holiness Code) or its redactor—first takes up three examples of incestuous or near incestuous conduct in primeval and patriarchal times, and then responds to both actual and hypothetical situations involving incest or related sexual matters posed by the stories about Abraham, Isaac, Jacob, and Judah. Although he gives no reasons for his assessment, Malcolm Clark is correct to characterize Leviticus 18–20 as "a purely ideal literary construct without institutional realization."[17]

LEVITICUS 18:6, 7

None of you shall approach to any that is near of kin to him, to uncover their nakedness: I am Yahweh. The nakedness of thy father, or the nakedness of thy mother, shalt thou not uncover; she is thy mother; thou shalt not uncover her nakedness.

The two earliest incidents of incestuous conduct in the Book of Genesis involve drunkenness, first Noah's and then Lot's. The two incidents have much in common: the role of wine, the initiative toward the parent from the son or daughter taking advantage of the drunken father, and the concern with future generations. The lawgiver looks at the two incidents together and uses them to set down the first rule of his series of rules on incest.

The first incident in the Bible that raises the issue of incestuous conduct is Ham's offense against his father, Noah (Gen 9:20-27).[18] Ham looks upon Noah's nakedness and informs his two brothers, Shem and Japheth, who carefully walk backward and cover their father with a garment. When Noah finds out that Ham has violated him (in some way that is not clear to us), he curses Ham to a life of enslavement to his brothers. Whatever the precise nature of the offense,[19] the Priestly lawgiver uses the incident to reflect on the potential sexual offense of a son against his father.[20]

The second incident pertinent to the rule occurs when Lot's daughters get their father drunk and lie with him in order to produce offspring by him. The lawgiver sets down the equivalent male offense, a son's intercourse with his own mother. This move on the part of the lawgiver is an example of how the link between a rule and a narrative can be of an indirect nature.

The rules are addressed to males, but we should be alert to the distinct possibility that in certain instances the masculine second-person pronoun, "thou," may include the feminine.[21] I am claiming that the lawgiver moves from Noah's situation, in which a son offends against his father, to Lot's situation, in which daughters offend against their father. There is thus considerable merit in reading the first part of the rule about the father to include an offense by either a son or a daughter. The language of the law is most appropriate if the lawgiver is considering the two offenses in the legends together. Ham looks upon a father's nakedness, and Lot's daughters uncover their father's nakedness. In expressing an offense against a father in terms of nakedness, the lawgiver encapsulates both offenses well. I think it likely that the use of the expression "to uncover nakedness" in the sense of sexual intercourse came first from the Priestly writer's focus on these two incidents.

If the language of the rule includes a daughter, then we have a rule prohibiting a daughter from instigating a relationship with a father. Ordinarily, it is the father's sexual advances on a daughter that are the problem; but no such formulation is found in the code.[22] The story about Lot's daughters would account for the reverse formulation in this rule.[23]

The rule gives more attention to an offense against a mother than to an offense against a father. The increasingly common attempt to read the rule as solely about sexual violation of a mother has doubtless been encouraged by the emphasis on her in the rule's formulation. The reason for the bias may well be the fact that in the narratives, the offense against the father is not in doubt, it is spelled out. In making a rule, however, the lawgiver has to postulate a corresponding offense against a mother. It is important to emphasize that the lawgiver uses the tradition less to condemn conduct described in it—after all, the tradition itself takes care of the obvious offense—than to bring out analogous conduct. The relationship between the law and the narrative is not a slavish one-to-one correspondence. It is rather a sensible exploration of the pertinent issues that the narrative raises.

LEVITICUS 18:8

The nakedness of thy father's wife shalt thou not uncover: it is thy father's nakedness.

The lawgiver takes up another offense from the patriarchal history. Reuben, Jacob's oldest son, lies with his father's concubine Bilhah. Again, as in the legends about Noah and Lot, the child violates a parent, in this instance a stepmother. (Leah is Reuben's mother.) The lawgiver generalizes from this patriarchal incident to include any wife of the father, even if the father has divorced his wife or is dead. The rule readily follows the previous one because in it the focus is also a father's wife, specifically, a man's own mother. The reason why the lawgiver would set down the offense even though it is explicitly cited in Genesis 35:22 is that from his point of view Jacob's condemnation is too mild. All the text says is that Jacob heard about it. Only at the end of Jacob's life does Reuben learn of a negative consequence, namely, that he has lost the right of the firstborn (Gen 49:4). The comparable rule in Leviticus 20:11 lays down a death sentence, as does Jubilees 33:1–17, whose author links both rule and story and raises the issue of Reuben's not receiving a capital sentence.

The rule describes the son's intercourse with the wife of his father as an uncovering of the father's nakedness. This focus on the father in the rule, and not on the stepmother, may well come from Reuben's father's own description of the incident. Jacob tells Reuben that it is against him that Reuben has offended when at the end of his life he assembles his sons together and addresses each in turn. In speaking to Reuben he takes up the matter of Reuben's sexual offense, but, interestingly, states it in a way that makes it appear that Reuben violated him. Thus Jacob says, "Thou wentest up to thy father's bed; then defiledst thou it: he went up to my couch" (Gen 49:4).[24] Jacob does not refer to the fact that a woman was involved.

In switching from the earliest history of the biblical ancestors to Reuben's escapade, the lawgiver typically ranges over the history of the generations. Where he finds a comparable example in a later generation, he will switch to that example, then return to the chronological sequence of events.

LEVITICUS 18:9–11

The nakedness of thy sister, the daughter of thy father, or daughter of thy mother, whether she be born at home, or born abroad, even their nakedness thou shalt not uncover. The nakedness of thy son's daughter, or of thy daughter's daughter, even their nakedness thou shalt not uncover: for theirs is thine own nakedness. The nakedness of thy father's wife's daughter, begotten of thy father, she is thy sister, thou shalt not uncover her nakedness.

The next three rules pose a very obvious puzzle. There is first a prohibition against intercourse with a half-sister, either a daughter of the same father or a daughter by the same mother from a previous marriage. There is next a prohibition against a man's relationship with a granddaughter. The third prohibition is again intercourse with a half-sister, this time more narrowly defined: she and her brother have the same father but a different mother.

Why would a lawgiver set down the same prohibition about a brother and a half-sister almost side by side? Why too, for that matter, does a rule about a man and his granddaughter come between these two almost identical rules about a half-sister? The conventional view is that we are reckoning with a code of laws patched together from different sources at some time in the history of ancient Israel.[25] There is another, more interesting solution—and, I might add, one more complimentary to the ability of ancient authors to set out rules in a way that made sense to them.

Patriarchal history continues to be the focus of these three rules. In the first, a man must not have intercourse with the daughter of his father's wife—a father's wife was the focus of the preceding law—or a daughter by his mother's previous marriage. This rule and the two following ones about grandfather-granddaughter relations and brother and half-sister look at actual and hypothetical aspects of the history of Abraham.[26]

The lawgiver first focuses on Abraham's marriage to Sarah. Abraham encounters problems during a sojourn in Egypt (Gen 12:10–20). On the occasion, Abram (his name at this point in time) says to his wife: "Say, I pray thee, thou art my sister" (v. 13). Abram is attempting to deceive the pharaoh in order to conceal that Sarai (Sarah's name at this time) is in fact his wife. He is motivated by his fear that the Egyptians will kill him to appropriate her. The hypothetical issue of a man's marriage to his sister arises from the story in the sense that a man who can say that his wife is his sister, even if she is not, poses the question, can a man marry his sister?[27]

This issue of marriage to a sister thus would have arisen even if we did not know from a later notice, in Genesis 20:12, that Sarai is indeed Abram's half-sister, the daughter of his father. In the first of his rules about the half-sister, the lawgiver generalizes from Abram's remark to the pharaoh, and he thinks of both the half-sister from the father and the half-sister from the mother. August Dillmann points out that the statement in Genesis 12:13 regarding Sarai as Abram's sister does not necessarily imply what we are told in Genesis 20:12, namely, that Sarah is the daughter of Abraham's father but not of his mother.[28] Nor does the genealogical notice in Genesis 11:29 about Abraham's father's lineage give this information. In other words, the lawgiver has the statement in Genesis 12:13 in focus, and he simply covers the two possibilities: marriage to a sister who is the daughter of one's father, and marriage to the daughter of one's mother. Of the daughter by the mother the lawgiver states that the prohibition applies to a daughter who has been born to the mother at home or abroad. Genesis 11:31 indicates that Abram's father, Terah, moved with Abram and Sarai from his home in Ur of the Chaldees to go abroad. Since we learn in Genesis 20:12 that Sarah's father is Terah, her mother would presumably have been from Ur. The point, however, is not Sarah's genealogy. It is the contrast between home and abroad, which the Genesis narrative brings out, that has prompted the geographical statement in the rule.

Why do we find the additional rule about the half-sister in the instance where she is solely the daughter of a father's wife? Why this prohibition again, which the lawgiver has included in the preceding rule but one? The answer is that he has under scrutiny the specific, later notice in Genesis 20:12 about Abraham's relationship to Sarah. Abraham (his name and Sarah's have been altered by this time) is again sojourning in foreign parts, the kingdom of Gerar this time, and again he fears that he will be killed on account of his wife. He resorts to the same ruse he tried in his previous visit to Egypt, and again the ploy comes undone. The foreign king, Abimelech, finds out that Sarah is Abraham's wife. In response to the king's discovery, Abraham informs Abimelech that Sarah is indeed his sister as well as his wife: "the daughter of my father, not the daughter of my mother, and she became my wife." It is precisely this relationship that the lawgiver prohibits, having laid out in his previous law but one the more general prohibition against marriage to a daughter of one's father or a daughter of one's mother.

The lawgiver's method of examining from a later ethical and legal stance information brought out in the narrative sequence explains why he repeats the prohibition. I might add that it is my contention that the legal material in the Bible constitutes the substance of the redactional activity that the Graf-Wellhausen theory claims is responsible for the makeup of the Pentateuch with its different strands, Jahwistic Elohistic, Deuteronomic, and Priestly. The relationship between the Deuteronomic and Priestly rules, on the one hand, and, on the other, the Jahwistic and Elohistic narratives is such that the strands form a much greater unity than critics have hitherto realized.

In between the two episodes about Sarah's sexual history with other men is the incident about Lot's daughters lying with their father. That incident was pertinent to the first rule prohibiting intercourse with a parent. The lawgiver looks at the incident again and uses it to derive his prohibition against a sexual relationship between a man and his granddaughter. This time he scrutinizes the incident in its wider context as part of the history of Abraham.

Lot is Abraham's nephew (the son of his brother Haran), so Lot's daughters are Abraham's grandnieces. Lot and his daughters are saved from the destruction of Sodom and Gomorrah because of Abraham's good standing with the deity (Gen 19:29). Their future husbands are not saved because they refuse to depart the threatened city. As a consequence of the destruction wrought on Sodom, the daughters reckon that they need their father for procreative purposes: "Our father is old, and there is no man in the earth to come in unto us after the manner of all the earth" (Gen 19:31).

The lawgiver has reflected on the reasoning of the daughters of Lot. There is no man on earth to impregnate them, they reckon. That is not true. If they mean that men from their kinship group are not available, that is not true either; there is their granduncle Abraham. To be sure, he is even more aged than their father, but as we learn from the account of Abraham's life at this time, he is perfectly capable of performing sexually at an advanced age. In their old age he and Sarah produce their son, Isaac. Abraham, then, could have come in to these daughters of Lot "after the manner of all the earth."

The lawgiver condemns out of hand the action of the daughters in resorting to sex with their father. The very fact that they get him drunk to begin with is an indication that they know their action is improper. For the lawgiver, on the other hand, the daughters' intercourse with their granduncle Abraham would presumably have been acceptable. Just as the lawgiver does not prohibit a union between a man and his niece—a relationship Abraham's brother Nahor had with his niece Milcah (Gen 11:27, 29)—so he would not prohibit a union between a man and his grandniece. As in Roman law, the relationship is too distant to trigger a prohibition.[29]

My submission is that the lawgiver derives his prohibition against a man having a relationship with a granddaughter from his examination of the episode of Lot's daughters. He has made the following move. He condemns a relationship of a daughter with a father, but would not condemn one between a man and his grandniece. He does, however, consider the relationship in between these two relationships. Can a man have a sexual relationship with his granddaughter? The lawgiver, prohibiting daughter and father, likewise prohibits grandfather and granddaughter.

Two other features of the material may also have been suggestive of a relationship between a man and his granddaughter. First, Lot is very old when the incident with his daughters occurs. Second, Lot's own father, Haran, died before Abraham and Lot migrated to Canaan. As Lot's uncle, Abraham took on the role of father to Lot as a result. In this light Abraham is very close to being a grandfather to these daughters.

There is no prohibition against a brother's intercourse with a full sister or a father's intercourse with a daughter, where the father is the target of the prohibition. There is, however, a prohibition against a man's having intercourse with his daughter-in-law (Lev 18:15). The reason why the prohibitions about a sister and a daughter are omitted is not solely that the lawgiver does not raise issues that no one questions, although this universal feature of early law codes is a factor.[30] The main reason for the absence of express prohibitions against intercourse with a full sister and a daughter is that the relationships in question were not ones that the lawgiver felt pressed to extrapolate from his scrutiny of the narrative material he worked with. The omission of a rule prohibiting a father's intercourse with a daughter may be surprising.[31] In that the incident involving Lot and his daughters is about the daughters' initiative and Lot's lack of it because of age and drink, the lawgiver has not bothered to look at the offense in terms of a father's initiative.

The inclusion of a rule about a man's having intercourse with his granddaughter when there is no rule about a father's intercourse with his daughter presents a major problem for those inquirers who automatically apply sociohistorical considerations to an understanding of biblical legal material.[32] J. E. Hartley, for example, proposes that "the reason for its [the rule about a daughter] absence may have been socioeconomic; that is, an Israelite would not think of severely reducing the marriage price his daughter could command by having relations with her."[33] It is difficult to believe that a father's lust aimed at a daughter would be deflected by thoughts of his bank account. Sexual passion just does not work that way. Hartley admits that his proposal does not explain the absence of a law against a brother–full sister union. Approaching these laws primarily in terms of social history is not a fruitful strategy. The laws were not set down to govern society, even though some of them may in fact have done so.

I turn now to a sequence of rules beginning with a prohibition against a man having a relationship with his daughter-in-law, which is followed by a rule prohibiting a man from taking his brother's wife. Then follows the extraordinary rule about a man's having sexual relations with a woman, her daughter, and her granddaughter.

LEVITICUS 18:15–17

Thou shalt not uncover the nakedness of thy daughter-in-law: she is thy son's wife: thou shalt not uncover her nakedness.

Thou shalt not uncover the nakedness of thy brother's wife: she is thy brother's nakedness.

Thou shalt not uncover the nakedness of a woman and her daughter, neither shalt thou take her son's daughter, or her daughter's daughter, to uncover her nakedness; for they are near kin: it is wickedness.

These three rules, I submit, were formulated in response to the story of Judah and Tamar in Genesis 38. Recall that Judah, one of Jacob's twelve sons, separates himself from his brothers and, living in Canaan, marries a Canaanite woman. Judah produces three sons by her. He marries the first of his sons, Er, to Tamar. God strikes Er down for some wickedness. There is no child by the union, and the second son, Onan, is obliged by the levirate custom to help Tamar to conceive so that she may raise up a child to his dead brother. Presumably for reasons of greed (Onan stands to gain if no son becomes heir to his dead elder brother), Onan avoids his obligation by ejaculating outside Tamar. Onan too is struck down by the deity. The obligation to fulfill the levirate duty then falls upon the youngest son, Shelah. But Shelah has not yet reached puberty. Moreover, from Judah's vantage point it appears that Tamar is the sinister force causing the deaths of his sons. Therefore when Shelah reaches sexual maturity, Judah, fearing for Shelah's life, does not involve him with Tamar. Tamar takes the matter into her own hands. She dresses as a prostitute and, with her face covered, seduces Judah as he is on his way to a sheep-shearing festival. After some months Judah is told that his daughter-in-law is pregnant by harlotry, and he pronounces a sentence of death by burning for her offense. As she is being led out to be burned, Tamar in her own defense produces objects that Judah gave to her at the time of their sexual transaction. Judah then acknowledges the rightness of her action; namely, producing an heir to her dead husband by a member of his family. By keeping Shelah from Tamar, Judah failed to fulfill this duty to his dead son Er. The story ends with Tamar producing twins.

The lawgiver sets down his rule against a sexual relationship with a daughter-in-law in response to Judah's dealings with Tamar: "You shall not uncover the nakedness of your daughter-in-law: she is your son's wife, you shall not uncover her nakedness." At the time of Tamar's ploy she is not actually married to any of Judah's sons. The point is, however, that whether or not Judah permits Shelah to consummate a marriage with her, Tamar is affianced to Shelah by the custom of levirate marriage. That is why she can be accused of harlotry.

The story itself brings out the taboo inherent in a relationship between a man and his daughter-in-law. Tamar does not approach Judah openly to obtain seed from him, but instead disguises herself and plays the harlot. The story, moreover, tells us that they never again have a sexual relationship after that one encounter. There is, then, a sense in which all the lawgiver does is spell out a rule that is implicit in the narrative. The narrative, after all, itself contains ethical and legal judgments. The lawgiver would simply be extending this process of judgment. He would be further encouraged to do so because the story in fact gives an ambiguous message. Judah states that Tamar, in getting seed from him, is "more righteous than I, inasmuch as I did not give her to my son Shelah." Judah's statement might actually imply that in some circumstances it is acceptable for a daughter-in-law to have a sexual relationship with her father-in-law. The lawgiver opposes any such relationship.

The next rule, against a sexual relationship with a brother's wife, also comes from reflection on that story. "You shall not uncover the nakedness of your brother's wife: she is your brother's nakedness." The story presupposes the custom of levirate marriage, in which a man in certain circumstances is obliged to have a sexual relationship with his dead brother's widow. Onan is unwilling to meet his obligation and conceals his unwillingness in an offensive way. Either the lawgiver opposes any union between a man and his brother's wife no matter the circumstances, thereby canceling the levirate custom, or the lawgiver views Onan's unwillingness as wholly appropriate for all Israelite men, except in regard to the levirate custom. I cannot decide which view prevails.

I turn next to the extraordinary rule prohibiting a man's sexual relationships with three generations of women in the same family: "You shall not uncover the nakedness of a woman and of her daughter, and you shall not take her son's daughter or her daughter's daughter to uncover her nakedness; they are your near kinswomen; it is wickedness." Again the story of Judah and Tamar is the key. A central feature of the story is that a woman, Tamar, has several sexual relationships within the same family. Although this story features a woman, in his rules the lawgiver addresses males. He therefore discusses a set of relationships for a man that approximates Tamar's experience.[34]

Tamar has a sexual relationship with a man of her own generation, but also with his father; that is, she has relations with two generations of men belonging to the same family. She is supposed to have a sexual relationship with another member of this family, Shelah. Shelah, however, has not yet reached puberty when the occasion arises. From the sexual point of view, the lawgiver would have considered Shelah's youth to have put him into a different generation from his dead brothers. Tamar's actual or potential sexual liaisons with what amounts to three generations of men in the same family inspire the lawgiver to set down a rule that prohibits a man from having sexual relations with three generations of women in the same family.[35]

If the rule is in any way meant to apply to real life, we must ask how realistic it is. In the world of antiquity a mother could be around forty, her daughter around twenty-five, and her granddaughter, like Shelah, around the age of puberty. Such a lineup would be quite exceptional, however.[36] When we take into account the improbable proposition that a man would seek a sexual relationship with all three generations, I think we have to reckon that the dramatic developments in the story rather than a real-life situation have triggered the lawgiver's thinking.

LEVITICUS 18:18

Neither shalt thou take a woman as a rival wife to her sister, to uncover her nakedness, beside the other in her lifetime.

The lawgiver next sets down a rule that is not about incest. A man must not marry two sisters while both are alive. It is easy to relate this rule to patriarchal history. Jacob is married to the two sisters, Rachel and Leah. These women are also his first cousins, but that particular degree of consanguinity is plainly not the reason for the prohibition. Presumably the lawgiver permits marriage between first cousins. The reason for the rule is the problem of rivalry between the sisters. The notable feature of Jacob's marriage to Rachel and Leah is precisely the rivalry between them in competing for his sexual services.[37] On one occasion one sister even hires him out to the other for a night's lovemaking (Gen 30:14–18).[38]

The history of patriarchal sexual relationships accounts, I contend, for the setting down of the series of rules in Leviticus 18:6–11 and 15–18. Where these relationships raise issues of incest, the lawgiver duly records his judgment. Where the stories raise issues other than incest, the lawgiver also proceeds to give his judgment. The lawgiver's method, then, accounts for the mixing together of laws to do with incest and laws not to do with incest. Any hypothesis about the nature of these rules has to account for such combinations of topics.

The lawgiver goes from the story of Tamar's marital history to the story of Jacob's when he sets down a rule about a man's marriage to two sisters after a rule about sexual relations with three generations of women. How do we account for this switch from one story to another? A fundamental procedure of the lawgiver is that he moves back and forth between the histories of the generations. What prompts him to do so is that time and again he finds that what occurs in one generation occurs also in a later or earlier generation. His procedure is exactly in line with how the biblical narrators themselves proceeded in setting out their narrative traditions. Typically these narrators recorded similar developments in the lifetime of each patriarch; for example, how each patriarch, beginning with Abraham, had a problem involving his firstborn son.

Tamar is married to first one brother and then, after he dies, to another brother. The lawgiver logically turns to a comparable marital setup in the preceding generation, namely, Jacob's. Jacob is married to two sisters, Rachel and Leah. Unlike Tamar's consecutive marital unions to two brothers, Jacob is married to each sister during the lifetime of the other. There are other features shared by the two stories. Tamar's marriages to the two brothers are disastrous. Jacob's own marriages founder—he hates Leah because he was tricked into marrying her, and Rachel, the one he loves, is barren. Onan's father instructs him, because of the levirate custom, to take Tamar as a wife. Onan spurns her. Leah's father instructs her, because of the custom to marry off the elder daughter before the younger, to become Jacob's wife. Jacob spurns her. Onan would never voluntarily have taken Tamar, nor Jacob Leah.

I conclude by considering the problem I set aside earlier. In introducing the sequence of rules I have just discussed, the biblical lawgiver expressly condemns the conduct of the Egyptians and the Canaanites, but says nothing about the similar conduct of his own ancestors. In the prologue to the rules in Leviticus 18:1–3 the Priestly lawgiver warns: "After the doings of the land of Egypt, wherein ye dwelt, shall ye not do: and after the doings of the land of Canaan, whither I bring you, shall ye not do." In the warnings that follow the presentation of the rules (Lev 18:24–30), the lawgiver again returns to the unacceptable conduct of the Canaanite inhabitants of the land and insists that the Israelites should not imitate it when they occupy the land of Canaan. One problem about these warnings is the difficulty of finding any evidence in the pertinent Near Eastern sources that the liaisons prohibited in Leviticus constituted a major feature of Egyptian and Canaanite life.[39] Further, it is hard to believe that Canaanite and Egyptian children were known for initiating sexual encounters with their parents or went in for relationships with three generations of women in the same family. I know of no scholar who addresses the discrepancy between the vices that Moses attributes to Egypt and Canaan and the actual social practices in those lands. Presumably the tacit view is that if we knew more about these societies, revelations of their outrageous ways would be forthcoming. I am skeptical, however, about the common assumption that these nations were indeed notorious for decadent behavior, and that the Israelites were reacting against them in the regulation of their own social life.

In every time and every place, it is typical for one group to blame another for sexuality that is deemed damnable. The Germans blamed syphilis on the French, the French on the Spanish, and the Spanish on Native Americans. Homosexuality has been termed the English disease; the term *bugger* means that it was the Bulgarians who engaged in homosexuality; and the word *sodomite* refers to the homosexual activity of the natives of Sodom. AIDS has been blamed on Africa. In a pre-Socratic Greek source we are told that the "Persians think it seemly that not only women but men should adorn themselves, and that men should have intercourse with their daughters, mothers and sisters, but the Greeks regard these things as disgraceful and against the law."[40] According to the Bible (sexual) harlotry started with the Canaanites (Genesis 34).

My scrutiny of the incest rules suggests that it was the behavior of the ancestors of the Israelites, not Egyptian or Canaanite behavior, that the lawgiver had in focus and condemned.[41] This conclusion should not be so unexpected when we recall that some of the rules do prohibit relationships actually found among the patriarchs. Why, then, did the lawgiver point the finger at the Egyptians and the Canaanites instead of at them? The answer is that the lawgiver had to view the behavior of the ancestors in light of their milieu. It is a universal phenomenon. Conduct barely acceptable in Denver is considered good enough in San Francisco.[42] The patriarchs did not have the laws of Moses to live by,[43] but instead were influenced by their Canaanite or Egyptian environment. That environment had to be taken into account in assessing their behavior. It is the lawgiver who inferred, in a way that I indicated was typical at all times and places, that Canaanite and Egyptian ways were beyond the pale and that the activities of the ancestors were more understandable as a consequence.

Abraham married his half-sister. The lawgiver probably inferred that such a union, offensive to him, simply reflected Abraham's deficient social and cultural setting, Mesopotamian in this particular instance.[44] He and Sarah were married before they migrated to Canaan. Abraham himself saw the need for his son Isaac to avoid a Canaanite marriage (Gen 24:3). Abraham's awareness of such an undesirable union would be evidence for the lawgiver that already in Abraham's time the Canaanites represented a harmful influence. Judah's relationship with his daughter-in-law occurred in Canaan, after he himself had married a Canaanite in Canaan. Moses prohibited the very union that his own parents had contracted—in Egypt (Num 26:59). For the lawgiver, then, it was the host cultures in which the ancestors lived, not the ancestors themselves, that his people must be warned about.[45]

The consensus of scholarly opinion has it that the Levitical lawgiver was himself living in a host culture, namely, Babylon. If this is so, it may be significant that he did not cite Mesopotamia as one of the cultures he deplored. To have done so would have been unwise. At the same time, however, if this social historical context is relevant to the rules, the lawgiver was in a coded way telling his fellow Israelites to avoid Babylonian ways.[46]

5 The Decalogue

From the time of Philo (born first century B.C.E.), readers of the Bible have regarded the Decalogue as enshrining the spirit of biblical law.[1] Thinking along similar lines, many modern scholars paint complex pictures of its origin and elaboration. They postulate different but unknown periods when various versions of the Ten Commandments supposedly affected ancient Israelite law and society. One persistent view is that the original Decalogue was quite different from the ones set down in Exodus 20:2–17 and Deuteronomy 5:6–21. Scholars postulate that the original Decalogue was concise and rhythmical—in short, that it was poetry.[2] They see the variations that exist between the Decalogue in Exodus 20:2–17 and the one in Deuteronomy 5:6–21 as evidence that the original Decalogue had been added to, had gone through stages of development over time.

One idea that appears to inform this view is a widespread misapprehension about ancient literary activity, specifically, that originally poetry was "language *tout court*, prose being the derivative and younger rival."[3] Scholars who think that the Decalogue existed in a poetical form are making the same error as those who think that all language first took the form of poetry. As David Daube states, "What needs to be realized here is that the illusion created by this topsy-turvy build-up of vocabulary, with 'poetry' identified long before 'prose,' still exercises a tremendous magic. The Encyclopedia Americana of 1981 contains several articles on Poetry, none on Prose; and the very first paragraph of the main article asserts that 'Poetry is . . . the earliest expression of primitive peoples. . . . It is both the most elemental form of human communication and the most sophisticated and subtle.' Apparently Adam, laid up with the flu, far from muttering 'Water,' declaimed 'Reach me the sky-born juice, my faithful Eve.'"[4] Underlying the tenacious view that the Decalogue goes far back in time and had a concise, rhythmical character is probably the same misunderstanding.

There is another explanation of how the Decalogue as a literary unit (not the individual items in it) came to be, and why it takes the forms it does in the two places where it occurs in the Bible. The activity of biblical scribes working closely with literary traditions is the key. To a greater or lesser degree, all narrative writing has built into it moral and legal judgments. This is particularly true of the narratives of the Bible. Some of these judgments are obvious, as when the deity declares himself or when Moses speaks on his behalf. Others are to be inferred. Those who set down the biblical laws first teased out issues implied in biblical narratives and then gave judgments on them. The Decalogue, which consists of a series of statements and rules, provides fine evidence that this process of judgment, probably undertaken by a scribal school, is what underlies the presentation of biblical law. Two narratives—the story of the golden calf and the stories of Adam and Eve, Cain and Abel—constitute the bodies of material out of which the two tablets of the Decalogue have been fashioned.

Before turning to the links between the Decalogue and these two narratives, I wish to draw attention to the closest parallel I have come upon to the process in question: the use of the Bible by the canonists.[5] They saw—although it is much more complicated than that, as I shall note—in the story of Adam and Eve general rules for how human justice should proceed if it was to properly convict a person for an offense.

From God's commandment to Adam, "Of the tree of the knowledge of good and evil, thou shalt not eat" (Gen 2:17), the canonists derived a rule that no one may be punished for an action that the criminal law has not previously defined and prohibited. The passage in Genesis 3:9 in which "the Lord God called unto Adam, and said unto him, Where art thou?" pointed to a requirement that in criminal procedure a defendant must be summoned before he can be lawfully punished. A citation is required. When God said to Adam: "Hast thou eaten of the tree whereof I commanded thee that thou shouldest not eat?" (Gen 3:11), the question indicated that a defendant must be told the precise nature of the crime he has been charged with. And when Adam replied to God ("And the man said"), some of the canonists saw this development as pointing to the origin of pleading. A defendant must be permitted to reply to any charge laid against him, even if he is certainly guilty of the offense. After all, he may be able to proffer, as up to a point Adam did, mitigating circumstances that would reduce the penalty appropriate to the offense. There was too the matter of the sentencing of the criminal. God pronounced his sentences on each of the culprits in the story. Moreover, God gave reasons for his judgments. A human judge must likewise speak his sentence aloud to the defendant and the court; and he must also give a reason for it.[6]

Two points might be made about the canonists' use of the Adam and Eve story. First, it showed a very sophisticated and detailed reading of the texts on their part. They would have noted that God must have known the whereabouts of Adam when he summoned him, yet God nonetheless asked Adam where he was. The apparently unnecessary question was evidence that procedure is important. Again, God must have known that Adam had committed the offense. Nonetheless in asking Adam whether he had committed it, God was careful to ensure that Adam knew exactly what the charge was.

Second, certain principles of justice and rules of judicial procedure would have been known to the canonists in some form or another when they read the Adam and Eve story. Unfortunately, we have little evidence of the makeup of existing procedural norms. The canonists turned to the Genesis narratives both to give clearer expression to such norms and, presumably, to lend further authority to them by anchoring them as far back in time as possible, and to the highest authority possible. In this instance they traced them to the prepast, so to speak—a feature that turns out to be characteristic of the rules in the Decalogue itself. It would be an error to think that the canonists were in any way naive when they linked legal norms to the Genesis narrative. What they did is what the biblical lawgivers had done before them—I am not suggesting that the canonists in any way knew how the biblical lawgivers proceeded—even if the aims of the two groups might have differed in many respects. The biblical lawgivers also worked with rules known to them (but, alas, not to us—unless a case can be made out that they were familiar with, for example, the laws of

Hammurabi), and they too chose to relate them to stories that were part of their cultural heritage.

THE STORY OF THE GOLDEN CALF (EXODUS 32)

The story of the golden calf in Exodus 32 tells how Moses comes down from the mountain with the Decalogue written on two tablets to find that the people have resorted to apostasy. Looked at from the perspectives of God and Moses, the judgments expressed in the Decalogue turn out to be integrally linked to the people's apostasy with the golden calf. I shall argue that, contrary to what the legend claims, the Decalogue did not exist prior to the incident of the calf, but rather the incident of the calf inspired the (first tablet of the) Decalogue.

While Moses is delayed on the mountain, the people wish to replace the Yahweh of the Exodus story, the god who brought them out of Egypt, with other gods who will guide them in their future journeying. Aaron is receptive to their request and crafts a molten calf out of gold he has collected from them. The people respond by proclaiming: "These be thy gods, O Israel, which brought thee up out of the land of Egypt" (Exod 32:4).

From the narrator's point of view this declaration is manifestly a challenge to Yahweh, because as the story unfolds, the narrator resolutely affirms Yahweh's significance. In the voices of God and Moses the narrator expresses his values and judgments on some, but by no means all, of the events of the story. This uncommented, or not sufficiently commented upon activity is what challenged the compiler of the Decalogue to formulate additional responses. The opening statement of the Decalogue expresses a counterstatement to the acclamation that the golden calf represents the gods that brought the people out of the land of Egypt. "I am Yahweh thy God which have brought thee out of the land of Egypt, out of the house of bondage" is the first statement or, consistent with the Hebrew description, word, of the Decalogue. The apostasy of the golden calf also calls for a prohibition: "Thou shalt have no other gods in preference to me" is the next statement of the Decalogue.[7]

The lawgiver also responds to the question of what form these other gods might take. In the example of the golden calf, the form of the god is that of an earthly animal. Since other forms are also possible, however, the rule is more comprehensive in scope: "Thou shalt not make unto thee any graven image, or any likeness of any thing that is in heaven above, or that is in the earth beneath, or that is in the water under the earth."

Other developments about the golden calf also demand response. Aaron builds an altar for it and proclaims the next day as a feast day on which the people should celebrate Yahweh. This idol, then, will have an altar in its honor and will enjoy the name Yahweh—a name that the narrator associates only with the invisible Yahweh of the events of the Exodus—and a day of celebration. These three aspects invite three responses: (1) "Thou shalt not bow down thyself to them, nor serve them [at an altar]";[8] (2) "Thou shalt not take up the name of Yahweh thy God in vain"; and (3) "Remember the Sabbath Day, to keep it holy." This sequence of statements in the Decalogue—worship, name, and special day—reflects precisely the sequence of the events in the narrative.

The purpose of the special day for the golden calf Yahweh is to celebrate its role in bringing the Israelites out of Egypt. Each of the authors of the two versions of the Decalogue in Exodus and Deuteronomy takes up one of two problems presented by this part of the narrative. First, the people celebrate a false god represented by the golden calf as the agent responsible for bringing them out of Egypt. Second, they celebrate what the narrator—and other biblical writers—regards as a man-made god.[9] In Deuteronomy the lawgiver takes up the first issue of who was responsible for bringing Israel out of Egypt. His Sabbath commandment emphasizes that it was the God Yahweh, not the golden calf Yahweh, who performed the miracle: "Keep the Sabbath Day to sanctify it, as Yahweh thy God hath commanded thee. Six days thou shalt labour, and do all thy work: But the seventh day is the Sabbath of Yahweh thy God: in it thou shalt not do any work, thou, nor thy son, nor thy daughter, nor thy manservant, nor thy maidservant, nor thine ox, nor thine ass, nor any of thy cattle, nor thy stranger that is within thy gates; that thy manservant and thy maidservant may rest as well as thou. And remember that thou wast a servant in the land of Egypt, and that Yahweh thy God brought thee out thence through a mighty hand and by a stretched out arm: therefore Yahweh thy God commanded thee to keep the Sabbath Day" (Deut 5:12–15).

The author of the Sabbath commandment in Exodus takes up the second issue, who is the true maker of everything that exists. "Remember the Sabbath Day, to keep it holy. Six days shalt thou labour, and do all thy work: but the seventh day is the Sabbath of Yahweh thy God: in it thou shalt not do any work, thou, nor thy son, nor thy daughter, thy manservant, nor thy maidservant, nor thy cattle, nor thy sojourner that is within thy gates: For in six days Yahweh made heaven and earth, the sea, and all that in them is, and rested the seventh day: wherefore Yahweh blessed the Sabbath Day, and hallowed it" (Exod 20:8–11). Unlike the rule in Deuteronomy, which affirms the God Yahweh over against the calf Yahweh in the role of rescuer from bondage in Egypt, this rule affirms the God Yahweh's power to create all things over against man's attempt to create a god.

The first part of the story in Exodus 32 (v. 1–6) is about wrongful actions, mentioned in the order in which one finds commentary on them in the Decalogue. The narrative itself details Yahweh's explicit judgments on these actions: the people "have corrupted themselves . . . they have made them a molten calf, and have worshipped it, and have sacrificed thereunto, and said, 'These be thy gods, O Israel, which have brought thee up out of the land of Egypt'" (Exod 32:7–8). Yahweh expresses the wish to destroy all the people except Moses and create a new people, starting over with him. Moses appeals to Yahweh's reputation, tells God that if he destroys the people he brought out of Egypt the Egyptians will hear of it and give him a bad name. Moses also appeals to Yahweh's promise to the patriarchs in Genesis that he would cause them to reproduce abundantly. The appeal is successful. The promise of continued reproduction among the Israelites still holds. This aspect of the narrative will prove significant, as I will shortly point out, in understanding why the next rule after the Sabbath command is the command to honor one's parents.

After Moses smashes the tablets, burns the calf, grinds it to powder, adds water, and has the people drink the concoction, he accuses Aaron of letting the people cause him, Aaron, to commit the great sin of the golden calf. Thus does Moses bring up the issue of Aaron's guilt. But Moses does not require that Aaron be punished. Rather, the focus is on the culpability and punishment of the people; the question of the negative consequences of Aaron's culpability is left hanging. The question of Aaron's responsibility is raised in another biblical account of the incident of the golden calf. In Deuteronomy 9:20 Yahweh himself expresses his anger with Aaron to such an extent that he seeks to kill him. Moses must intervene to save Aaron.

Only two items of the Decalogue make the point that negative consequences may flow from an offense. One instance concerns the threat of punishment to a person who uses Yahweh's name for a vain purpose: "For Yahweh will not hold him guiltless that taketh his name in vain" (Exod 20:7; Deut 5:11). Because Aaron is not punished in the story of the calf for his offense, in particular that aspect of it which is entirely due to his own initiative when he proclaims the name Yahweh over the calf, it is important that guilt be attributed to him nonetheless. The nonpunishment of Aaron for his offense is precisely the type of issue that invites a response in the form of a judgment. The Deuteronomic account of how Yahweh is going to destroy Aaron is one example of a response (Deut 9:20). The compilers of both the Decalogues took the same path as the Deuteronomist in addressing the issue of Aaron's guilt in Exodus 32.[10] The view that the person who misuses God's name will be held accountable may correspond to the view expressed in Exodus 32:33: "Whoever has sinned against me I [Yahweh] will blot out of my book."

Another development in the same story involves dire consequences for the promoters of apostasy. Moses appeals to those among the people who are loyal to Yahweh, and the Levites step forward. At his command they slaughter some three thousand of the people with their swords. Moses then appeals to Yahweh to forgive the rest of the people for their sin of worshipping the calf. Yahweh's response is complicated. He will blot out of his book those who have sinned, he plagues the people, and he anticipates that in the future he will visit their sin upon them.

One other item of the Decalogue takes up the issue of negative consequences of apostasy. Those who worship idols will find that "I Yahweh thy God am a jealous God, visiting the iniquity of the fathers upon the children unto the third and fourth generation of them that hate me" (Exod 20:3–6; cp. Deut 5:7–10). This prediction about future iniquity follows from Yahweh's threat in the story. The future iniquity that the author of the Decalogue has in mind is the worship of the calf by later generations of Israelites. In scanning the history of the Israelites one finds a recurrence of calf worship during the reigns of King Jehu and his three sons. The Deuteronomic narrator of the Book of Kings singles out sons of Jehu to the fourth generation as wrongly committed to the use of the calves. In actuality, while 2 Kings 10:30 refers (Jehu is being addressed) to sons of the fourth generation, 2 Kings 13:2 (Jehoahaz), 14:24 (Jeroboam), and 15:9 (Zachariah) encompass in fact only three generations of Jehu's sons. Just as Yahweh guarantees this history of succession in Jehu's family (2 Kings 10:30), so Yahweh, the ultimate cause of all that happens in the world, visits the sin of the calf upon three or four generations of a leading family in Israel. The Decalogue, like the story of the calf itself,[11] anticipates this particular development.

The Levites' slaughter of some three thousand offenders is a positive action from the point of view of the narrator of the story of the calf. The Decalogue sets alongside the anticipated outbreaks of idolatry in future Israelite life an affirmation that Yahweh will show "mercy unto thousands of them that love me and keep my commandments." Why, one must wonder, does Yahweh not say that he will show mercy to everyone who loves him and keeps his commandments? Why does he use a curiously specific number—namely, thousands—to enumerate the number of those who will be loyal to him? A recent commentator glosses over these questions by asserting that the word 'alaphim (thousands) really means a thousand generations, that is, at all periods of time in the future Yahweh will show mercy to those loyal to him.[12] No doubt that is the meaning that theologically one would expect. But the text should be kept intact. It is significant as it is because it refers to the Levites' slaughter of the apostates. In the setting of the calf story, Yahweh is about to destroy all the people with the exception of Moses. In the event, that does not happen because of Moses' appeal. Moreover, it turns out that the Levites prove loyal to Yahweh by obeying his command to kill, "slaying every man his brother, and every man his companion, and every man his neighbour" (Exod 32:27). We are told that three thousand die (v. 28). It follows that Yahweh, instead of destroying the Levites along with the rest of the people, showed mercy to them because they chose to express loyalty to him. Since they managed to kill three thousand of the people, there must have been thousands of them. Hence the statement in the Decalogue about Yahweh's mercy to thousands is an accurate anticipation of Yahweh's preferential treatment of the Levites in the incident of the golden calf.[13] The Decalogue thus takes after this quite particular development in the story.[14]

The narrative in Exodus 32:15, 16 refers to the Decalogue itself. Moses has just returned from the mountain with God's written tablets, two in number, implying two sections to the Decalogue. When we turn to the substance of the Decalogue in either of the versions, Exodus 20:2–17 or Deuteronomy 5:6–21, each of the rules in its first section has been violated in the most specific of ways by the Israelites. There is, therefore, a detailed link between the actions of the people and this part of the Decalogue. This can be no coincidence. There are two possibilities. Either the narrator of the story of the golden calf composed it with a view to illustrating how the items of the Decalogue might be violated, or the compiler of the Decalogue, despite historical reports that the Decalogue existed before the making of the golden calf, reflected on an existing narrative and extracted the contents of the Decalogue from it. Since a major feature of the presentation of all biblical law is that God and Moses accurately and miraculously anticipate problems before they arise, the problem of the Decalogue existing prior to the incident of the golden calf is more apparent than real.[15]

The former alternative—that the narrative is based on the rules—can be discounted because the art and artifice required to compose a story to match the sequence and detail of the individual items of the Decalogue are beyond the bounds of possibility. The other alternative—an author has opinions about a story he knows and gives judgments that constitute commentary on it—is more true to life. What reinforces this second alternative is that the compiler of the Decalogue incorporated so many particularities of the story into its items.

The Decalogue has two tablets. If the first brings out the wrong-doing involved in the worship of the golden calf, the second is also likely to be based on a past development. This is indeed the case. Moreover, the significance of the offense in the narrative underlying the second tablet turns out to be remarkably similar to the significance of the offense of the calf.

THE STORY OF ADAM AND EVE, CAIN AND ABEL (GENESIS 2–4)

The second tablet of the Decalogue begins with a focus on the first family ever, and particularly on Cain, the first son ever to commit an offense. He murders his brother, Abel. Before I turn to the history of the first family, I must first explain why the lawgiver shifts from one narrative history to another, and why in switching to the Genesis narrative the lawgiver begins with Cain's offense, and not with Adam and Eve's offenses.

Why, in the first place, were the two stories—the golden calf and Adam, Eve, Cain, and Abel—chosen for the purpose of compiling the Decalogue? The answer is that each concerns not just a unique development, but a first-ever crucial development. The story of the golden calf is the first outbreak of actual idolatry in the history of the nation. So pervasive does the problem of idolatry become at later times in Israelite history that there is a compelling motivation to grapple with its origins. The Adam, Eve, Cain, and Abel story, in turn, represents the very beginnings of human life and conduct, the time when God's moral code was established. The compiler's derivation of this code from such beginnings explains why he has the Decalogue delivered in a setting that recalls the beginnings of the world. Thus when God prepares to present the tablets to Moses in Exodus 19, wonders of creation are on display. God speaks, and elemental forces of creation accompany his pronouncements. Among other manifestations of divine power, there is a voice from heaven, thunder and lighting, smoke and fire, and the descent of the deity to the top of a mountain.

Why is there a switch from the story of the golden calf to the story of Cain and Abel, Adam and Eve; or, alternatively, why does the rule about honor to parents come after the commandment about the Sabbath? First and foremost in this regard is the issue raised by the Israelites' creation of a god in Exodus 32: namely, is there any sense in which human beings can be said to enjoy the capacity to create that is associated with God? The lawgiver notes that only by producing children do humans approach the creative powers of God. That is why he turns to the topic of honoring parents, and in particular to the situation within the first family ever. One honors parents as one's progenitors, as one honors on the Sabbath the Creator of all life. As Philo puts it, "Parents, in my opinion, are to their children what God is to the world, since just as he achieved existence for the non-existent, so they in imitation of his power, as far as they are capable, immortalize the race" (*De Specialibus Legibus* 2.225; cp. *Quod Deterius Potiori insidiari solet* 54; *De Vita Mosis* 2.209).

Central to both the rule about the Sabbath and the rule about honor to parents, then, are the notions of creation and procreation, respectively. Procreation plays a major role in the incident involving the golden calf. When God decides to destroy the Israelites and begin over again with Moses, the latter tells God that destroying the people he has just brought out from Egypt will give him a bad name among the Egyptians. Moses appeals to God's promise to Abraham, Isaac, and Jacob that their offspring would multiply mightily and become possessors of the land of Canaan (Exod 32:13). The appeal succeeds. Behind it is the view that reverence for progenitors transcends national boundaries.[16] God, it is implied, agrees with Moses that the Egyptians would subscribe to this view. A prime illustration of the international character of the view comes out in the rule in Deuteronomy 21:10–14: an Israelite who has taken captive in war a woman he wishes to marry must let her first mourn her non-Israelite parents for a month. The fundamental concern with procreation in Exodus 32 is a major factor in the lawgiver's focus on Cain's failure to revere his progenitors. Just as God tacitly agrees with Moses that there should be no dishonor of the first patriarchs, Abraham, Isaac, and Jacob, and their wives by destroying their descendants, so too Cain should not have dishonored the first ancestors, Adam and Eve, by destroying their son Abel.

Both the Adam and Eve story and the golden calf story in fact share interesting features. First and foremost is the similarity of the offenses. In the Genesis story God is jealous that the human beings have become godlike ("Behold, the man is become as one of us"; Gen 3:22). In the Exodus story similar jealousy is aroused because human beings have created a god. Each offense involves wrongful eating—from the tree of the knowledge of good and evil in Genesis that conferred godlike knowledge on the humans, and the eating (and drinking) to celebrate the man-made god in Exodus. Each development prompts a judicial-like inquiry—God's questioning Adam and Eve about the offense of eating from the forbidden tree; Moses' questioning Aaron about his culpability for making the golden calf. In each instance the party questioned attempts to evade responsibility for the misdeed—Adam directs attention away from himself to Eve, and Eve likewise from herself to the serpent; Aaron from himself to the people. In both cases the sword is involved in punishing the culprits: the Cherubim wield a sword to ensure that no one approaches the tree of life; and the Levites, special representatives of God like the Cherubim, wreak havoc among the guilty with their swords. Structurally, just as the story of Adam and Eve follows the story of the six-day creation followed by God's rest on the seventh day (Gen 1–2:3), so the story of the golden calf follows the account in Exodus 31:12–18 about how the Sabbath is a sign that the people should reverence God for creating the world in six days and resting on the seventh.

I turn to the first rule in the second tablet of the Decalogue—the command to honor parents—in order to account for its specific formulation in each version of the Decalogue. As already noted, Cain is the first son ever to commit an offense, and the lawgiver had reason to turn to that offense after he brought out the various issues in the story of the golden calf. Cain murders his brother Abel. Both sons came from their mother, Eve, with Yahweh's assistance (Gen 4:1). Apart from the obvious offense of the murder, an accompanying major offense is that Cain, by killing their son, dishonors the parents who created that son. There is an immediate negative consequence for Cain. He is banished from working the ground, which he had tilled as his vocation until then. There is a further negative result. Because he is banished from the land (ground), he becomes a fugitive and a wanderer on the earth. As such he is faced with the threat of being murdered himself.

Counsel about a son's relationship to his parents in light of Cain's relationship to his might well take the two forms one finds in the two versions of the Decalogue. The Exodus version, "Honour thy father and thy mother: that thy days may be long upon the land [literally, "ground"] which Yahweh thy God giveth thee" (Exod 20:2), reflects the fact that Cain's punishment meant that he could no longer work the land. Once we relate the substance of the rule about honoring parents to the story of Cain, we no longer have difficulty in seeing why a lawgiver would link honoring parents to a son's living long upon the land (ground). It is not otherwise a very obvious link. The Deuteronomic version of the rule takes a slightly different form. One is to honor one's parents, "That thy days may be prolonged, and that it may go well with thee, in the land [ground] which Yahweh thy God giveth thee" (Deut 5:16). Again the Cain story explains why this version of the rule speaks specifically about living a long life. Cain had to live under a threat of death after he left his plot of ground to become a fugitive and a wanderer upon the earth. Death at an early age because of his offenses (murder and dishonor of his parents) was a real possibility.

In extracting rules from stories the lawgiver does not find it necessary to repeat the obvious offense in the story. The process of producing moral and legal counsel from a story is more sophisticated than reiterating a point already made in it. From the story it is obvious that the narrator regards the offense of murder as wrongful. If one is going from story to law it is superfluous to spell out a rule about murder. Yet "Thou shalt not murder" is the next rule in the Decalogue, and there is a specific reason why this is so. Cain is not put to death for his murder of Abel. The issue of a capital penalty for him is not even addressed, as any reader, ancient or modern, might expect it to be. Instead, and this makes the matter even more surprising, Yahweh responds sympathetically to Cain's complaint that the punishment he has received is a threat to his life. This threat has nothing to do with his crime, but only with the peculiar nature of his punishment. Cain complains that his banishment is too much for him to bear. Someone will come upon him and slay him as he wanders the earth (Gen 4:14). Responding positively to the complaint, Yahweh places a protective mark on Cain to ensure that he is not himself murdered. It is from this development in the narrative that the lawgiver derives the rule about murder, not from Cain's murder of Abel itself. Yahweh's action implies the rule.

The next development in Cain's life is his marriage (Gen 4:17). At one level the story reads as biography. At another, deeper, level—the one important to the storyteller—the story ponders fundamental aspects of human life. One can detect this second level by noting that Cain marries a woman whose existence is problematic, to say the least, if one reads the story as biography. On the surface level the only woman around is Eve, Cain's mother, and she is certainly not under consideration as his wife (nor is the daughter attributed to her by Saint Augustine).[17] At the other level the story probes the origin of the institution of marriage. The recounting of the life history of the first humans is really secondary to such probing.[18]

The story has already brought out in a quite explicit way this deeper aspect of things—evidence that such probing is the point of the storytelling. When describing how the woman first came from the man, how Eve came from Adam's rib, the storyteller anticipates future human life and spells out the fundamental nature of the institution of marriage. Significantly, Cain is the focus. As laid out in Genesis 2:24, he, not Adam, is the first son ever to leave his father and his mother to cleave to a wife. Such a development is related to the origin of the woman from the man. Marriage thus reflects the nature of creation itself. A man's cleaving to his wife recalls how at creation the woman came from the man with a view to her being his partner. She came from the man's body, and whenever a marital union occurs it mirrors, even reestablishes, this original unity of man and woman.[19] At the mythical level, then, when Cain marries he reaches into his own body, so to speak, to do so. Future interference with such a union—for example, when a man has sex with another man's wife—is an offense against the created order. A rule, "Thou shalt not commit adultery," is necessary to protect not just the institution of marriage but the order of creation itself. The lawgiver proceeds similarly to the storyteller at his second, deeper level.

No adultery is committed in the Genesis narrative, but one must recall that there is no direct correspondence between narratives and the laws derived from them. The lawgiver focuses on issues that are but suggested or implied in the narratives. In regard to the offense of adultery, the lawgiver brings out the implication of what is stated about the marital union in the narrative. The implied view is that because God created the first man, Adam, with Eve in some sense part of him, this original unity of the male and the female requires the protection of the one flesh of the marital bond.[20]

Cain is the first son ever to marry. In doing so, he is the first to fulfill the notion about marriage that the narrator of the Genesis story expresses at the creation of Eve from Adam, namely, "Therefore shall a man leave his father and his mother, and shall cleave unto his wife: and they shall be one flesh" (Gen 2:24). Cain's parents are, however, the first married couple, and the lawgiver soon shifts his attention to their deeds. Immediately after the description of how a son leaves his father and his mother to marry, the story relates how the first man, Adam, and his wife, Eve, are naked and not ashamed. This leads into the description of how at one point in their history a sense of shame comes over them because of their nakedness. It happens because they eat of the fruit of the tree of the knowledge of good and evil, of which God has commanded them not to eat.

Although it is not spelled out in such terms, Adam and Eve have in fact stolen something. The object stolen is fruit. This simple theft brings in its wake a multitude of complications. The narrator is taken up with the troubling implications of the theft, but the lawgiver chooses to focus on the act of theft itself. Hence he sets down the rule "Thou shalt not steal."

As a consequence of their wrongful appropriation of the fruit, a sense of shame comes over Adam and Eve. They cover themselves and hide among the trees in the garden when they hear God walking there. On God's asking where Adam is, Adam tells about his fear because he is naked. This is no offense, but when God asks why they know about nakedness and whether they have eaten of the tree of which they were told not to eat, Adam and Eve give distorted responses. Adam downplays his own culpability by drawing attention to Eve's role in the theft, and Eve in turn puts the blame on the serpent, who knew the significance of the tree's nature. The picture presented of the overall scene is that of a judge in a court of justice putting a question to someone who was present at the scene of the offense and is targeted as culpable for an act of theft. Fundamentally, their responses are attempts to place the blame for what they did on someone else.[21] The wrongdoing in their responses is not lying as such, but consists of words that point to someone else's culpability. The rule that is derived is consequently not a condemnation of lying in general, but brings in the notion of testimony from one party who was a witness to another's deed: "Thou shalt not bear false witness against thy neighbour" (Exod 20:16), or in the words of Deuteronomy 5:20: "Thou shalt not respond as a misleading witness in regard to thy neighbour." Once the rule is read against the background of the Adam and Eve story, the problem of why the rule is not a blanket condemnation of lying but has a narrower, legal bias to it is solved.

God holds all three participants in the theft guilty and punishes them: the man and the woman for the actual deed of stealing, and the serpent for his role as instigator. God's reaction underlines his rejection of their spoken testimony.

The story does not end with the punishments for the culprits. God is concerned that the same offense will be repeated with the other tree in the garden ("lest he put forth his hand, and take *also* of the tree of life, and eat, and live for ever"; Gen 3:22). The anticipation that there will be a repeat offense implies that this tree too will be looked upon as desirable and will be coveted for its conferral of eternal life. God thwarts the offense by expelling the couple from the garden. They are left with a sense of coveting and desire for something they can never acquire. Just as the punishment for the offense of taking from the tree of the knowledge of good and evil determined the course of future life for the man, the woman, and the serpent, so the human desire for whatever is seen to offer a better way of life will also complicate future human existence. Although it does not involve desire for an object, the next development after the conclusion of the Adam and Eve story is the problem of desire faced by Cain because of God's acceptance of Abel's sacrifice. God warns Cain about the power of desire (Gen 4:7), but he fails to heed the warning. The concern about Cain's handling of his emotions reveals that the problem of human desire is a perennial one that demands attention. Genesis 3:20 explicitly points to the future: Eve is the mother of all living.

Both the story and the Decalogue focus on the male. In the longer term, the problem that will confront the man after his expulsion from the garden will be his desire for whatever he sees as helping him to improve his lot in life. His destiny has been determined because he appropriated the knowledge of good and evil. Henceforth he will have problems with where to live, with sexual desire because of his awareness of female nakedness, and with an agricultural life made difficult by land which, unlike the fertile ground of the garden, will not be readily cultivable. Already in the story, God's clothing Adam and Eve is a recognition of the future problem of sexual desire.

The lawgiver takes stock of the problem of the man's future and issues a rule condemning coveting in matters relating to home life, sexuality, and agricultural life; that is, coveting as spelled out in the climactic rule in the Decalogue: "Thou shalt not covet thy neighbour's house, thou shalt not covet thy neighbour's wife, nor his manservant, nor his maidservant, nor his ox, nor his ass, nor any thing that is thy neighbour's" (Exod 20:17). The comparable rule in Deuteronomy 5:21, which contains both the verbs "to covet" and "to desire," as in Genesis 3:6, adds the neighbor's field.

The lawgiver does not find it necessary to produce a rule about coveting when considering the theft from the tree of the knowledge of good and evil. The narrator makes it clear that Adam and Eve's desire and covetousness are wrong. The lawgiver instead draws out what may be overlooked when the virtually identical offense is about to recur, namely, the prospect of Adam and Eve focusing their desire on the tree of life. The storyteller gives no attention at this point in his narrative to the inner aspect of the offense, perhaps because the event is thwarted. The lawgiver, however, picks up on the fact that the event's failure to come about should not conceal the fact that the inner feelings remain and constitute a problem.

The Decalogue furnishes a model of how all biblical laws came to be formulated. The laws were not just incorporated at certain points in a narrative history (for example, the Decalogue into a description of the Exodus from Egypt); they have an integral relationship with that narrative history.[22] The study of biblical law is thus an expansive field because it involves a study of biblical literature as well.

The narrative history and the legal material share the same spirit. Whether narrative or law, each focuses on significant beginnings, and each ranges back and forth over recurring patterns of conduct throughout the generations. In regard to the narratives, for example, the history of the patriarchs up to and including Moses and his generation moves forward in time, and the narrator records parallel developments. But sometimes the narrator refers back in time. Thus the narrator of the story of the Exodus recalls the promise to the patriarchs (Exod 3:6); likewise the narrator of the story of the golden calf (Exod 32:13).[23] The narration of the Adam and Eve, Cain and Abel history gives both the forward progression of events and backward references. Cain's marriage cannot be understood without the recognition that there is a sense in which his wife comes from his own body, as did Adam's wife from his body. In historical reality Cain appears to marry an independently existing woman, but in mythical time she exists as a part of him. Biblical history gives prominence to the notion that a particular generation repeats, or is made to repeat, what happened to a previous one.[24] Cain's marriage may furnish an example.

The punishments in the story also reveal the narrator's turn backward to what previously occurred. They take the form of reversals of previously existing conditions. The woman will experience pain in producing offspring whereas previously she had come painlessly from the man during a deep sleep. The man will experience a life of hardship and constant awareness of the need to search for food and shelter, whereas previously his life was one of ease and plenty. The serpent will become the most despised, the lowest of creatures, whereas previously it was a creature higher than the animals, and higher, in the sense of more godlike because of its awareness of good and evil, than the woman and the man in their primitive, animal-like state.

The lawgiver also proceeds forward in time, picking up problems that he comes upon in the narrative history, forward too in that if he notes a comparable problem in a later generation, he will take up the aspect there presented, either in the law he is drafting or in a separate law, before he too turns back to a parallel development in a previous generation.

The general bias of biblical narrative writing is similar to the general bias of the laws. Many narratives are etiological in character. They take up what is presumably a contemporary concern for the narrator and trace the issue back to the beginnings of the nation. Israel's superiority over the Edomites, for example, is the point of the story about the twins in Rebekah's womb (Gen 25:19–26) and how an oracle comes to her telling her that one, Jacob (Israel), will usurp the other, Esau (Edom). When the lawgiver sets out a rule he too presumably expresses a contemporary concern, but like the narrators of biblical stories he traces it back to some development in the early history of his nation. Alas, we have no evidence of what the contemporary concerns of each may have been.[25]

Another important characteristic shared by biblical laws and narratives is that both incorporate matters that occur in different generations.[26] The law of the king in Deuteronomy 17:14–20, for example, recognizes the loyalty of the Levites in the incident of the golden calf (Exodus 32) and incorporates aspects of the tradition of Israel's first king, Abimelech (Judg 9:1–6), of the people's request to Samuel to appoint a king (1 Samuel 8), and of Solomon's multiplying horses, wives, silver, and gold (1 Kings 10, 11).[27] The story about the Moabitess Ruth marrying into an Israelite family incorporates features from the story of her first ancestor, Lot, and his daughters (Gen 19:30–38) and from the story of Tamar's marrying into an Israelite family (Genesis 38).[28] The story of Esther incorporates features from the story of Joseph (Genesis 37–45) and from the story of Saul and the Amalekites (1 Samuel 15).[29]

All the biblical stories can be subjected to the kind of ethical and legal scrutiny I have laid out. Contrariwise, although this is a more difficult process, a story may be composed to support a rule. The story of Susannah and the elders or Abraham's sacrifice of Isaac (Genesis 22) may be examples, illustrating, respectively, a rule about the need to separate witnesses and a rule about the substitution of animal sacrifice for human.[30] It is, however, difficult to argue that these two stories provide much evidence that the illustration of the rule may be the motive for the composition of the story. Even more difficult, if not impossible, is to compose a story that incorporates all the details of a rule.

While any story might yield rules along the lines already indicated, the stories of the golden calf and of Adam and Eve, Cain and Abel yield rules of a kind and sequence that are peculiar to their idiosyncratic features. The story of King David's adultery (2 Samuel 11) might yield rules about adultery (although the offense being obvious, it would not be necessary to formulate a rule), murder (because Uriah's death in battle is a cover for David's murder of him), and theft (but again, the rich man's theft of the poor man's lamb is too obvious), but it would not yield the same rules as the Adam, Eve, Cain, and Abel material does, or in the sequence that material determines.

To account for the origin of the Decalogue is to surmise that a scribal school brought its knowledge of rules about idolatry, the vain use of Yahweh's name, and Sabbath observance to bear on the tradition about the golden calf. The scribes proceeded to formulate specific rules in response to the particularities of that incident. The process is perhaps best observed if one supposes that the kind of offenses cited in Hosea 4:2 were brought to bear on, for example, the particularities of the Adam, Eve, Cain, and Abel story. The offenses in Hosea 4:2 are swearing (but not of the specific kind, when Aaron uses Yahweh's name in reference to an idol), lying (but with no reference to a witness as in the more limited situation in the Decalogue), murder, stealing, and committing adultery. Moshe Weinfeld has matters the wrong way round when he claims that it is "clear that during the times of Hosea the prophet (eighth century B.C.E.) it [the Decalogue] was already existent (Hos 4:2; cp. Jer 7:9)."[31] The offenses cited by Hosea are of such common occurrence that one cannot make that claim without further argumentation. Resemblance tells one nothing about priority of composition. Moreover, Weinfield makes no attempt to explain why, if Hosea is citing the Decalogue, the language differs, the sequence of the items is not the same, and two of the items, swearing and lying, are more general in scope than the corresponding items in the Decalogue.

Assertions about the uniqueness of the Decalogue date back hundreds of years. Manifestly, the individual items are not unique; they have many parallels in other material in the Bible. What is unique about them is solely the way in which they were brought together to form a literary unit. Rules about murder and stealing originate in a different world of experience than do rules about the Sabbath and idolatry, and it is difficult to imagine why they would be set down together. It is less difficult to understand if one considers that the lawgiver worked on two narrative histories that inspired the diverse issues in question. This process accounts for the joining together of the individual items. There is consequently no need to puzzle over why rules that do not ordinarily belong together in the world of experience somehow came together in the Decalogue. An appreciation of how the narratives are conduits for the rules is crucial in revealing the factors that account for the origin of the Decalogue.

The claims commonly made for the uniqueness of the Decalogue do not hold up. In a recent representative study, Weinfeld makes a number of assertions. The Decalogue's commandments, he says, are meant for everyone in a way that is not true for other biblical rules. "No punishment is prescribed and no details or definitions are given." They constitute a set of brief and concise, basic obligations. They set out "religious and moral principles."[32] None of these assertions is accurate. The rule about false witness against a neighbor, unlike a rule forbidding lying, is not concise in wording and applies only in specific circumstances (directly contrary to Weinfeld's claim that like the other items in the Decalogue it is not "dependent on specific circumstances").[33] The rule about images supplies many details along the lines of a definition of what constitutes a graven image. A rule such as "Thou shalt not murder" is not a moral or religious principle, unlike, for example, a call to reverence all life. Presumably, Weinfeld's desire to elevate the rule about murder to a principle is what makes him include suicide within its scope. He does so parenthetically with no comment, apparently unaware that nowhere in either Old or New Testament is there even a suggestion of a prohibition against suicide.[34]

The claim that the Decalogue lacks sanctions is wrong. The rule against using Yahweh's name for a vain purpose is explicit in telling that the culprit will not go unpunished. The command to honor parents implies that the son who does not will find the land unproductive and will not live long. Some light is cast on why the rules about murder, adultery, stealing, and false witness have no sanctions attached to them by noting the role of punishment in the narrative about Adam, Eve, Cain, and Abel. The rule about honor to parents that precedes these rules contains the implied penalty: loss of attachment to the land and a shortened life span. The rule has Cain's punishment in focus. What is interesting to observe about the lack of explicit penalties for murder, adultery, stealing, false witness, and coveting is that Cain's murder of Abel does not result in death for Cain—the later penalty for intentional homicide—but in consequences related to his expulsion from the land he once tilled. Anyone who murders Cain is faced with sevenfold vengeance at heaven's hand. The theft from the tree, the misleading responses under questioning, and coveting all have consequences, but of a kind the lawgiver cannot translate into sanctions compatible with the needs of later Israelite legal culture. In this light, the gulf between a mythical account of the beginnings of human life and the later realities of Israelite culture is too great for the lawgiver to bother to attach specific sanctions to these rules.

6 An Eye for an Eye, and a Tooth for a Tooth: The History of a Formula

The formula "life for life, eye for eye, tooth for tooth," and variations on it, has no parallel in ancient Near Eastern sources of law. It is unique to the Bible. Near Eastern codes have penalties such as "If a citizen has destroyed the eye of one of citizen status, they shall destroy his eye" (CH 196), but no corresponding "life for life, eye for eye," and so on. The formula occurs in Exodus 21:22–25, the law about the death of a pregnant woman during a fight, and in Deuteronomy 19:15–21, the law about a capital penalty for a false witness. Then, puzzlingly, the formula is broken up in the one other place it occurs in the Old Testament. In Leviticus 24:18 the phrase "life for life" is detached from the death of a person and is applied to restitution in the instance where one man kills another's beast. The one responsible for the killing is to give life for life; that is, to replace the dead beast with a live one. Offenses that cause disfigurement come under the formula "fracture for fracture, eye for eye, tooth for tooth."

There is an even more puzzling aspect to the matter. A rule about murder is set down just before the rule about killing a beast. This homicide rule reads, "And he that killeth any man shall surely be put to death" (Lev 24:17). There is no reference in the rule to the phrase "life for life." It has been separated not just from the rest of the formula but also from the wrongful death of a person.

There is a yet larger puzzle about the Levitical rules, well recognized by interpreters. The rules about murder, restitution of an animal, and disfiguring injuries make their appearance, bewilderingly, in the context of a case about blasphemy. Nothing in the description of the blasphemy leads one to expect any link with the substance of these rules. Interpreters speak of interpolations, but they can provide no reason why the rules should have been inserted in the midst of—

not even at the end of—the discussion about what to do with a blasphemer. A proper reading of the rules in Exodus and Deuteronomy, in which the talion formula appears, solves all of these puzzles, and also casts light on why in early Jewish legal sources, in the famous Jesuanic statement about an eye for an eye, and in the Mekhilta (a second-century c.e. commentary on Exodus) the part of the formula about an eye for an eye and a tooth for a tooth is no longer attached to the part about life for life.

The formula as it appears in both the Exodus and Deuteronomic rules has, I contend, been totally misunderstood. I shall concentrate initially on the Deuteronomic rule in order to note its relevance to what turns up in Leviticus 24. The explanation of the formula in the Deuteronomic rule applies equally to the rule in Exodus about the pregnant woman.[1] Deuteronomy 19:15–21 reads:

> One witness shall not rise up against a man for any iniquity, or for any sin, in any sin that he sinneth: at the mouth of two witnesses, or at the mouth of three witnesses, shall the matter be established. If a false witness rise up against any man to testify against him apostasy; then both the men, between whom the controversy is, shall stand before Yahweh, before the priests and the judges, which shall be in those days; and the judges shall make diligent inquisition: and, behold, if the witness be a false witness, and hath testified falsely against his brother; then shall ye do unto him, as he had thought to have done unto his brother: so shalt thou put the evil away from thy midst. And those which remain shall hear, and fear, and shall henceforth commit no more any such evil in thy midst. And thine eye shall not pity: it shall be life for life, eye for eye, tooth for tooth, hand for hand, foot for foot.

It is universally thought that the formula in the Deuteronomic (and the Exodus) rule refers to retaliation in kind depending on the offense: a life for a life, an eye for an eye, a tooth for a tooth, a hand for a hand, and a foot for a foot. To be sure, some interpreters read back into the biblical rule the later Jewish interpretation that monetary damages are meant.[2] And some critics claim that the formula in both the Exodus and Deuteronomic rules has little connection with the crime under consideration (the death of the pregnant woman and false witness, respectively), rather that somehow, but one is not told why, the formula has become a generalized, proverbial statement loosely attached to the issues in the two rules.[3] It requires little comment that neither of these views—monetary damages are meant, a proverbial principle is being applied—comes anywhere near addressing the issue of the origin, language, and substance of the talionic formula.[4]

In fact, the formula means exactly what it says. It is about retaliation of a precise kind, but, and this is the point, it refers solely to an offender who has received a capital sentence. It means a life for a life—to be followed by the systematic mutilation of the offender's corpse. The formula begins with the top of the body, the eye, and works its way downward to the foot. The picture conveyed is that of a single body.

No corresponding penalty has yet turned up in Near Eastern law codes. The closest parallel I am aware of is the anatomizing of executed persons in eighteenth-century England. The preamble to the Murder Act of 1752 states, "It is become necessary that some further Terror and peculiar Mark of Infamy be added to the Punishment [of hanging]." This further punishment took the form of the criminal's corpse being given over to surgeons for public dissection. Peter Linebaugh points out that "except for a minority of surgeons and sympathetic observers, dissection was considered less as a necessary method of enlarging the understanding of *homo corpus* than as a mutilation of the dead person, a form of aggravating capital punishment."[5]

There is abundant proof for reading the biblical formula this way; that is, as expressing an intensification of the death penalty itself, "eine Verschärfung der Todesstrafe."[6] The Deuteronomic code explicitly refers to one such practice: sometimes a criminal is not just executed, his body is then hung on a tree for the living to behold and consider (Deut 21:22, 23).[7] Other biblical texts refer to comparable practices; for example, in 2 Samuel 4:12, after the offender is executed his hands and feet are cut off and the corpse hung (cp. Josh 10:26; 2 Samuel 21). After his death at the hands of the Philistines, Saul's head is cut off and his body is pinned to a wall (1 Samuel 31).

It is remarkable that this simple solution to the meaning of the full formula, "life for life," etc., has never, so far as I am aware, been considered. The reasons for this failure are many and interesting. For example, since the turn of last century the tendency has been to give a kindly interpretation to the formula in order to oppose the common perception that Old Testament law is somehow summed up in the notion of literal vengeance of an eye for an eye.[8] The formula in this reading is that the lawgiver meant to put a check on the limitless vengeance to which the society in question supposedly resorted. "Far from encouraging vengeance it limits vengeance and stands as a guide for a judge as he fixes a penalty suited to the crime."[9] The lawgiver intended only one eye for an eye, nothing more. There is no support for this view in any of the pertinent texts. Some rules, for example, Deuteronomy 25:1 ("If there be a controversy between men, then they shall come unto judgment"), instruct the disputing parties to avoid self-help and take their dispute before a court of law. In neither the rule about the pregnant woman nor the one concerning the false witness is there any such instruction.

In passing, it is worth questioning the common assumption that ancient societies were uncontrollably violent,[10] which probably derives from misguided notions about their primitiveness. It will owe much to a distorted reading of the sources caused by a failure to appreciate the profound role of the contrariness of things. One typically finds such contrariness showing up in matters of speech and early law codes. Only the remarkable gets attention; the unremarkable goes unnoticed.[11] To some extent, the same phenomenon applies to the record of incidents in the ancient sources—violent events may have been set down precisely because they were so out of the ordinary. In many countries today a national newscast will report a murder, but in the United States such an item of news is rare precisely because the murder rate is so high.

The Levitical legislation has also contributed to the failure to realize that the formula in Exodus and Deuteronomy applies to an executed criminal. That legislation does indeed refer to offenses that cause disfigurement to a living person. Consequently, its significance has been read back into the other two texts where the formula occurs.

In Leviticus 24, however, the formula has been broken up. It is no longer "life for life, eye for eye," etc.

There is one major clue in the text of the Deuteronomic law that should have signaled the correct reading of the formula. The law is about a false witness who accuses another of *sarah* (Deut 19:16). In every other biblical text where this word is found it means an offense against the deity, specifically, to turn against him, to reject him.[12] Interpreters are aware of this specific meaning but nonetheless feel constrained to claim that in the Deuteronomic rule about false witness the word instead appears to have some general sense of wrongdoing.[13] Perhaps they have opted for this dubious meaning because they have made up their minds that the talionic formula refers to various types of offenses.[14]

Interpreters do not question the assumption that they are dealing with a general formula of talion, despite the fact that the Deuteronomic law about the man who falsely accuses his bride of not being a virgin on her wedding night offers no support for their position (Deut 22:13–21). The charge against the woman is a capital one: if upheld, she is stoned to death at her father's house. If the charge turns out to be untrue, the husband's penalty is not death, a result one might have expected if the common view of the talionic formula had merit. Instead he has to pay money to the girl's family, he receives what might be a physical beating, and he is told he cannot divorce her. There is thus nothing especially talionic about the penalty he receives for his false charge.

The fact of the matter is that in Deuteronomy the law about false testimony refers to a quite specific instance of someone testifying that someone else has, in some sense, rebelled against God. The lawgiver has in focus a particular incident known to him, namely, the trial of Naboth in 1 Kings 21. The link between this incident and the formulation of the law provides compelling evidence for the view that the talionic formula is about the intensification of the death penalty. This same link also solves other problems in the law, for example, why the law dictates that a case of false witness automatically comes before a central tribunal and not first of all before a local court. A preceding law in Deuteronomy 17:8–13 states that a case should be referred to the central tribunal only if it is too difficult to decide at the local level.

King Ahab seeks to acquire Naboth's vineyard because it is adjacent to the royal palace. Naboth demurs on the ground that it is ancestral property and that this family tie puts him under an obligation to retain it. The Deuteronomic law that immediately precedes the law on false witness is precisely about such an obligation: "Thou shalt not remove thy neighbour's landmark, which they of old time have set in thine inheritance" (Deut 19:14). In other words, this particular rule, which seems so unconnected with the following rule about false witness, upholds Naboth's position, and once read as a direct response to his problem explains why the rule about ancestral boundaries and the rule about false witness are set down together.

The need for the lawgiver to respond to another legal feature of the narrative accounts for the statement about witnesses that stands at the beginning of the law about the false witness. That statement is to the effect that two or three witnesses are necessary in any legal proceeding. This general statement has also contributed to the misinterpretation of the following part of the law, about the false witness. It encourages the view that because it is a general statement, the following part of the law must also be general in character: all cases of false witness are to be punished according to the appropriate penalties for the alleged offenses.[15]

There is a quite specific reason, however, for the inclusion of the general rule about witnesses at the beginning of the law about false witness. Its inclusion affirms that the resort on the part of Ahab's wife, Jezebel, to two witnesses in Naboth's trial was in fact proper according to Mosaic legislation. The topics found in the biblical law codes are topics that arise in the narrative histories. These topics became the focus for the composition of the laws of Moses because his laws had not been formulated when the Book of Deuteronomy was produced. Jezebel's use of proper judicial procedure required especial scrutiny because she throws a cloak of legality over her move to be rid of Naboth.

It is indeed the king's spouse, Jezebel, who takes the matter of the acquisition of Naboth's vineyard in hand and instigates the offense against him.[16] She writes letters in the king's name—with, it is to be inferred, his tacit approval—and sends them to the leading men of Naboth's city. She requests that they conspire together to have Naboth convicted of the crime of cursing God and the king. In other words, the alleged crime is *sarah*, rebellion against God. She further tells them to find two thugs to testify to Naboth's wrongdoing. The leading members of Naboth's local community so proceed. Naboth is "set on high" at an assembly in his local city, as if in an honored position, but his false accusers, in collaboration with the local elders and nobles, have him convicted. The king confiscates Naboth's vineyard, he is stoned to death outside the city, and, most important to keep in mind, dogs ravage his corpse.

Why does the Deuteronomic rule have a case of false witness involving *sarah* automatically referred to the central tribunal instead of, initially at least, taken care of at a local level? The reason is patent. The rule has the totally lawless situation in Naboth's local community in focus. The judicial officials of his town participated in setting him up for false conviction. The lawgiver's position is that in light of this incident in Israelite history, such a development must never again occur in any local town. The rule is an ideal construction.

The rule concerns an attempted crime but does not consider a completed one. The Pharisees and Sadducees debated the interpretation of this rule at a very early period in Jewish legal history. The Pharisees opted for punishment only if the crime was attempted, the Sadducees only if it was accomplished.[17] The Pharisaic interpretation, despite the seeming oddness of the view—punishment only if the attempt is made—is the correct one. The rule assumes that the lawlessness seen in the Naboth incident will not reach the climactic stage because the central tribunal will always be able to examine the witnesses so well that any false testimony will be detected.[18] The idealistic view is that such serious false testimony will never get beyond the stage of attempt.

I return to the aftermath of Naboth's execution. It is a commonplace that where the weak seek legal redress from the powerful, the law has but fringe relevance at best.[19] In ancient law, for example, there is resort to the use of the curse as a mechanism to influence whatever conscience those with power who commit an offense might have: "Cursed be he that removeth his neighbour's landmark. And all the people shall say, Amen" (Deut 27:17). Or religion may address the problem. Thus, after a crime by the powerful has taken place, there is the claim that some kind of hidden justice is at work despite appearances to the contrary. The deity in the guise of the prophet Elijah takes on this role in dealing with the wrongdoing of Ahab and Jezebel. Heaven engineers the means of punishment for their misdeeds, and therefore the punishment mirrors the nature of the offenses. Each culprit's subsequent death is relevant to why the punishment in the Deuteronomic law takes the form that it does.

Ahab meets his death on the battlefield. His implication in the offense against Naboth determines not just that he must die but how his death comes about. Although commentators have not observed them before, there is a remarkable number of correspondences between the events surrounding Naboth's death and those surrounding the death of Ahab. In other words, the major feature of the narrative history in 1 Kings 22 is precise retribution along the lines of Wisdom 11:16: "*Per quod quis peccat, per idem punitur* [By what things a man sinneth, by the same also he is tormented]." The correspondences in question represent a biblical author's notion of divine punishment worked out long after the event.

First, Naboth dies because Ahab desires his ancestral property; Ahab himself dies in a battle to acquire a city, Ramoth-Gilead, that once belonged to his country (1 Kings 20:34).[20] Second, a local court trafficking in lies convicts Naboth; a heavenly court trafficking in lies engineers Ahab's death. At this court God puts a lying spirit into his four hundred prophets in order to misinform Ahab that he should proceed because the battle will have a positive outcome.[21] In reality, the battle will go against Ahab. When these prophets speak a falsehood with one voice, it is equivalent to the unanimity of deceit that prevails at the city court when Jezebel, the elders, the freemen, and two scoundrels proceed falsely against Naboth. The spirit that puts the falsehood into the four hundred prophets corresponds to the role of Jezebel in getting all the city to testify falsely against Naboth. Ahab does not know what is going on in the earthly court; he is likewise unaware of the proceedings in the heavenly one. Third, the one prophet, Micaiah, who does tell Ahab the truth about his forthcoming fate on the battlefield mocks Ahab in a manner that corresponds to the mockery of the king by Naboth, who allegedly had shown contempt for Ahab. When Ahab singles out Micaiah and asks him how the battle will turn out, Micaiah, knowing that it will lead to Ahab's demise, nonetheless lies initially and mimics the optimistic but wrong prediction that the other four hundred prophets have given to the king.[22] Fourth, the two base fellows, sons of Belial in Hebrew, who bring the decisive witness against Naboth stand for deviants in society, types fundamentally lawless, characters who represent everything contrary to general orderliness.[23] In terms of what they accomplish, their equivalent is the nameless Syrian soldier on the battlefield who deviates from orders. Instructed to shoot only at the Israelite enemy's leader, he fires a chance arrow that fatally strikes down Ahab, who has disguised himself as an ordinary soldier.[24] Fifth, at the town meeting to determine Naboth's fate, he is set on high among his townspeople—from his viewpoint a place of honor. The reverse is the case. He is convicted of a capital crime, of having cursed God and king. Ahab on the battlefield, anticipating—because he has taken stock of Micaiah's report of the proceedings of the heavenly court—that he will be safe from enemy fire if he disguises his royal status, dresses as a lowly member of the army. His reversal of status proves fatal. This reversal mocks his own position as king and, carrying God's curse, recalls Naboth's alleged offense against him.

Interpreters have been blind to all of the above correspondences. They have been misled by the account of how Ahab repents in response to Elijah's condemnation of what befell Naboth. Elijah in turn responds by declaring that evil to Ahab's house will not befall him in his own lifetime but will descend in his son's lifetime. This statement has to be interpreted narrowly; only a certain kind of punishment will not befall Ahab—namely, the loss of hereditary rights in his own lifetime. The violent death of his son sometime after Ahab's own death occurs, it is to be understood, because Ahab acquired Naboth's ancestral property, in consequence of which his own son and heir would lose property. From this perspective the punishment fits the crime, because with his heir's death Ahab's family loses hereditary succession to the kingship. Significantly, when Ahab's son dies violently at the hands of Jehu, his body is cast onto the plot of ground that Naboth once owned (2 Kings 9:21–26).

Commentators have failed to comprehend two things. First, Ahab's offense as spelled out by the prophet Elijah is a double one: "Hast thou killed, and also taken possession?" (1 Kings 21:19)—murder and wrongful acquisition of another's property.[25] When Ahab dies on the battlefield, his death, far from being a heroic and honorable one, as one commentator remarks,[26] represents mirroring punishment for Naboth's murder. Second, the composer of these narratives had to work with the historical facts available to him. One such fact would be that Ahab did not die in connection with any offense his family committed against Naboth's family, but did indeed die on the battlefield. Consequently, the composer of the saga had to work out both aspects of the retribution for Ahab's offense against Naboth by turning first to Ahab's death on the battlefield and then to the death of his son at the hands of Jehu (the latter death also representing a historical datum).

The Deuteronomic lawgiver sets out his penalty for the false witness in response to the precise retaliation that characterizes the narratives. In them, heaven's justice proceeds without regard to problems that earthly justice has to deal with (definition, proof, practicalities, and the like). Despite these drawbacks, one system often exerts influence on the other: law influences religion, and religion influences law.[27] Expressions of earthly justice are transferred to the deity or fate,[28] but sometimes there is a transfer back—as illustrated by the penalty laid down by the Deuteronomic rule about false witness.

It is important to note that the narrator of the story of Naboth sustains his interest in talionic punishment when he describes the aftermath of Ahab's death. After Naboth's death, dogs lick the blood from his corpse (1 Kings 21:19). After Ahab's death, dogs lick the blood that spilled onto the chariot he rode in and in which he received the fatal blow from the arrow.[29] Moreover, harlots wash themselves in this same blood. This aspect of Ahab's death is something that interpreters have never been able to make sense of, but surely it recalls his wife's decisive involvement in Naboth's death.

In the description of Jezebel's own death (2 Kings 9:22) reference is made to her harlotry, the point of which is the seductive charms of her foreign religion. Even the gesture of washing clothes can have associations with mourning.[30] The harlots who wash themselves in Ahab's blood recall the role of Jezebel in the chain of events leading to Ahab's death. Even though she is not physically present at the pool where Ahab's bloodstained chariot is washed, and is not an actual harlot, nonetheless as a member of a wider category of harlots she is a decisive link in that chain.[31] The presence of the real harlots at the pool, involved as they are in the final gesture of Ahab's end, is a commentary on his ill-fated involvement with a foreign wife. Not only does she exercise her wiles on him when she proceeds against Naboth, she is also a harlot in some transferred sense because of her origin.

The penalty of a life for a life, an eye for an eye, and so on in the Deuteronomic rule comes from the lawgiver's focus on the spectacle of Naboth's corpse.[32] After Naboth is put to death outside the city, as Jezebel instructs, the dogs proceed to their grisly work. Biblical dogs were not the modern, domestic variety. They would have torn Naboth's corpse to shreds.[33] So too the culprit in the rule deserves not just execution but execution followed by a comparable tearing apart of the corpse. Decisive support for this conclusion comes from the description of Jezebel's own death.

Like those of her husband's death, the events surrounding Jezebel's death and its immediate aftermath recall in a mirroring way what happened to Naboth. When King Jehu comes to execute her, she is positioned high up in her palace and has made herself up—the narrator is possibly pointing to her association with harlotry—by painting her face and adorning her head. Her elevated position recalls Naboth's honored one just before his demise when he is "set on high among the people" (1 Kings 21:12). When Jehu asks the members of Jezebel's household to show their loyalty to him, two or three eunuchs respond and throw her out a window. Their number, two or three—a curiously imprecise notice—recalls the requirement of a proper number of witnesses that Jezebel fulfills in proceeding against Naboth.[34] After Jezebel is dead, Jehu gives orders that she be buried. In the interim, however, her body is subjected to gruesome mutilation: "And they went to bury her: but they found no more of her than the skull, and the feet, and the palms of her hands" (2 Kings 9:35).

J. A. Montgomery speaks of Jezebel's demise in the following terms: "The ghastly details of the end of Jezebel's remains are petty, but historical."[35] Perhaps, but the much wider perspective of how heaven's inexorable law of precise retribution functions primarily determines the outcome. Even the detail about how Jehu goes indoors and eats and drinks after Jezebel is thrown to her death may not be a passing detail, but intended to recall Jezebel's first move ever in bringing about Naboth's own ghastly end. When her husband tells her about Naboth's unwillingness to sell him his vineyard, Jezebel's words to him are, "Arise, and eat bread, and let thine heart be merry: I will give thee the vineyard of Naboth the Jezreelite" (1 Kings 21:7).[36] In any event, what happens to Jezebel's corpse is due punishment for what happened to Naboth's. It is important to note that the narrative history recounts what happened *after* each death. Ahab dies from an arrow wound, and the dogs drink his blood; and a fall kills Jezebel, after which the dogs eat her. Such intensified, disgraceful death is the feature of the formula that the lawgiver incorporates into his law about what is to be done to the false witness.[37]

The accounts of the deaths of Ahab and Jezebel reflect not just the historical record that lay before the biblical author, but also his notion of retributive justice. Ahab's body is not mutilated after death, whereas Jezebel's is. Jezebel is directly involved in Naboth's end, and because Naboth's corpse is mangled, hers is too. Ahab's role in the murder, on the other hand, is less direct. He tacitly goes along with his wife's actions. Consequently, the dogs lick the blood not directly off his body but from the chariot in which he was killed. Ahab's indirect role also accounts for the detailed attention to the planning that precedes the battle in which Ahab dies. That planning recalls the planning that went into Naboth's trial because Ahab's offense is that he permitted his wife to proceed against Naboth as she chose. Ahab's permission to her and its results invite retribution in kind.

I turn now to a major change the formula underwent and to the bewildering puzzles with regard to its use in the Levitical legislation that I mentioned above. The formula is unaccountably broken up and appears, with no link to context, in the midst of a case that requires a decision about a blasphemer.[38]

A long-standing, well-recognized problem in the study of biblical law is the tantalizing nature of the relationship between the legal material in the Book of Deuteronomy and the comparable material in the Book of Leviticus. Similar rules, often narrow in scope, appear in both, but they are different to the point that interpreters speak of tension between their two sources. This judgment, however, has never been much more than an impression. The link I aim to establish between the case of the blasphemer in Leviticus and the law of false witness in Deuteronomy may cast new light on the general problem.

Suppose that the Levitical lawgiver setting out the case involving blasphemy had before him the Deuteronomic law about the false witness, and suppose further that his procedure was the same as the Deuteronomist's. He similarly focused on incidents in the nation's history, in this instance also on Naboth's execution.[39] If these assumptions are in order, new light is cast on the rules in Leviticus 24. For one thing, this scenario explains why the case is one involving blasphemy. Naboth is accused of this offense, and he is put to death for it. The accusation is false, but the punishment for the crime is appropriate according to the Levitical lawgiver. Just as the Deuteronomic lawgiver affirmed in the initial part of his rule about false witness that Jezebel's resort to two witnesses in fact conformed to correct procedure, so the Levitical lawgiver affirms that the sentence for blasphemy was also a correct Mosaic judgment.

The actions against Naboth are fundamentally lawless. Part of that lawlessness, however, consists of covering up the crime with correct judicial procedures and outcomes; namely, the use of the law of witnesses and the capital sentence for blasphemy. I assume that in Naboth's time these rules would have enjoyed proper legal status. They probably had not, however, the underpinning of Mosaic authority, and in light of Jezebel's crookedness there was need for it. The creation of the biblical law codes and many of the legends about Moses provide such underpinning. In this process of inventing past authority for later needs the lawmaker takes up a legal issue in a narrative and makes a judgment on it as if Moses himself was the judge. One example of the phenomenon is the institution of kingship that arose long after the time of Moses. "Moses" anticipated the issues involved and laid down certain requirements in light of a crisis of leadership in his own time (Deut 17:14–20).[40] Another example is the worship of the golden calves by the northern kings, beginning with Jeroboam (1 Kings 12:25–33). Moses gave his judgment on their use of the calves in the legend that tells how he condemned his brother Aaron for making a golden calf at the time of the Exodus from Egypt (Exodus 32).

While the incident about the blasphemer in Leviticus 24 may have some roots in a historical tradition—it is attributed to the time of Moses—it primarily addresses the issue of the legality of a death penalty for blasphemy in the later incident involving Naboth. A pointer in this direction is that the legislation immediately following the judgment about the blasphemer concerns the issue of the sacrosanctity of ancestral property (Leviticus 25), the issue that led to Naboth's execution for blasphemy.[41] Like the incident of the golden calf in Exodus 32, in which Moses also gave his judgment on the golden calves in 1 Kings 12:25–33,[42] the incident of the blasphemer in Leviticus 24 is the occasion on which Moses also gave his judgment on the punishment for blasphemy that arose with Naboth in 1 Kings 21.[43]

In the incident in Leviticus 24 the blasphemer is the son of an Israelite woman and an Egyptian. Their pedigree presumably reflects the historical setting: namely, in the wilderness after the Exodus. Among those who have accompanied the Israelites out of Egypt are some of mixed ancestry (Exod 12:38).[44] The mother is a Danite, a priesthood rejected as illegitimate by the Jerusalemite priesthood (1 Kings 12:25–33, 13:33, 34). Both the story of the golden calf in Exodus 32 and the story of the Danite blasphemer in Leviticus 24 may reflect a negative attitude to the tribe of Dan.[45]

Jezebel chooses to accuse the native-born Naboth of the particular offense of blasphemy and cursing the king. It is someone of her foreign background, however, who is more likely to blaspheme. The reason for the formulation of the rule in Exodus 22:28 ("Thou shalt not revile God, nor curse the ruler of thy people")—the rule Jezebel uses to convict Naboth—is the recognition that when the foreign group, the

Hivites, are absorbed by Jacob's clan, they might well curse the Israelite God and the ruler who has replaced their ruler (Gen 34:2, 35:1–5).[46]
Leviticus 24 is thus quite realistic in setting out a case that involves
the culprit's foreign background. The rule in Exodus 22:28 lacks a
sanction, whereas Leviticus 24 is very much taken up with the question of the appropriate sanction for the blasphemer. As already noted,
what happens to Naboth sharply raises the issue of the validity of the
capital sentence he received.

Most suggestive of the interconnectedness of the Levitical material
about blasphemy, the Naboth story about a false allegation of blasphemy, and the Deuteronomic legal material about false testimony is
that the Levitical lawgiver bewilderingly incorporates into his judgment on the blasphemer rules about murder, the killing of someone's
animal, and assaults that result in the victim's disfigurement. Why is
there a rule about homicide in Leviticus 24:17? Jezebel's offense is the
murder of the falsely accused blasphemer, Naboth. His death is a judicial murder, not a judicial execution. So the switch in focus from
blasphemy to murder in Leviticus 24 could have come from the legislator's taking stock of Naboth's demise for his alleged blasphemy.

The Deuteronomist concentrates on the offense of false witness,
which leads him to formulate, very understandably, a punishment
comparable to what the falsely accused Naboth received, namely, intensified death. The Priestly lawgiver recognizes that the false witness
in question is in reality a murderer, and he sets down a general rule
about homicide, namely, that the murderer should be put to death.
There is no hint, however, of any intensification of the death sentence.
Yet, if the offenses that the Priestly lawgiver cites immediately after
his homicide rule are included (bovicide and disfiguring injuries), it
can be seen that both lawgivers share a focus on precise retaliation in
kind. There is, however, a tantalizing difference.

The Deuteronomic talionic formula applies to a dead criminal: "life
for life" means that the life of a criminal is taken because he took the
life of his victim; "eye for eye" means that the eye is removed from the
criminal's corpse because the criminal mutilated, or let be mutilated,
the corpse of the victim. And so on. The Priestly lawgiver, on the other
hand, applies the talionic formula, as best he can, to the living: "life for

life" is not applied to the homicide but means that a live beast is given for a dead one that has been killed by a person; "eye for eye" means that the eye of a living person is removed because he caused the loss of an eye in another living person. And so on.

Does the Priestly lawgiver accept the Deuteronomic judgment on the false witness and find another use for the formula? And does he not know about the existing rule regarding assault (Exod 21:18, 19), which does not entail injuries in kind but rather the payment of monetary compensation? The only way to make sense of these tantalizing links is to assume that the Priestly lawgiver stands opposed to the intensified death penalty in any situation. He nonetheless takes up the formula that had been applied to an executed criminal and reapplies it to bovicide and disfiguring injuries. It is almost impossible otherwise to figure out how he moved to these topics from the topic of homicide.

For the Priestly lawgiver, then, a murderer is to be put to death, but subsequent systematic mutilation of his corpse is not in order. It is this stance that explains why this lawgiver, breaking up the talionic formula as used by the Deuteronomic lawgiver, applies it in the way he does. The Priestly lawgiver does not, as might have been expected, apply the first part of the formula, "life for life," in his homicide rule. Instead he applies it to the case of a person killing someone else's animal. This part of the formula, moreover, no longer means that if someone takes the life of an animal, the life of one of his animals will in turn be forfeited. The application of talion in regard to the loss of an animal means that a live animal will replace the dead one. This change from a focus on homicide to a focus on bovicide is most puzzling unless one assumes a negative reaction to the original Deuteronomic use of the entire formula to apply to an executed criminal.[47]

The assumption that the Priestly lawgiver reacts negatively to the Deuteronomic application of talionic punishment to an executed criminal also explains why he turns to the topic of assaults that cause bodily disfigurement. Taking up the topic of the disfigurement of a human body from the Deuteronomic rule about the false witness, he opposes the systematic mutilation of a dead body. Instead he reapplies the part of the formula about bodily disfigurements to a living person. As is common with the Priestly lawgiver, there is a tendency to generalize specific aspects of existing legal formulations. In this instance, he substitutes "fracture for fracture" for "hand for hand, foot for foot," but keeps "eye for eye, tooth for tooth."[48]

The basis of the Priestly lawgiver's objection to the intensification of the death penalty is probably his enormous interest in ritual law, a branch of biblical law very much concerned with the contagion contracted by touching dead bodies (Leviticus 21; Num 6:6–12, 9:6–11, 19:11–22, 31:19; cp. Lev 19:28). To cut up the dead body of an executed criminal, as the Deuteronomic rule requires, is indeed contact with impurity. This repugnance would explain why the Priestly use of the talionic formula is as far removed as possible from association with death. The Priestly lawgiver applies it, it is worth repeating, by having a live animal replace a dead one and by having a disfiguring injury done to a live person but not to a dead one.

The conflict between the rule in Exodus 21:18, 19, in which the penalty for assault is monetary compensation, and the rule in Leviticus 24:19, 20, in which the penalty is physical injury for physical injury, should not be explained on the grounds that each rule reflects different periods in the history of Hebraic law. There is no evidence of any kind that these rules describe the living reality of Israel's sociopolitical life. There is, however, detailed evidence that the rules are scribal, hypothetical responses to different issues that arise in the narrative histories. The rule makers were not particularly interested, perhaps not at all interested, in consistency between one rule and another. The rule in Exodus 21:18, 19 is a construction inspired by the brothers' assault on Joseph,[49] and the rule in Leviticus 24:19, 20 is a construction inspired by the hypothetical issue raised by the Deuteronomist's reaction to the offense against Naboth; namely, if cutting up a corpse is unacceptable, is there scope for penalties involving mutilation?

A concern of Leviticus 24 is that the laws apply equally to both the Israelite and the foreigner living within Israel. The Naboth story again illumines this aspect. The criminality of Jezebel is central to the story. She is a foreigner committed to her Sidonian religion, but as King Ahab's wife her status is that of an Israelite (1 Kings 16:31–33). The narrator leaves no doubt that Jezebel, who deceitfully presents herself as zealously upholding the Israelite law against blasphemy

(Exod 22:28), is culpable for her offenses; in a way she is doubly culpable because of her foreign background. The lawgiver expresses this judgment in his general statement in Leviticus 24:22, "Ye shall have one law for the alien and for the citizen: for I am Yahweh your God."

Several issues arise with regard to the later history of the talionic formula. Why, for instance, is the Levitical rule about disfiguring injuries not taken up except by Philo (*De Specialibus legibus* 3.33, 34), a certain group of Sadducees known as the Boethusians, and, to a lesser extent, Josephus (*Antiquitates Judaicae* 4.8.35.280)? Two interrelated reasons come to mind. First, from a practical point of view there is manifestly enormous difficulty in carrying out such surgical operations (an eye, for example)—a difficulty not faced if the one to be mutilated is a corpse. Second, the Levitical stance, and the other exceptions, may be as hypothetical as the stance represented by the Deuteronomic rule about the execution of the false witness. The Levitical interest in the topic of bodily disfigurement probably represents a particular Priestly interest—for example, the notion that bodily perfection reflects the idea of holiness—rather than a concern with law enforcement.[50] The Levitical language used to speak of such mutilating injuries is "If a man cause a blemish in his neighbour . . . " (Lev 24:19). For the Priestly writers, physical blemishes carried important consequences in other areas of life. A priest was automatically disqualified from his vocation should he have any one of a range of bodily blemishes (Lev 21:17–23). Blemished animals could not be offered as sacrifices (Lev 22:20, 21, 25; Num 19:2).

The talionic formula came to stand for monetary compensation for injuries received. The reason for this is again relatively easy to explain. In the Book of the Covenant the rule for the infliction of bodily injuries is payment for the victim's time off from work because of the injury and for having him restored to health (Exod 21:18, 19). In neither this code nor in the Deuteronomic code is the talionic formula applied to physical injuries to a living person. In both codes the formula applies to mutilation after death.

A digression is in order for the Deuteronomic rule about the woman who loses her hand because she grabbed the testicles of her husband's opponent during a fight (Deut 25:11, 12). Her punishment is physical mutilation, but not because she inflicted physical injury. Unlike the examples of physical damage to the man's genitals by the woman in the Middle Assyrian rules (MAL 8), the biblical rule is not about any actual physical injury to the man. The concern is solely with the shamefulness of her action. The rule is, however, in some sense talionic in character. The term for "hand" in this instance is not the usual Hebrew term *yad*, but *kaph*, which can mean both the palm of the hand and the female genitalia.[51] Her offense consists in the shamefulness of grabbing a man's genitals, and the rule, happily a hypothetical one, conveys the heinousness of her action. What exactly is intended by the allusion to her own genital region is disputed. Lyle Eslinger comes down firmly on the side of a clitoridectomy and reads the rule as damage to a man's genitals in turn paid back by damage to those of the woman.[52] I think that a literal cutting off of the hand is the sense, and that the lawgiver is drawing attention to the nature of her offense by using the term *kaph*.

The Pentateuch became the sacred constitution of the returning exiles from Babylonia in the time of Ezra and Nehemiah. Presumably the authorities resolved the contradiction between the requirement of disfiguring penalties for bodily injuries as laid down in Leviticus 24 and the requirement of monetary compensation in Exodus 21:18 by opting for the latter. They were, after all, faced with practical issues of law enforcement. The evidence from Tannaitic sources (from about 150 B.C.E. to about 200 C.E.), for example, the Mishnah and the Mekhilta, points to monetary compensation as the rule in practice (*babylonian Baba Kamma* 83b–84a; Mekhilta on Exod 21:18).

There are exceptions. The Boethusians appear to have favored actual retaliation.[53] Apart from their reputation for harshness,[54] they probably opted for the Levitical rules about literal talion because their ties to the Priestly aristocracy were long-standing and deep. In their straightforward, rational approach to Scripture they would have observed the contradiction between the rule about assault in Exodus 21:18 that lays down monetary compensation and the Levitical rule about literal talion. Having done so, they would have chosen the legal heritage to which they considered themselves especially linked, namely, the Levitical.

The priestly background of Josephus—he was a member of one of the great priestly families—may explain why he too expresses the view that a man who mutilates another should be mutilated in the same manner (*Antiquitates Judaicae* 4.8.35.280). He represents a unique position, however, in that he has a mutilating penalty apply only if the victim does not accept monetary damages. While it is possible that Josephus's position is an attempt to reconcile the contradictory biblical texts, it is worth noting that in his early life he experimented with both the Sadducean and Pharisaic sects. In the end he went over to the Pharisees, who came down firmly on the side of monetary compensation for bodily injuries.[55]

The position of Jesus in regard to the formula "an eye for an eye," etc., has nothing to do with opposition to mutilating penalties in force in the criminal law of his time, as David Daube has shown.[56] For one thing, the criminal law then did not allow mutilation, which had long since been replaced by fines. In his counsel about turning the other cheek (Matt 5:38, 39) Jesus is not concerned with law reform, but with ethical and spiritual understanding. In the face of humiliation he counsels meekness instead of going to court to seek a monetary award. Even though Jesus quotes the formula "an eye for an eye and a tooth for a tooth," he is not in fact opposing literal talion. The illustration he uses for the offense, a slap on the face, is an excessively weak one. The focus on such a mode of striking is evidence that he deals not with assault but with insult, because a slap on the face is the standard description of such a delict in antiquity. The English word *insult* originally meant a physical action, an assault, but from the seventeenth century it came to be confined to nonphysical action.[57] So too Matthew's narrowly focused use of the formula no longer means physical action, but nonphysical in the sense that no visible injury is the result.

Daube argues that around the time of Jesus, Tannaitic law extended the law of assault to include insult, with the consequence that monetary compensation could be demanded not just for physical injury, for incapacity to work, for medical expenses, and for pain, but also for an insult to one's person (200 suz if slapped with the front of the hand, 400 if with the back). Jesus' position represents opposition to the idea that one should receive money for such an intangible injury. From a legal point of view, his position is a conservative one, indicating that he was uncomfortable with a new development. A modern parallel to his attitude would be the widespread negative public reaction to a child who takes his parents to court because they boxed his ears.

I would add a further consideration as to why the formula "an eye for an eye," etc., comes to signify insult. Already in its use in both Exodus and Deuteronomy the formula specifies actions that intend insult. They are visited upon the dead person in order to disgrace him. Conceivably, the formula still retained something of this terrible disgrace in the time of Jesus.

Daube notes that the talionic formula that Jesus quotes omits the part about "life for life." The reason, he claims, is that in line with the Tannaitic law of the time, the part about "an eye for an eye, and a tooth for a tooth" no longer referred to literal talion, whereas "life for life" still did. I would instead argue that because Pharisaic jurisprudence used the Levitical formula to signify what the rule about assault in Exodus 21:18, 19 lays down—namely, monetary penalties—it is the Levitical formula that Jesus quotes. That formula already had "life for life" separated from "eye for eye," etc.[58]

Only in Matthew is the talionic formula the basis for the delict of insult. In later Jewish law, the rule about the immodest woman in Deuteronomy 25:11, 12 is, remarkable as it may appear, the scriptural basis for the delict, not the talionic formula.[59] The reason for the change is probably the desire on the part of the Rabbis to separate offenses that involved actual damage to a person from those that involved the abstract and spiritual notion of indignity inflicted on someone. Jewish law in the times of Jesus and Matthew had not yet broken through to this desirable jurisprudential distinction. The Deuteronomic rule about the immodest woman proves useful in working with this kind of distinction, because the woman's offense did not cause physical damage but injury in the sense of insult. The Rabbis probably also chose to base their rule about insult on the rule about the woman's shaming action because the latter had likely become a dead issue in their time.[60]

7 Life/Death

About to confront death, Moses addresses his people. After giving them his laws, he presents his followers with a clear-cut choice: "See, I have set before thee this day life and good, death and evil. If thou obeyest the commandments . . . then thou shalt live and multiply in the land which thou art entering to take possession of it. But if thine heart turns away . . . thou shalt not live long in the land. . . . I call heaven and earth to witness against you this day, that I have set before thee life and death, blessing and curse . . . therefore choose life, that thou and thy descendants may live, loving Yahweh thy God, obeying his voice, and cleaving to him, for that means life to thee and length of days, that thou mayest dwell in the land" (Deut 30:15–20). Proverbs 8:35, 36 has a similar perspective: the one who finds wisdom finds life and favor from God; the one who hates wisdom loves death. Adherence to the laws will give life to the Israelites; failure to adhere will lead to death.[1]

This view about living a just life is a radical one reminiscent of the view embodied in the ancient Egyptian notion of the scales of justice. After death, a man is weighed in the nether world against truth. He is represented by his heart, which is placed in one dish; in the other is truth in the form of a feather. The result is either perdition or salvation. There is no compromise.

David Daube thinks that the notion underlying the scales of justice has had profound influence on the ways justice actually operates. "Justice as a living phenomenon contains an element that is averse to finer differentiations, quite apart from practical difficulties. The symbolism of the scales expresses a deep-rooted tendency to see no shades between black and white, to admit no degree of right and wrong, to allow no distribution of loss and gain among several litigants, to send a party away either victorious or defeated."[2] As an example of what he means, Daube points out how Roman law and its modern descendants award to a man the fruits he draws because he honestly thinks he is the proprietor when in fact he is not. This is unjust to the real proprietor. English law gives the fruits to the proprietor, and this is unjust to the bona fide possessor. A less black-and-white notion of justice would require a sharing between them.

As embodied in both the Egyptian scales of justice and in Moses' peroration as he approaches death, the notion of justice as an all-or-nothing affair had, I wish to argue, a profound influence on the way biblical lawgivers actually constructed laws. One of the keys to understanding many a biblical law is to note that the lawgiver tried to forestall the blurring of the mutually exclusive categories of life and death.   .

Consider the prohibition "Thou shalt not boil a kid in its mother's milk" (Exod 23:19, 34:26; Deut 14:21b). Why ever not? To this day, the very same dish is served in the Middle East, and its Arabic name so describes it: *laban ummu.* The prohibition has had profound influence on Judaism. It is the basis for the system of *kashrut,* of separating meat dishes from dairy.

There is no dietary reason for the rule. Eating a young animal cooked in its mother's milk does not harm the health of the consumer. Ambiguity about life and death is in fact the issue underlying the rule. The aim of the lawgiver is to keep life and death apart. The crucial move in understanding the rule is to inquire why it specifies the mother's milk, and not milk in general. Interpreters of the injunction all stress its problematic nature, but the solutions they offer indicate their failure to grasp the problem.

When modern inquirers are puzzled about a matter, they often turn to ancient sources. Exegetes have taken this route in regard to the kid law. While rejecting Philo's view that the law is a humanitarian one, they fasten onto Maimonides' view that the prohibition is anti-idolatrous in character, that it is directed against a Canaanite practice.[3] A Ugaritic text of the thirteenth century B.C.E. is adduced as evidence for the existence of such practice.[4] The text is faulty in parts, but scholars generally agree that the reference is to a fertility rite that entails boiling a kid in milk. The connection between the biblical prohibition and the social reality behind the Ugaritic text is patently speculative. Moreover, scholars' ready acceptance of the parallel shows their failure to grasp the puzzling element in the biblical prohibition. There is one major difference between it and the Ugaritic text. The biblical rule concerns boiling a kid in its mother's milk, the Ugaritic text refers simply to milk. T. H. Gaster rightly points to this difference as constituting a decisive objection to the use of the Ugaritic text to illuminate the biblical rule.[5] Gaster suggests on the basis of comparative folklore that the biblical rule is about the superstitious fear of tampering with the milk of the she-goat and thereby rendering it harmful in some magical way.[6] He too has difficulty in understanding why the rule specifically mentions the mother's milk, but he plausibly gets round the problem by claiming that the mother's milk was more likely to be used, or, alternatively, that people would more readily believe that harm to the animal resulted when the dam's milk was used. Gaster, hovering around the problem, likewise fails to locate it.

The crux of the matter is simply that the Israelite is prohibited from cooking the dead kid in the very milk that had been used to sustain its life. In real life such a jarring juxtaposition of life and death can trouble the human observer, hence the prohibition. Philo, in fact, is the one commentator who comprehends the true reason for the law. Modern scholars, however, pay attention only to his more general humanitarian explanation and ignore his particular reasoning. Philo states, "For he [Moses] held that it was grossly improper that the substance that fed the living animal should be used to season and flavour the same after its death, and that while nature provided for its conservation by creating the stream of milk and ordaining that it should pass through the mother's breasts as through conduits, the licence of man should rise to such a height as to misuse what had sustained its life to destroy also the body which remains in existence" (*De Virtutibus* 143–4).[7]

A number of other Deuteronomic laws embody this concern with keeping life and death separate. The clearest example of such a law is Deuteronomy 12:16 (cp. Lev 17:10–14)—an Israelite must not eat the blood of a slaughtered animal, for the blood constitutes the soul or life of the animal.[8] The role ascribed to the blood parallels the role ascribed to the milk. Just as an Israelite should not consume dead animal flesh with its lifeblood, so he should not prepare for consumption a dead kid in the milk that once gave life.

The Deuteronomic lawgiver ascribes similar notions of life to both the first fruits of the ground and to the agricultural triennial tithe (Deut 26:1–15); and he is similarly taken up with ensuring that such agricultural produce has no association with death. This produce represents the divine gift of new life in the new land the Israelites are about to possess. The person who dedicates the tithe has to declare that not only has he refrained from consuming it while mourning the dead, but he has not offered it to the dead for their consumption. The command to dedicate the first fruits and the prohibition against cooking a kid in its mother's milk are set down together in Exodus 23:19 and 34:26—some indication that similar thinking may inform each rule.

The rules set down alongside the prohibition about the kid in Deuteronomy 14:21 are also concerned with sharply distinguishing between life and death. The kid law comes immediately after a law that prohibits the Israelites from eating the flesh of an animal that died a natural death. S. R. Driver, noting that the corresponding law in Leviticus 17:15, 16 is placed immediately after a prohibition against eating blood, states that the reason why the Israelite must not eat this kind of dead beast is because the animal's blood would not have been satisfactorily drained from its body.[9] When the blood is not properly drained off, the dead animal constitutes an abhorrent mixture of life and death. The animal can be sold to a foreigner, though. Unless one attributes malevolence to the ancient Israelites, the sale to the foreigner is testimony to the fact that the issue is not one of health. Rather it is about this seemingly curious concern to keep life and death apart.

Another law motivated by that concern is Deuteronomy 14:1: the Israelites are not to cut themselves or shave between their eyes on account of the dead. The usual explanation for the law is that the Israelites must not do what the Canaanites do, namely, mourn the dead in this way. But as the texts in Isaiah 15:2, and 22:12; Jeremiah 16:6,

41:5, and 47:5; Ezekiel 7:18; Amos 8:10; and Micah 1:16 well bring out, this was the standard Israelite way of mourning the dead. Commentators get around the difficulty by claiming that the Deuteronomic rule was ignored or was not known.[10] The more likely explanation is that the Deuteronomic lawgiver, especially alert to such matters, recognized that these mourning customs constitute an entanglement of life and death in the living person. As S. R. Driver puts it, the actions of the mourner "imprint upon their person the visible tokens of death."[11] The lawgiver's concern to avoid death impinging on life appears to be the explanation for why he opposes a customary Israelite practice.

The three laws—make no marks on one's body for the dead, do not eat an animal that died a natural death, and do not cook a dead kid in its mother's milk—are found in the same section of Deuteronomy 14:1–21. Between the mourning law and the other two laws come the lists of animals, fish, and birds, some of which may be eaten and some of which may not. Although other criteria help to determine which creatures can and cannot be eaten, a major precept seems to be that creatures that kill other creatures are forbidden.[12] Their killing (and eating) habits in no way meet the requirement of separating out life in the form of blood from the dead prey. Attached to the two laws about mourning the dead and not eating a dead animal (Deut 14:1, 21) are the words: "For thou art a holy people unto Yahweh thy God." The meaning is that the Israelites are to separate themselves from the surrounding peoples. If the Israelites keep life and death in all their manifold forms apart, they will both enhance this cultural difference and give content to this notion of sanctity.

There is a series of five laws in Deuteronomy 21 in which the concern to keep life and death apart plays a significant, if complex, role. A law about removing the blemish to the land caused by the victim of a murder, the assailant not being known, is followed by a law about the procedure for marrying a foreign woman who is a captive of war, and who, if the marriage does not work out, must be treated with dignity. This law is followed by an inheritance law that upholds the right of the firstborn son to a double portion of his father's estate. Then comes a law about a son whose disobedience to his parents brings him a sentence of death. Finally, there is a law about a criminal whose body, having been hanged on a tree after his execution, must be buried before nightfall. In terms of legal topics there is no link between one law and the next. This lack of sequential logic seems to justify the consensus of opinion that the laws in question, coming from different historical periods and sources, were brought together by a haphazard editorial process. In fact, the matter is quite otherwise.

I shall not here go into detail on why the lawgiver picks up on the topics he does except to point out that, as usual, they came to his attention through his scrutiny of certain narrative traditions.[13] The important point for this discussion is that the traditions in question are characterized by someone's failure to recognize who is and who is not an enemy. The rule about the blemish to the land caused by a homicide comes from a story in 2 Samuel 20. David's army commander Joab murders David's other commander, his fellow Israelite Amasa, while both are in pursuit of David's enemy, the rebellious Sheba. The sight of Amasa's blood-soaked body in the highway causes the Israelites to stop and gape. To avoid this, Amasa's body is thrown into a field and covered with a cloth. The lawgiver picks up on this particular development in setting down a rule about a slain body found on Israelite land.

The next rule, about an Israelite's acquiring a woman taken captive in war with a view to making her his wife, is, like the previous one, inspired by a tradition about enmity within a group related by family ties. Laban accuses his son-in-law, Jacob, of taking his daughters, Rachel and Leah, "as captives taken with the sword" (Gen 31:26). Jacob does not view his action in this light, but Laban nonetheless moves to ensure that his daughters will be treated properly in keeping with their status as wives of Jacob, not as captives in war. The following rule about a man's failure to recognize the right of his firstborn son by a wife whom he hates is inspired by Jacob's hatred of his wife Leah (Gen 29:31, 32), who gives birth to Reuben, his firstborn son. Again the lawgiver takes up the topic of hostility wrongly directed. Just as Laban claims that Jacob treats his daughters as war captives because of Jacob's enmity directed at him, so there is the concern that a firstborn son like Reuben might be discriminated against because of a father's hatred of the mother. The law of the disobedient son follows the law about the right of a firstborn son because the lawgiver looks at the wrongful hostility directed at Esau on account of Rebekah's favoritism to his brother, Jacob. The lawgiver examines the situation to see if there might ever be grounds for treating someone like Esau as not worthy of the right of the firstborn son. The fifth rule in the series expresses concern about the exposed corpse of a criminal. In focus in this instance is how enmity against King Saul is directed at his sons, who are put to death and their corpses exposed (2 Samuel 21).

The five laws in Deuteronomy 21 have a striking feature in common, namely, the interplay between life and death. The lawgiver turns his attention to situations involving death, each of which is connected with wrongdoing. There is the body of a man murdered in the open country with the consequence that the land is defiled; there is the woman who must be allowed to mourn her parents before her Israelite captor can marry her; there is the father who, contemplating his death, wrongly seeks to deny his firstborn son his proper claim to a double share in the inheritance; there is the son who brings a death sentence on himself for his abuse of his parents; and there is the executed criminal whose hanged body would defile the land if not removed before nightfall. No uniform feature about these deaths emerges. There is justified death and unjustified death, contemplated death and death associated with war. There is also the notion of intensified death.[14]

What also stands out in these rules is that alongside the focus on death is a focus on life in some particularly enhanced sense. There is the abundantly fertile, newly possessed land; the woman about to enter a marital union in a cultural setting new to her; the birth of a firstborn son; sonship; and the new land again. The marked interplay between life and death is a feature shared by the five laws. I shall look at each in turn.

THE SLAIN MAN (DEUTERONOMY 21:1–9)

When the nation of Israel inherits the land, it receives the gift of life in diverse forms. The land's productivity is extraordinary (Deut 6:3, 10, 11), and day and night, from the beginning of the year until the end, providence cares for it and watches over it (Deut 11:12). Crops, animals, and humankind prove abundantly fertile (Deut 7:13–14, 8:8, 13, 11:15). Long life on the land is in prospect because there will be peace, security, and rest from enmity. In return for such life-enhancing benefits the Israelites are obliged to maintain the land in a state of purity. Certain offenses will mar such a state. The body of a person murdered by an unknown assailant is a horrible blot on the land, precisely because this land represents the manifestation of the deity's conferral of life on the Israelites. In his opening sentence the lawgiver throws into relief such a blemish: "If one be found slain in the land which Yahweh thy God gives thee to possess . . ." (Deut 21:1).

The clearest indication that the law gives prominence to the polarity of life and death is the ceremony necessary to absolve the nation of guilt for that particular offense to the land. The elders of the city closest to the scene of the crime have to slaughter a young heifer that has not been worked and has not pulled in the yoke, by breaking its neck at a site on the land that has not been plowed or sown, and where there is perennial running water.[15] What stands out in regard to both the heifer and the plot of land is their untapped vitality.[16] The piece of land represents potential fertility, and the young heifer, in the words of C. F. Keil, is "in full and undiminished possession of its vital power."[17] Yet the animal is struck down at this spot. As dramatic as the case of the man slain in the open country is this example of death being visited upon life.

Some scholars hold that the animal is a substitute for the unknown murderer, the breaking of its neck representing his punishment.[18] The influence of their own legal culture gets in the way of their appreciating the strange aspect of this law.[19] There is no concern with the assailant in the law. If those scholars were correct, one would expect a member of the victim's family to participate, either himself or in cooperation with the elders, in the killing of the heifer. But there is no mention of the victim's family and their need to redeem the blood of their relative. The law is not concerned with the murderer's offense as such, nor is it concerned with what is more frequently met with in other law codes (CH 24, for example)—namely, the legal liability of the occupiers of a territory to compensate the relatives of the victim.[20] The law's concern is solely with the abhorrent mixture that is the consequence of the crime: innocent blood on the new land.

The ceremony, involving as it does the disturbing conjunction of life and death, is necessary because it serves to focus attention on what has occurred.[21] The killing of the heifer represents the slaying of the victim. The heifer is to be slain on land that is especially fertile because it is unplowed and beside an ever-running stream. The special nature of the site of the slaughter serves to remind the Israelites of the special nature of the entire land that God gave them. In interpreting the law, it is crucial to pay attention to the alleged historical circumstances in which all of the laws were promulgated. Just before his death, Moses proclaimed his laws so that they would take effect in the new land. The distinctive character of both the heifer and the uncultivated ground, plus the dramatic slaughter of the animal at this spot, serve to highlight not just the killing itself, but its significance in the new communal environment.

Many commentators wrongly assume that the animal's blood is shed.[22] Breaking the neck can produce blood, but it need not, and this particular mode of killing (presumably by a well-struck blow) strongly suggests that it was chosen specifically to avoid bloodshed. The use of *halal* (to pierce) to refer to the murdered man in the law leaves no doubt that blood was spilled at his death. The best way to appreciate that no blood is shed when the heifer is sacrificed is to take seriously the statement that follows its death. The elders wash their hands over it and declare, "Our hands did not shed this blood, neither did our eyes see it shed." If the animal's blood has flowed, this statement makes no sense.[23] While the lawgiver finds it is necessary to bring together life and death in order to highlight the horror to the land caused by the slain body on it, he nonetheless shows sensitivity by not adding more blood to the land by shedding the heifer's blood.

THE CAPTIVE WOMAN (DEUTERONOMY 21:10–14)

The law of the foreign captive woman dictates that a period of one month must elapse before the Israelite warrior can consummate their marriage. For her, this lapse of time is not one of joyous anticipation of a wedding, but quite the opposite, a time to mourn her father and mother. She does so by shaving her head, paring her nails, and removing the clothes she wore when taken captive. When captured she was, the law informs us, a woman of beautiful appearance, but in this state the reverse is more likely to be true. The contrast is as startling as the juxtaposition of the forthcoming wedding and the required mourning period.[24] Although some commentators are unsure how to interpret the actions required of her, there can be no doubt about their association with mourning.[25] The role played by clothes in connection with death is well documented.[26] The vow of a Nazirite, male or female, is made void by contact with the dead, and is shown to be so by the person's shaving his or her head (Num 6:2–9). The paring of nails in mourning is attested in Arabic sources.[27]

The lawgiver recognizes that the customary practice of acquiring a female captive in war is fundamentally wrong. Just as an Israelite humbles (*'innah*) an unbetrothed Israelite woman by taking her without her father's consent (Deut 22:28, 29), so too does he humble (*'innah*) the foreign woman.[28] The woman's parents will never see her again. The day of their deaths will not be known to her. It is not likely, in the case of the mother, at least, that they died in the battle. The honor owing to parents requires that at death their children mourn them. The state of uncertainty as to their fate is a concern of the lawgiver. He notes that the Israelite warrior who is intent on enjoying the woman sexually is liable to overlook her relationship to her parents. The lawgiver insists that she undergo a period of mourning before the Israelite consummates a union with her. The result is that she mourns parents who may well be alive. An Israelite woman who has been acquired without proper ceremony may not be divorced by her Israelite husband (Deut 22:29). The captured foreign woman may be divorced, but the lawgiver denies the husband the right to treat her as a slave and sell her should he do so.

To mourn the living is an odd and disturbing act.[29] It involves the undesirable coming together of death, in the form of her mourning, and life because of the likelihood that at least one of her parents still lives. This odd juxtaposition is given vivid expression. Previously the lawgiver prohibited any physical disfigurement as a sign of mourning (Deut 14:1). But here he requires the woman to cut off her hair and pare her nails. She has to do what the lawgiver considers fundamentally wrong, namely, in S. R. Driver's phrase,[30] imprint upon herself "the visible tokens of death."[31] The reason is to express the fact that she mourns parents who might not be dead. This disturbing confusion is not her fault, but the result of her capture in war. There is wrongdoing here that the lawgiver does not, or more likely cannot, proscribe.[32] He does not conceal the offense, rather he gives it dramatic expression by the form of mourning he requires of the woman.

There is a pronounced parallel between this law and the preceding law about the slain man. The dead man on the new land represents an unwelcome impinging of death on life, in acknowledgment of which the elders of the nearest city must slaughter the heifer at an especially fertile site. The forcible removal of the woman from her homeland, while acceptable because of war, nonetheless involves dishonor in her separation from her parents. The separation causes a bewildering overlap of life and death. From one viewpoint the parents are alive, from another viewpoint—hers—they are dead. By way of recognizing what has occurred, the lawgiver requires the captive woman to symbolize this confusion by the ritual imprinting of death on her living person. The unknown factor in each of these laws—the unidentified assailant and the uncertainty about a parent's death—brings about the need for ceremonial rites. Ceremonies often grow out of the need to cope with the unknown.

The contrast between life and death that shows up in the ritual mourning comes to even more dramatic expression in the fact that the woman goes from, as Ecclesiastes 3:4 has it, "a time to mourn" to "a time to dance," in the form of her nuptials. Such a juxtaposition in time of lamentation and wedding celebration lends to the law a startling element similar to that found in the preceding law about the slain man. Should this wedded state not last and her Israelite husband decide to dismiss her, he must not treat her as a captive of war and dispose of her as a slave. Nothing resembling war is to characterize the settled life of this community.[33] The period of mourning for her parents and the proper wedding procedure establish her honor in her new community.

PRIMOGENITURE (DEUTERONOMY 21:15–17)

A custom typically invites little or no reflection on the part of those involved in it. The firstborn son has a different standing from all other siblings precisely because he is the firstborn. He receives special treatment even though he and his father may lack a conscious awareness of their unique relationship. A customary practice in ancient Israel was for the firstborn to receive a double share of his father's estate. Ordinarily when a father contemplates his family's future after his death, his firstborn son's special status is a matter of course. Sometimes, however, a complication may exist to disturb what is taken for granted. One such is in a polygamous setup in which the first son is the issue of a wife whom the husband hates. In that situation the customary right of the firstborn may be threatened.

The lawgiver is disturbed by such a possibility: "If a man have two wives, one beloved and another hated, and they have borne him children, both the beloved and the hated; and if the firstborn son be hers that was hated: Then it shall be, when he maketh his sons to inherit that which he hath, that he not make the son of the beloved firstborn before the son of the hated, which is indeed the firstborn: But he shall acknowledge the son of the hated for the firstborn, by giving him a double portion of all that he hath: for he is the beginning of his strength; the right of the firstborn is his" (Deut 21:15–17). The lawgiver thus seeks to prevent the overthrow of a time-hallowed right. To bring out the potential wrong he juxtaposes two opposites: life and death. At the very moment when the father distributes his goods and wealth in contemplation of death, the lawgiver reminds him of something he should not need to be reminded of, namely, that his firstborn son is special because he is "the first fruits of his strength" (reṣit 'ono). This son represents the supreme example of the father's procreative power. This is true both in a past sense, because he was conceived at the height of the father's virility, and in a future sense, because this son will preserve in a preeminent way his father's name and memory, his ongoing "life."[34]

Like the law of the slain man and the law of the captive woman, which dramatically illustrate death coming into contact with life in order to recognize and come to terms with an offense, this inheritance law sets down the jolting but justifiable juxtaposition of "a time to die" with "a time to be born" (Eccles 3:2) in order to forestall an offense.

Ecclesiastes 3:1 states, "For everything there is a season and a time for every matter under heaven." The statement implies that one might expect and hope for a separation of the two opposites, the time of birth and the time of death.[35] The moment of the firstborn son's birth should have determined his special status with his father, and hence the matter should not come up at the moment when his father is anticipating his own death.[36] Ecclesiastes 3:8 states that there is "a time to love and a time to hate." The father in the law has the misfortune to be married to a woman he hates as well as to one he loves.[37]

THE INCORRIGIBLE SON (DEUTERONOMY 21:18–21)

The next law concerns a son who will not obey his father and his mother. They chastise him, but if this has no effect, something dramatic takes place: his parents, who gave him life, themselves hand him over to the authorities for capital punishment. No law illustrates so forcibly how this lawgiver views certain kinds of wrongdoing as a clash of life and death.

In Greek drama there is opposition to the idea of a father's seeking vengeance against his son. Antigone declares that it is not right for a father to do so, no matter how guilty the son (Haemon) may be (Sophocles' Oedipus Coloneus, ll. 1189–91). David is totally reluctant to avenge himself on Absalom (2 Samuel 18, 19). A new perspective on the biblical law of the incorrigible son comes from noting how, in line with the preceding laws, there is again the dramatic conjunction of life and death. A son who owes his life to his father and his mother is handed over by them to a death sentence. The unexpected role played by the mother in the legal proceedings becomes more understandable in light of this special perspective.

The parents charge their son before the elders with being a glutton and a drunkard. They had chastised him, probably by physical means, in an attempt to save his life, just as in Proverbs 23:13, 14 the sages counsel a parent to save a wayward son's life by physically chastising him. Like the lawgiver, the sages too couch their reflections on human conduct in terms of life and death. In this same context in Proverbs (v. 20), the sages take up, in language identical to that used in the law, the problem of a son's drunkenness and gluttony. Both lawgiver and sage share the same tradition of wise counsel.[38]

THE HANGING CORPSE (DEUTONOMY 21:22–23)

The last law in the series of five provides a concrete example of death in the midst of life. As a disturbing but necessary action to deter crime, the dead body of a criminal is hanged on a tree. By night, however, when only God sees, the dead body constitutes an abhorrent sight to God, whose eyes alone are upon the land day and night to confer upon it life and good (Deut 11:12). To prevent the loss of such benevolence, the body has to be buried before nightfall.

There is interesting overlap between the first and last laws. The hanged body in open view compares with the slain victim in open country. The visible demonstration of death in the midst of life is justified in the instance of the hanged body, but not in regard to the slain victim. The victim's presence on the land nonetheless requires, in the form of the slaughter of the heifer at the special spot of ground, a corresponding demonstration of death visited on life. A further comparison is noteworthy. The polluting presence of the murder victim on the land would have its analogue if the criminal's body remained on the tree after dark. Should it do so, the lawgiver warns, the land would be defiled. Also noteworthy is that in each instance the pollutant becomes invisible to the human eye: the blood that has gone into the ground and the criminal's body left after nightfall.

These five laws provide interesting examples of the conflict of law with principle. From some higher perspective certain actions are fundamentally wrong—slaughtering the heifer, marking the body in mourning, having to remind a dying man of the identity of his firstborn, delivering one's own child over for capital punishment, and hanging a corpse—but the lawgiver nonetheless sanctions them. On account of expediency or because of the need to compromise with ineradicable human sinfulness, he knowingly incorporates into his laws commands or permissions that the ideal order of things would not tolerate.[39]

In each of the above laws there is a requirement that life and death come together in the recognition of an offense. This is such an unusual principle in the construction of biblical rules that there can be little doubt that one lawgiver is responsible for both their construction and their arrangement, even though this idea runs contrary to the commonly accepted one.[40] What is the explanation for this way of looking at wrongdoing on the part of the Deuteronomic lawgiver?

Part of the explanation lies in the broader perspective that encompasses his laws. The choice between life and death that he (Moses) offers after he gives the laws implies acceptance of one and rejection of the other. There can be no room for compromise, for obedience to some commandments and disobedience to others; there can be no mixing of life and death. What is fascinating is that one can observe how a particular lawgiver actually works with a basic concern in constructing his laws. He holds that wrongdoing among the Israelites threatens the people with death. In sharp contrast, their settled existence in the new land represents the deity's conferral of life. All the more so, then, does any wrongdoing bring about a clash of the two opposites.

Fundamentally, the primary concern of the lawgiver is that life and death do not in fact impinge on each other. Insofar as natural death and nonhostile killing (slaughtering animals for food) occur and constitute no wrongdoing, death inevitably exists in the community. Where these types of death are found, the lawgiver is especially keen to ensure that they do not impinge too closely on life. That is why he prohibits eating any flesh with the blood still in it, eating an animal that has died a natural death, making marks on one's body when mourning the dead, boiling a kid in its mother's milk, offering the triennial tithe of the land's produce to the dead, and consuming it while mourning.

To keep life and death apart in these examples is to prevent even the appearance of wrongdoing, whereas in the examples of the five laws in Deuteronomy 21 (slain man, captive woman, primogeniture, incorrigible son, and hanged man) it is the very conjunction of life and death that draws attention to the gravity of the wrongdoing.

The larger explanation for the lawgiver's seemingly curious focus on matters of life and death lies in his recognition that their overlap is disturbing and undesirable, yet in life the overlap exists. In Roman Egypt prosperous Egyptians kept in their homes the embalmed corpses of their relatives, their faces covered with portraits from their lifetime. Keith Hopkins comments, "To us it seems macabre for the dead to inhabit the homes of the living."[41] In recent times, much disquiet has arisen from the necessity of precisely defining the moment of death so that organs from the dead can be transplanted into the living. Spontaneous heartbeat is no longer a sufficient indication of life; a person is dead only when there is an irreversible cessation of brain function. Responding to the development, the Jesuit scholar John Mahoney, writing to the *London Times* (February 3, 1975) expresses concern, "For it is in the interests of society that death, as justice, must be seen to take place."[42] One unacknowledged reason why there is opposition to capital punishment has to do with unwillingness to confront the offender's forthcoming death. To think about it arouses discomfort because it is a reminder of one's own death. Samuel Johnson's remark that "when a man knows he is to be hanged in a fortnight, it concentrates his mind wonderfully" applies not solely to the criminal. Most profound of all, there is a sense in which the figure of Noah in the story of the flood (Genesis 6–9) represents every one of us. At any one moment in time death on a staggering scale occurs in the created world. Yet we survive. The Deuteronomic lawgiver both shares and exploits our disquiet about the juxtaposition of life and death.[43]

8 Law in the Narratives: Retribution

The discussion about the formula "life for life, eye for eye, and tooth for tooth" in chapter 6 brought out the considerable role of retribution in biblical narratives. Time and again the retribution takes the form of a punishment that mirrors the original offense, which means that a great deal of reflection has gone into the nature of the offense. Abimelech, the upstart king in the period of the Judges, achieves his position by ruthlessly ridding himself of his seventy brothers, slaughtering all of them (with one exception) "upon one stone" (Judg 9:5). His punishment: he is mortally wounded when a woman drops a millstone on his head (Judg 9:53, 54). Absalom defies his father's royal authority and sets in motion a rebellion against King David. He dies because Joab, the commander of David's forces, defies the king's authority and refuses to spare Absalom's life (2 Sam 18:5, 10–15).

Biblical authors often relate how the offender experiences retribution by some form of the same offense. The form depends on what aspect of the offense the author has under scrutiny. Judah's punishment for his role in the disposal of his brother Joseph (Gen 37:26–35) takes two forms. From Jacob's point of view, his son Joseph is dead. Retribution befalls Judah when he loses sons himself in his dealings with Tamar, the woman his firstborn son marries (Genesis 38).[1] Later, in Egypt, Joseph causes Judah to pledge that he will become a bondman to him and remain in a foreign land, Egypt (Gen 44:33). This fate mirrors what befell Joseph himself after Judah got his brothers to go along with his scheme of selling Joseph into slavery (Gen 37:26–28).

Another example of double retribution is Jacob's punishment for deceiving his father, Isaac. With his mother's help, Jacob tricks his father by taking advantage of his blindness. As a result, Isaac gives the blessing of the firstborn to Jacob, the younger son, and not to the elder son, Esau (Genesis 27). Jacob in turn is tricked by Laban, his mother's brother. On Jacob's wedding night, when he cannot see properly because it is dark and he is drunk from feasting, Laban substitutes his elder daughter, Leah, for the younger daughter, Rachel, so that Leah and not Rachel becomes his wife (Genesis 29). Jacob receives further retribution for another aspect of his offense against Isaac. He uses Esau's garments to deceive his blind father into thinking that he, Jacob, is Esau. Isaac's anguish is visited upon Jacob when his own sons use Joseph's blood-soaked garment to convince him that Joseph is dead (Genesis 37).[2]

Three episodes about Kings Saul and David exemplify, in a way that has not previously been recognized, how retribution for certain offenses has a marvelously subtle mirroring character. There is a joke about an incident at sea involving a captain and his petty officer that illustrates the kind of retribution at work in the biblical narratives. The captain of a ship puts down in the logbook one day, "Mate drunk all day." The next day the mate gets his own back when he records in the logbook, "Captain sober all day." Such a precise way of paying someone back for an offense, where a reversal of meaning does the trick, is one of the commonest features of biblical narratives about retributive justice. The puzzle about the two conflicting accounts of how King Saul dies can be solved once one sees this type of retribution at work.

SAUL'S DEATH (1 SAMUEL 31, 2 SAMUEL 1)

Saul, wounded in battle and not wishing to be made sport of by the Philistines, takes his sword and falls on it (1 Sam 31:4). David Daube warns against reading later views about suicide into this biblical episode.[3] The word *suicide,* coined from Latin but not previously existing in that language, made its appearance first in English and then in French in the seventeenth century. Walter Charleton introduced the term in his translation of the *Ephesian Matron* from the *Satyricon* of the Latin writer Petronius. Its coinage was probably a joke at the expense of John Donne. Charleton, not caring for Donne's views, may have intended an outrageous pun, namely, "the killing of a pig," from *sus, suis* (pig). Such punning was fashionable, and Charleton knew his philology. In his tractate *Biathanatos* (published after his death around 1644–47 but written about 1607), Donne very cautiously argues that taking one's life might be justified in certain circumstances. The prevalent terms used to speak of the deed—self-murder, self-destruction, self-slaughter—all implied culpability, and the deed was indeed condemned as utterly wrong.

While there is criminal homicide, there is also justifiable homicide, as in self-defense, and there is even commendable homicide, as in war. Donne wanted a neutral term that could cover instances where killing oneself might not be viewed as wrong and introduced the term *self-homicide.* If it had not been for Charleton's sly dig at Donne's conception, this term would probably have come to prevail because of Donne's standing in English literary tradition. Charleton's coinage, *sui-cide*—he used a hyphen—would not have caught on but for the interest of the French Jesuit Abbé Pierre Desfontaines in odd words in the English language. Voltaire in turn took up the word, and because of his popularity in England it became accepted in English.

Two features stand out in an examination of the various words used to refer to suicide in Greek, Latin, Hebrew, German, French, and English. First, in the ancient sources the act is initially viewed as a form of killing before it is viewed as a form of dying. The conception of the act as a mode of dying betokens a more subjective way of thinking about it. The greater reflection involved is a phenomenon especially noteworthy in Greek development, which in turn exerted enormous influence on all other traditions, even Hebrew.

Second, the development of the concept indicates the use of neutral expressions for the act in Greek, Roman, and Hebraic (including both Old and New Testaments) antiquity; harsher expressions in the Middle Ages; followed by gentler ones with the advent of humanism. Daube notes how Saul's suicide is described in a concrete, objective way. He takes his sword and falls on it. The act is a form of killing. When David laments the deaths of Saul and Jonathan, he says that "in death they were not divided" (2 Sam 1:23). Jonathan was killed in battle by the enemy; he did not die by suicide. There is consequently no recognition or hint of the difference between the father's death and that of the son. The linguistic evidence as well as the immediate context of Saul's suicide indicate little or no reflection on the matter.[4]

A good deal more has to be said, however, about Saul's suicide, and the issue is one that ties in to a major problem about the death of Saul. There are, in fact, two accounts of Saul's death, and they contradict each other. The first, in 1 Samuel 31, tells how in the battle with the Philistines Saul faces certain death at their hands. He asks his armor bearer to kill him with his sword, but the armor bearer refuses and Saul kills himself. The second account, in 2 Samuel 1, is different. An Amalekite who is the son of a sojourner within Israel is a member of the Israelite camp during the battle with the Philistines. He reports back to King David, who has just returned from a successful campaign (against the Amalekites), on the final moments of Saul's life. Saul, facing imminent death at the hands of approaching Philistine warriors, requests of the Amalekite that he slay him. This the Amalekite does. Having told David what transpired, he hands over to him Saul's royal crown. Rather than commending him for its delivery, however, David has him slain because he killed "Yahweh's anointed" (2 Sam 1:14).

The standard approach to resolving the contradictory accounts of Saul's end is to claim that the first is accurate and the second is a fabrication by the Amalekite servant. Interpreters who take this way out have the utmost difficulty in coming up with evidence that the Amalekite is lying.[5] The view that he is lying plainly diminishes the Amalekite's own standing, and it also diminishes the biblical author who bothers to recount such a fabrication. From the Amalekite's point of view, if his story is true, he genuinely believes that he is doing a fine thing both in carrying out Saul's wishes and in bringing the crown to the new king, David. From the narrator's point of view, the actions of the Amalekite on behalf of Saul are the stuff of tragedy and therefore worth recording. A man fully believes that what he is doing measures up to the finest conduct, only to learn that there is a terrible flaw in his actions. Interpreters who take the view that the Amalekite is lying are solely concerned with the resolution of the discrepant historical reporting. They are not alert to the marvelous subtlety and sophistication of biblical literature.

The key to solving the problem of the two accounts of Saul's death is to observe how they relate back to two offenses committed by Saul. The first offense occurs when Saul, under orders to slaughter every living creature that belongs to the Amalekites (1 Sam 15:3), fails to do so and spares Agag, the king of the Amalekites, and the best of their animals. For this failure to obey the prophet Samuel's authority, Samuel informs Saul, he will lose his crown.

How Saul dies is, I suggest, made to relate to how he disobeys a particular law. Samuel's order to slay the Amalekites is based on a law that comes to expression in Deuteronomy 25:17–19: the Amalekites are to be exterminated.[6] The report of Saul's death in 2 Samuel 1 recounts how the Amalekite servant responds to Saul's request to put an end to his life. This report concentrates on Saul's disobedience to the law calling for the total extermination of the Amalekites. Nothing belonging to this group was to be kept alive; there was to be no overlapping of life and death. How appropriate that because he chooses not to slay the highest member of the Amalekite tribe, he, the king of Israel, meets death at the hands of a lowly Amalekite camp follower. How appropriate, moreover, that Saul actually asks the Amalekite to slay him. Saul's offense was permitting some life to remain after his rout of the Amalekites. His end, in turn, is a strange overlapping of life and death in that just sufficient life remains for him, the king of Israel, to request the Amalekite to have done with it.

There is support for the interpretation that this particular account of Saul's death relates back to the infraction involving the Amalekites. In 1 Samuel 15:28 Samuel tells Saul that because he failed to kill King Agag, the kingship will be taken from him and given to his neighbor, namely, David. In 2 Samuel 1:10 the Amalekite servant does precisely this when he brings to David the royal insignia—the crown and armlet—from Saul's body. It is the fulfillment of Samuel's prophecy. There is also the correspondence between Agag's expectation that his life will be spared ("Surely the bitterness of death is past"; 1 Samuel

15:32) and the Amalekite servant's expectation that his deed will put him in good favor with the new king. Each dies nonetheless.[7]

The account of Saul's death in 1 Samuel 31 is equally subtle. In this instance the death relates back to Saul's offense in seeking out a medium to call Samuel from the dead (1 Samuel 28). Unable to obtain advice about a forthcoming battle with the Philistines from dreams, divinatory lots (Urim), or prophets, Saul goes to a woman of Endor who is a medium. Such activity is forbidden by law, and thus he proceeds to break a rule he previously enforced (1 Sam 28:3, 9). He consequently chooses to disobey a commandment (Deut 18:11) that involves the abhorrent mixing of life and death. He, a living Israelite, by means of the medium of Endor reaches into the realm of death. Ghosts, by definition, inhabit the zone between life and death.[8] The woman too is culpable. Her comment, "I have taken my life in my hand" (1 Sam 28:21), refers to the consequences of her misdeed. Her words imply that she is close to giving her life away as one delivers over something in one's hands. In verse 9 she rebukes Saul for involving her: "Why then are you laying a snare for my life to bring about my death?"

For Saul, two fearful consequences follow from his offense of bringing up Samuel from the dead: he learns from Samuel's ghost exactly when he is going to die—the next day he and his sons will fall on the battlefield (1 Sam 28:19)—and when the occasion comes round he does not wait for death to take him, but seizes death himself. With suicide one chooses exactly when one dies. Instead of a slow ebbing away of his life, Saul consciously closes the gap between life and death. Saul's suicide is thus viewed not as wrongdoing in the way that certain actions involving the failure to keep life and death apart are regarded, but as the inevitable outcome of his interference in the realm of death. The manner of his end reveals heaven's inexorable law of retribution at work, which means that in his case life and death should come together. His suicide mirrors a misdeed deserving of death and is seen as acknowledging and highlighting the offense at Endor.[9] Death was coming to Saul from a situation (battle) not in his control. By interfering in its inevitability, however, he unwittingly made of his situation a self-imposed punishment for his offense.

While it is true that an immediate reason is given for Saul's act of killing himself—namely, the Philistines would kill him and make sport of him (1 Sam 31:4)—a wider perspective prevails. The suicide is disturbing, undesirable, yet necessary, because inscrutable providential governance requires that every wrongdoing receives its ultimate just desert.[10] The comparable account of Saul's end in 1 Chronicles 10:13, 14 is more explicit in relaying the wider perspective: "So Saul died for his transgression which he committed against Yahweh, even against the word of Yahweh, which he kept not, and also for asking counsel of one that had a familiar spirit [the woman of Endor], to inquire of it; And inquired not of Yahweh: therefore he slew him, and turned the kingdom unto David the son of Jesse."

The two accounts of Saul's death may not have much, or anything, to do with discrepant historical reporting.[11] Each account seeks to make the punishment fit the crime, and the narrator(s) has probably introduced some license. The fact that the central concept is such a fundamental one as the interplay between life and death allows for a fairly easy adjustment to reports about the nature of a man's death, in this instance on the battlefield.

I think it likely that each account was more or less from the outset linked to a preceding tradition about a misdeed of Saul. There is an adumbration of such a link in the tradition about the medium of Endor, and it predicts the death of Saul on the battlefield. While there is no prediction of the actual suicide, Saul's refusal to eat after hearing the terrible news about his forthcoming death foreshadows that he would readily be done with life. The tradition also cites Saul's earlier infraction of failing to put down the Amalekites totally. There is thus reflection on Saul's death and his offenses in this tradition. It is but a short step to the realization that closer links between his actual death and the specific nature of his misdeeds might be sought.

The two accounts of Saul's end would have been shaped according to the character of his offenses. If the inspiration for this process is the view that an offense will in its own peculiar but inevitable way meet with its matching penalty, and if details about the actual death of Saul were lacking, the resulting contradiction between the two accounts is less puzzling, as is the recording of each together in the Book of

Samuel. As exercises in the working out of the nature of retribution, both cover the ground. This aim, I submit, has taken precedence over any biographical or historical aim the author may have had.

Where earthly justice cannot handle the problem of punishment, an author is all the more likely to undertake the task of working out appropriate retribution at some other level. The offense of failure to exterminate a group enemy is not likely to be handled by an earthly court, and necromancy is typically a secret offense that is liable to escape detection by the public authorities. Neither of these offenses in the Deuteronomic code has a sanction attached. Someone concerned about due punishment for these offenses would have to resort to the view that a broader perspective prevails. Someway, somehow, there is an ultimate sorting out from above.

KING DAVID'S ADULTERY (2 SAMUEL 11)

King David, walking one evening on the roof of his palace, sees Bathsheba bathing herself, conceives a desire for her, inquires who she is, learns that she is the wife of Uriah the Hittite, sends for her, and has intercourse with her.[12] Pregnancy ensues. In order to make it appear that Uriah is the father of the child, David summons him back from the battlefield, where he is engaged in a war against the Ammonites. David asks Uriah for a report on how the battle is faring, then sends him home to make love to his wife. The problem is that Uriah observes the customary rule that one does not have sexual relations while on military duty.[13] David is alert to this restraint, and that is why he resorts to language with a double meaning. He tells Uriah to return to his house and wash his feet (2 Sam 11:8), meaning the genital feet (in Hebrew as in other languages, "feet" has this transferred sense).[14] Uriah does not take the hint and instead sleeps outside the palace door.

No doubt if Uriah had openly protested David's order, David needed say only that he meant for Uriah to wash his feet in the literal sense. That Uriah did understand David's remark in a sexual sense is indicated by his response to David when the latter asks him why he has not returned to his house. Uriah replies that in light of the fact that his companions are all engaged in warfare, "Shall I then go into my house, to eat and to drink, and to lie with my wife?" David tries again the next day to have Uriah return to his wife and plies him with drink, but Uriah does not go. David then resorts to sending Uriah back to the battlefield as if he is an honored emissary bearing messages from the king to Joab, the commander of the armed forces. In reality, the letter he carries contains his own death sentence. The message to Joab is that Uriah should be placed in the hottest part of the fighting so that he will die at enemy hands. (David was himself once the object of such a ploy. King Saul sent him into battle with the promise that Michal, his daughter, would be David's reward, but the move was really an attempt by Saul to have David killed [1 Sam 18:20–25].)

Joab does as he is bidden, and Uriah dies in battle. Bathsheba mourns his death, and then she and David become husband and wife. The child is born but becomes sick and dies. Bathsheba again conceives and Solomon is born. So far as the historical record is concerned, all of the above data, from the adultery to the account of Solomon's birth, may well be accurate.

I wish to concentrate on the interpretation that has been imposed on the probable historical facts, in particular on the legal and ethical aspects of the narrative, which are no less engaging than the literary ones.[15] There are many such aspects. For example, a view expressed in the Book of Deuteronomy is that if one keeps the commandments, blessings and life will ensue; if not, curses and death will befall the malefactor (Deuteronomy 28). The narrator of the court history, sharing the same view and applying it to David, interprets David's adultery as the end of his rise to power and favor and the beginning of an inexorable decline.[16] The story might also lend itself to working out different stages in the history of the law of adultery. The death penalty for the offense is aimed at David but not at Bathsheba. It may be that the story reflects a stage in the law of adultery when the public authorities regarded the man, but not the woman, as culpable. The law looked away from the woman's role, her fate being left to her offended husband, inapplicable in Bathsheba's case because of Uriah's death in battle. In the absence of the Deuteronomic law requiring both the man and the woman to be put to death for adultery (Deut 22:22), the woman's position might seem the more fortunate one. However, as David Daube argues, while this may be true in terms of her physical survival, from all other angles the lack of penalty simply reflects her lowly status.[17] When the law finally chose to take account of the woman's role in adultery, society was conferring personhood on her, a step forward in terms of the history of women's rights. To be sure, society typically exacted a high price: women paid for the advance by coming under a capital sentence for adultery.

Whether or not the narrative can be used to yield historical knowledge about developments in the law of adultery is a question, I think, we have to leave open. What can be analyzed with more assurance is the actual judgment on David's adultery that is recorded in the narrative. The prophet Nathan, who somehow finds out about the offense, tells David what turns out to be a parable. A rich man has many flocks and herds, in contrast to a poor man who possesses but one ewe lamb. The man has an especially intimate attachment to the lamb; it is like a daughter to him, but that attachment ends when the rich farmer takes the lamb in order to serve it to a traveller.

When Nathan recounts this story to David, on the surface he is not telling a parable; he is calling for the king's legal judgment. We know little about the Israelite kings' role as judges, other than that they did now and then hear cases.[18] What Nathan asks David to judge is an offense about the theft of an animal. The interesting aspect of the case lies solely in the wildness of David's judgment. He pronounces a sentence that calls for fourfold restitution of the animal, a reasonable judgment in line with the one laid down in the collection of rules in the Book of Exodus (21:37), but then, remarkably, he goes quite overboard and also places the offender under a capital sentence.[19]

The explanation for the harshness of David's judgment is twofold. First, he fails to observe an elementary rule for any judge who hears a case, namely, to get at the legal facts and disregard extraneous features not pertinent to these facts. In the same collection of rules in the Book of Exodus about the theft of an animal there is a rule that bears all the marks of an address to judges: "Thou shalt not favour a poor man in his cause" (Exod 23:3).[20] Nathan's prosecutorial skill in relaying the circumstances of the poor man whose lamb has been taken by the rich man so sways David's emotions that he gives the wrong judgment.

Second, and more profound, the reason why David's emotions cause him to give the wrong judgment in the case of theft is because of his prior offense against Uriah. His emotions got the better of him then, too, and resulted in his taking another man's wife. The penalty for adultery was death. When his emotions are again put to the test in judging the case of the poor man's lamb, David gives the wrong judgment in regard to the lamb—but the right one in regard to the person the lamb represents, Bathsheba.

In line with its original Greek etymology, the term *parable* means the throwing of something alongside something else, an account of one event shedding light on another. Nathan's parable of the theft of the lamb is really meant to bring to David's mind his appropriation of Bathsheba. Its cleverness is of a very high order and warrants further comment.

Many critics find the contents of the parable problematical when they try to align its details with the particulars of David's conduct. I find no such difficulty. The parable points solely to David's adultery; it says nothing about his consequent evil against Uriah. For some critics the parable's omission of David's role in Uriah's death points to a fractured relationship between the story about the lamb and David's offenses. It would, however, be a mighty task for any composer of parables to effectively include both the veiled depiction of David's adultery and a veiled account of how he eliminated Uriah. Moreover, it was surely sufficient for David to be judged on his adultery alone. That offense entailed a capital sentence, and once David recognized that it was this offense Nathan was on about, he would immediately have known that his eradication of Uriah had to be added to the offense of adultery. As the parable stands, it is a model of simplicity and ingenuity in accomplishing a risky political task. Someone without secular power not only communicates to someone with supreme power about his tyrannical ways, but has the tyrant damn himself.[21]

The rich man and his many flocks stand for David with his many wives. The association between women and domestic animals—there are similar associations for men—is evidenced elsewhere. For example, the name of Jacob's wife, Rachel, means "a ewe," and their daughter, Dinah, is in focus in the legal proverb about how as the daughter of an ox she was (sexually) plowed by the son of an ass—by Shechem, the son of Hamor, or "Ass" (Deut 22:10; Gen 34, 49:5–7). When Samson declares that the men of his city could not have solved the riddle he gave them unless they had plowed with his heifer, he is referring to their seducing his wife into giving the solution. The poor man and his one ewe lamb represent Uriah and his sole wife, Bathsheba. How much we should deduce from the notion of the lamb as an intimate family pet— certainly we can infer the existence of animals as pets—and like a daughter who sat on his lap is problematical. It would not have done to suggest a sexual relationship between the man and his animal.[22] From a broader perspective, we should not be too surprised to find in the general culture an older man's young wife described as being like a daughter. This might be especially so in polygamous setups such as David's own, which may have included daughters of around the same age as the younger wives.

Interpreters have been at a loss to comprehend the reference in the parable to the traveller (*helekh*) who had to be catered to.[23] In fact, that is one of the most significant links between the parable and the narrative about David and Bathsheba. The term used, unique to this context, is derived from the verb *halakh* (to walk). It refers back, and hence the uniqueness of the term, to the initial action that set in motion all the subsequent events—namely, when David walks on the roof of his palace and his sexual desire travels in the direction of the naked Bathsheba.[24] Biblical literature elsewhere thinks of desire in this way.[25] We noted above how David's wrong judgment in the case of the theft of the animal is linked to his initial lack of control of his emotions in satisfying his desire for Bathsheba.

The rich man has the ewe lamb prepared for the satisfaction of the traveller's appetite. No attention is drawn to the fact that the lamb would first have been slaughtered. The focus is on the lamb as food. The parallel between sexual appetite and appetite for food is well established in biblical material. In Proverbs, the lips of a loose woman drop honey (Prov 5:3), a man has to drink water from his own well

(Prov 5:15), and bread eaten in secret is pleasant (Prov 9:17). The way of an adulterous woman is that she eats, wipes her mouth, and says, "I have done no wickedness" (Prov 30:20). All these are sexual references. The Rabbinic interpretation of the statement in Genesis 39:6 that Potiphar left all that he had in Joseph's hand, that Potiphar "knew not aught save the bread which he did eat," may be accurate in getting at the original meaning of the odd statement (*Genesis Rabba* on 39:6). The Rabbis understood the statement about the bread to mean that only Potiphar's wife was off-limits to Joseph.

One other link between the parable and the narrative is worth mentioning. Nathan has David unwittingly pronounce a judgment of death on himself for his theft of the ewe lamb, that is, Bathsheba. David's unwittingness corresponds to Uriah's when David had him carry to the front a message that contained his own death sentence.

One consequence of David's adultery is that the child Bathsheba conceives by him becomes ill and eventually dies. The narrator interprets its death as punishment for David's adultery. The principle of punishment that underlies this judgment is manifestly not the principle of communal responsibility; namely, that the child is somehow tainted by and hence also answerable for the offense of adultery.[26] Rather, the principle is individual responsibility. David alone is held responsible for the offense, but he is punished indirectly by the loss of a member of his household, a form of punishment that David Daube terms "ruler punishment."[27]

A most interesting aspect of the child's death is David's peculiar behavior both before and after it dies. While the child is ill, David mourns greatly, as if it is already dead. He stops eating and lies on the earth all night. When the child dies, his servants fear that he will take his mourning to such lengths that he will do himself harm. David's conduct, however, proves to be the opposite of what they fear. He washes, anoints himself, changes his clothing, and eats again.

Two comments might be made about his conduct. First, we should link David's inappropriate emotions both before and after the child's death to the role of his emotions when he sought his sexual encounter with Bathsheba, and again when he overreacted to the man's theft of the animal. Second, there emerges a striking view of wrongdoing that is also found in other laws and narratives of the bible. According to this view, an act of wrongdoing mixes matters that relate to death and those that relate to life. Often the punishment will bring out the nature of the wrongdoing. An amusing story from a small upstate New York town serves to illustrate the phenomenon. A certain youth got the daughter of an Italian immigrant family pregnant. The Italian father sent a tuxedo to the youth with the message, "Wear this at your wedding or your funeral." He wore it at his wedding.[28]

In biblical material the failure to keep the two opposites, life and death, apart often constitutes an offense. The prohibition at the heart of the system of *kashrut* against boiling a young animal in its mother's milk—the very milk that gave life to the animal before it was slaughtered—is infused with the notion that life and death should be kept apart.[29] David's grievous mourning when the child is alive and his life-affirming behavior when it dies may point to the wrongdoing surrounding its birth. David's offense is that he had Uriah killed in order to make it appear that Uriah is the child's father—a horrifying use of death to cover for the origin of life.

The consequences of David's adultery also show up in two incidents involving his other children: when his son Amnon violates his daughter Tamar, and when another son, Absalom, avenges the misdeed and slays Amnon. Tamar is Amnon's half-sister, and he conceives a great desire for her. Like David, his father, he wants immediate gratification. Unlike Bathsheba, Amnon's object of desire is in fact available to him should he fulfill certain formalities. The narrative presupposes that a marriage between a brother and his half-sister is possible, that is, that such a union has not yet come under the Levitical lists of prohibited degrees of consanguinity. The narrator states that Amnon humbles ('*nnah*) her. *To humble* is a technical legal term, wrongly translated in most versions as meaning that he forced her.[30] Rather, it refers to his failure, as the text elsewhere spells out, to consult her (their) father with a view to arranging a marriage.

At first glance, David's role in both Amnon's seduction of Tamar and Absalom's subsequent slaying of Amnon seems a peripheral one. Amnon, feigning illness, seeks an opportunity to gratify his sexual appetite and asks David for permission to have Tamar come to his private quarters and provide him with food. There is again the association between food and sexuality. In any event, we are not only meant to recall David's seduction of Bathsheba but, more to the point, we are meant to see that he unwittingly sets up his own daughter to be seduced. Such a development is the inevitable consequence of David's wrongdoing. The inscrutable workings of providence visit a mirroring retribution on the offender, and members of a family are but instruments in heaven's hands to accomplish the retribution.

Amnon succeeds in his seduction of Tamar. Unlike David, who loves and marries Bathsheba, Amnon's attitude is quite the opposite. After he seduces Tamar, "The hatred wherewith he hated her was greater than the love wherewith he had loved her" (2 Sam 13:15). That hatred will lead to his murder. Again, it is David who, unwittingly, sends Amnon to his fate. Another son of David, Absalom, seeks and obtains permission of his father to have Amnon join him at a sheep-shearing festival. There, Amnon, in a drunken state reminiscent of his feasting with his sister, is slain.

A most peculiar feature of the narrative again indicates how David's original misdeed determines subsequent events. David mourns the loss not of the dead son, Amnon—"for he was comforted concerning Amnon, seeing he was dead" (2 Sam 13:39)—but of the living son, Absalom, who takes refuge in another part of the country after Amnon's murder. David's soul longs for Absalom and mourns for him day in and day out. Surely we are meant to recall David's strange conduct when he mourns for his love-child by Bathsheba when the child is yet alive, but is unconcerned after it dies.[31]

David's emotional attachment to Absalom brings disaster to father and son. The disastrous developments all relate to David's original offenses against Uriah. What happens to Absalom is intended to recapitulate what happened to Uriah. The way the narrator links the two lives is remarkable. David has Uriah return to Jerusalem because of a woman, Bathsheba. Uriah stops short of going to his home, although David wants him to go. After Absalom takes refuge because of his murder of Amnon, David has him return to Jerusalem on the advice of a woman, the so-called wise woman of Tekoah.[32] Absalom stops short of entering his father's house because David, in contrast to his wish for

Uriah, does not want him to take that final step. In each instance, David compounds an offense. By having Uriah return to Jerusalem, David is covering up his adultery. By having Absalom return, David is setting aside Absalom's murder of Amnon.

Another noteworthy contrast is between Nathan's fictitious case about the theft of the lamb and the story the woman of Tekoah tells David about the threatened death of her one remaining son who has murdered his brother. Nathan's aim is to have David convict himself of his wrongdoing, whereas the woman of Tekoah aims to have David discount Absalom's murder of Amnon. By thus overlooking Absalom's offense, David prepares the ground for the punishments that Nathan predicted would befall him: the violation of his concubines and the violence of the sword brought down on his own household (2 Sam 12:10–12).

One more contrast is worthy of attention. When Uriah stops short of going to his own home, the reason is his loyalty to Joab and his fellow soldiers who are camped in the open field. David wants Uriah to offend against that commitment. When Absalom, by contrast, tries to return to his father's house, he offends against Joab by setting Joab's field of grain on fire, which he does in the hope of pressuring Joab to convince David to receive him in person. David's refusal to have Absalom in his presence is what prompts Absalom to offend. The overall significance of these contrasting developments is that Uriah, by not going to his house, brings disaster on himself and future disaster on David. Absalom, by insisting on going to his father's house, brings disaster on himself and his father.

After David receives him, Absalom rebels against David's authority and succeeds in forcing him from his kingship in Jerusalem. Absalom symbolically makes claim to the throne by setting a tent on the roof of the palace and, in full view of the public, lying with each of his father's ten concubines (2 Sam 16:20–23). Such temporary accommodation is perhaps the equivalent of the accommodation needed by the "traveller"—identified, we recall, as David's sexual desire—in Nathan's parable. In any event, Absalom's display of sexual prowess recalls the secret seduction of Bathsheba by David when he let his desire wander from that same roof in the direction of the bathing Bathsheba.

What David does in secret, Absalom does in the open; and where David's sexual desire is dominant, Absalom's is, we can infer, not a factor. His is a political act; no emotions override his judgment. The fact that Absalom's sexual activity occurs within the family of David reminds us that David's adultery is, in the nature of things, a violation of a family tie.

David's hotblooded adultery is followed by his coldly calculated disposal of Uriah. When David takes up arms against his upstart son, Absalom, his emotional state is again cause for wonder. He makes a request, wholly inappropriate in the midst of a decisive battle, that Absalom be treated well: "Deal gently for my sake with the young man, even with Absalom" (2 Sam 18:5). In contrast stands his callous treatment of Uriah. In any case, Joab ignores the request and has Absalom killed. Absalom's offense is that he defied his father's authority. He dies because Joab defies David's order to deal gently with him.

Absalom's death is a humiliating one. Riding his mule in the midst of a forest, he gets his head caught in the bough of a tree as the mule passes on. As he hangs suspended there, between "heaven and earth," Joab casts three darts at him, then has his servants put an end to him. It is remarkable that an enemy leader should be so accessible, and consequently so easily disposed of. Absalom's fate recalls Uriah's similarly humiliating death in battle. Uriah, one of David's best warriors (2 Sam 23:8, 39), was all too easily killed because he fought too close to a wall.

Joab compares Uriah's death with the humiliating death of the first king of Israel, Abimelech (Judg 9:50–57). Abimelech, Joab recalls, speaking on behalf of David (2 Sam 11:21), died after a woman drops a millstone on his head. Joab's (David's) comparison of Uriah's death to Abimelech's death is an apt one because it brings out the fact that a woman played a role in each. Soldiers actually killed Uriah, but it was his commander, Joab, who deliberately placed him in such a vulnerable spot. Joab in turn took his orders from David, who gave them because he had committed adultery with Bathsheba. The chain of causation thus leads back to her role in the adultery. This comparison between Uriah's death and Abimelech's provides us with the only evidence that the narrator regards Bathsheba as culpable for her part in the adultery. It cannot surprise that the narrator's interest in causation extends to details of the saga. The entire narrative is a magnificent exploration of the role of cause and effect in human affairs.

Not only Uriah's fate but Absalom's too may be compared with that of Abimelech. Both Abimelech and Absalom are guilty of fratricide. Abimelech slaughters seventy of his brothers with the exception of one, Jotham, and Absalom has Amnon slain. Each becomes king by underhanded means. Each dies a humiliating death. Each is associated with imagery involving trees. In Jotham's parable about how the trees seek to appoint a king to rule over them, the worthy trees, those representing the status quo (olive, fig, and vine), disdain the position. Derisively, it is offered to the bramble (Judg 9:7–15). The inferior Abimelech is the person whom the parable targets. As for Absalom, his suspension from a tree signifies the ignominious end to his reign as king.

When David awaits the outcome of the battle, his sole intent is to hear how his son has fared. When he learns that Absalom has been killed, he utters his famous dirge, "O my son Absalom, my son, my son Absalom! would I had died for thee, O Absalom, my son, my son!" (2 Sam 19:1). In its immediate context, it is a heartrending lament. In a wider context it is the judgment that Absalom's death is the one David should have suffered for his offenses. David continues to mourn Absalom, a state of emotion that his subjects regard as quite inappropriate. The consequence is the breakup of his kingdom. David's mourning for Absalom is but a continuation of the emotional turmoil he has felt from the moment he let his eye fasten on Bathsheba.

I conclude this discussion with some final observations about the legal and ethical aspects of the entire story. The profound view of how David is paid back in similar coin for his adultery and subsequent disposal of Uriah is what makes the story such a compelling one. Heaven, we are to believe, works this way in the pursuit of justice. What might appear to be innocent, certainly unwitting, actions on the part of David are really predetermined by his earlier guilty actions. A modern reader is reminded of Freud's claim that what appear to be accidents, errors, and tragic occurrences are often masks for semi-intentional harm on the part of those involved.[33] The biblical perspective is well expressed in a classical Vietnamese saying (from the *Tale of Kieu*): "Happiness or misfortune is prescribed by the law of Heaven, but their source came from ourselves." Heaven has David send Tamar to her seducer, and heaven has David send the seducer to his death at the hands of his brother.

The historical fact that David got away with his act of adultery and elimination of Uriah no doubt determined the narrator's quest for other ways to suggest that wrongdoing meets with its just deserts. Alas, in interpreting the events of this story, the ancient writer(s) presents a view of justice that is profoundly unsatisfactory. The actors in the drama of unfolding retribution are but instruments in heaven's hands, mere objects to satisfy a craving for justice. Tamar is sexually violated in order to pay back David for his adultery. Her brother Amnon behaves in ways that are both morally and legally wrong, but not to the extent that he deserves to die; certainly he did not deserve to die as he did at the hands of his brother Absalom. The fates of Amnon and Tamar are tied to David's action to cover up his adultery. The craving for justice reveals right values, rises to the heights in suggesting a unified view of all human action, but also depicts justice as cold, impersonal, and antihuman.[34] The topic is the enormous one of the tension often latent in the claims of religion as against those of the law. The law is not in a position to punish for some offenses, but religion insists on it. The narrator writes from the viewpoint of an ideal religious and moral order because the legal order fails to visit consequences on David for his wrongdoing.

I have shown elsewhere that biblical lawgivers oppose the kind of justice found in the narrative sources of the Bible. Where these sources describe vicarious penalties, the lawgivers set down penalties directed at the culprit only. The inspiration for the formulation of the majority of biblical laws is the lawgivers' focus on the legal and ethical problems thrown up by narrative sources such as the saga of David's rise and fall. One example of a legal construction that derives from the David saga is the Deuteronomic law about the criminal whose body is to be hung up for public exposure after his execution (Deut 21:22, 23).[35] In this rule the lawgiver refers not just to a man who has been executed, but unnecessarily, for the drafting of a law, to the execution of a man who "has committed an offense worthy of death." This redundant statement is his reaction to the fate of the sons of Saul whom David hands over to the Gibeonites for execution (2 Samuel 21). These sons are not punished for any offense they committed. They are put to death and their bodies exposed because the Gibeonites are avenging Saul's offense against them.

Biblical lawgivers often construct rules after the fashion of proverbs, particularly proverbs that encapsulate a feature of a story. A prime illustration of this process is the way biblical rules about the Passover enshrine aspects of the story of the Exodus. A characteristic feature of Nathan's parable is precisely that of the relationship between biblical laws, especially those in the form of legal proverbs, and their narrative sources. As I discussed in chapter 3, rules forbidding sowing a vineyard with two different kinds of seeds, plowing with an ox and an ass together, and putting on *shatnez* (wool and linen together) all constitute clever, cryptic judgments on patriarchal conduct. Nathan's parable about a ewe lamb that stands for Bathsheba is a cryptic judgment on David's conduct with her.

9 Law in the Narratives: Dispute Resolution

In a historic lecture at Saint Paul's Cathedral in London, David Daube began by saying that "all history-writing transfers features of one event or one great personage to another, and, indeed, much history-acting is in imitation of previous occurrences. Whoever nowadays writes about Napoleon is likely to lend him some traits of Caesar, and Napoleon himself—not to mention de Gaulle—would on occasion look to that example. This general phenomenon, that history, whether reflected upon or in the making, harks back to history, is enormously accentuated in New Testament times because, in the then prevalent view, Old Testament events and personages were largely a prefigurement of things to come."[1] This phenomenon is no less pronounced, although less attention has been given to it, in the way events in the Hebrew Bible are recounted.

There is a sense in which even the world is re-created after the flood. Lot's drunkenness is like Noah's in that members of the immediate family abuse the paterfamilias. Abraham has a problem about who, Isaac or Ishmael, is to have the right of the firstborn, and this problem recurs for Isaac when Jacob wins out over Esau. Jacob denies the right to Reuben and confers it upon Joseph, whose firstborn son, Manasseh, is in turn displaced by Ephraim. Or again, Jacob's role as a slave (or quasi-slave) of Laban and Esau (on meeting up with him, Jacob addresses Esau as a servant addressing a master; Gen 32:18, 20, 33:5, 8) has its parallel in Joseph's role as a slave in Egypt; and his experience is in turn repeated in the later lives of all the Israelites in Egypt. Problems of deception in male-female relations recur: Abraham has a problem because his wife is beautiful to behold, and he gives out disinformation that she is his sister and not his spouse; his son Isaac has the same problem with his wife, Rebekah; Jacob wants the lovely Rachel as his wife but is duped into marrying her not-so-beautiful sister, Leah; his son Joseph is faced with the problem of the scheming wife of Potiphar. Or again, generation after generation, a king's religious stance in regard to a quite specific kind of unacceptable worship is judged in light of a predecessor's stance.

The story of the Exodus provides a further illustration of how someone writing about one historical episode harks back to a preceding event and personage. The writer links, in a way that has not been observed before, the event of the Exodus and its aftermath, in which Moses is the foremost player, to the immediately preceding event of Egypt's experience of famine, in which Joseph is the central figure.

First and foremost, we can observe the link between the two episodes by noting that the destiny of both Joseph and Moses is to rescue their fellow Hebrews from hardship: famine in Joseph's case, enslavement in Moses' case. The less momentous links discussed below are also quite striking.

Moses is saved from the river by Pharaoh's daughter, who belongs to a foreign nation. His name, given to him when he grows up, supposedly reflects this rescue: "Because I [Pharaoh's daughter] drew [mašah] him out of the water" (Exod 2:10). He ends up a member of an Egyptian family, not with his own Hebrew family (although his mother, unbeknown to his adoptive mother, is his nurse).

Joseph is taken from the pit, his life saved by a group of foreigners, Midianites, but he too ends up a member of an Egyptian household. He later acquires an Egyptian name, Zaphenath-paneah, and just as Moses' name is associated with the action of Pharaoh's daughter in drawing him out of the Nile, so Joseph's Egyptian name is associated with the action of Pharaoh himself in elevating Joseph to a high position in Egyptian society. Both Joseph and Moses escape death: murder for Joseph at the hands of his brothers; drowning for Moses because of Pharaoh's decree. A close relative—Joseph's brother Reuben, Moses' sister Miriam—plays a part in delivering each from death. When each eventually dies, a very similar formula is used with regard to the future of their descendants in the land of Canaan (Gen 50:24; Deut 34:4).[2]

His fellow Hebrews treat Moses with hostility because they think he is setting himself up as a ruler and judge over them (Exod 2:13, 14). Joseph arouses the hostility of his brothers because of his dreams: "Shalt thou indeed reign over us? or shalt thou indeed have dominion over us?" they complain (Gen 37:8). As a sequel to the respective attacks on their standing among their fellow Hebrews, Moses and Joseph end up in a neighboring country, Joseph in Egypt, Moses in Midian. In that foreign setting each marries the daughter of a priest: Joseph marries Asenath, daughter of Potiphera, priest of On (Gen 41:45); Moses marries Zipporah, daughter of Jethro, priest of Midian (Exod 2:16–22). Each union produces two sons.

During his residence in Egypt, each outdoes his Egyptian counterpart in specialized tasks and reveals his superiority to the native born. Joseph interprets Pharaoh's dreams when the Egyptian magicians and wise men cannot (Genesis 41). Moses (in conjunction with Aaron) outdoes the Egyptian "wise men and the sorcerers; . . . the magicians of Egypt," in secret arts (Exod 7:11).[3]

The role of imitation common to all history writing goes some way toward explaining why these links exist between Joseph and Moses. An author selects incidents and developments for presentation because they are reminiscent of—or made reminiscent of—what has occurred before.[4] There are, however, other specific factors at work in biblical historiography. Writing about the origins of German nationalism, J. J. Sheehan refers to how "the apostles of nationalism were able to create a historical memory of 'liberation' which projected their own enthusiasms on to the nation." He further states, "As is always the case with patriotic myths, the historical memory of liberation took many forms and had many different heroes."[5] The account of ancient Israel's liberation from enslavement in Egypt is, mutatis mutandis, less a product of historical fact than of the historical imagination of writers expressing their own beliefs and enthusiasms. What I wish to suggest is that the writer (or writers) who elevates Moses to such a supreme position in the legend about the origin of his nation does so by linking him to Joseph as one hero to another, not just through the universal process of viewing one period of history as a reflection of a preceding one, but in another, quite specific and sophisticated way.

Critics claim that the legend about Joseph exerted no further influence on biblical literature. D. B. Redford speaks about the "virtually complete silence of the rest of scripture on the subject of the Joseph story. The romanticized hero of the Genesis story almost never appears elsewhere in the Old Testament outside Genesis and the first chapter of Exodus."[6] M. Niehoff puzzles over the (alleged) fact that in late antiquity the biblical Joseph enjoyed great popularity among Jewish interpreters, in contrast to his "rather insignificant role . . . in the shaping of Israelite religion."[7] This common view about the supposed lack of influence of the Joseph story on other biblical material does not stand up to critical scrutiny.

J. L. Kugel's comments are curiously uncritical in regard to his assessment of Joseph in the Genesis account itself. At one point he says that Joseph "eschews revenge and hatred," that his virtue is supreme. Yet he also refers to Joseph's "intrigue with their [the brothers'] grain sacks," and says, "If he [Joseph] does arrange things so as to give his brothers a scare or two along the way—well, a reader most likely feels that this is only justified in view of their earlier misconduct."[8] Such claims about Joseph's unquestioned virtue are not justified. The fact is that in at least two instances the writer of the Exodus narrative, taking stock of Joseph's actions, adopts a religious ethical stance that results in a negative judgment on Joseph.[9]

THE MANNA STORY (EXODUS 16)

When Joseph's brothers come to Egypt to obtain food during the famine, Joseph's power to confer life or death looms over them time and again. On their first visit to Egypt, for example, the disguised Joseph accuses the brothers of the capital crime of spying.[10] Unbeknown to his brothers, Joseph is intent on pursuing retribution because of their original offense against him. To this end he later engages in a transaction with them that involves deception on his part. After he sells them grain, he has the money they paid to him replaced in their sacks of grain when they are not looking (Gen 42:25).[11] Ordinarily, deception in a transaction of this kind takes the form of cheating the recipient out of the full amount of the commodity he has paid money for. Joseph, however, has his own reasons for choosing to torment his brothers in such a contrary manner.

After the Exodus from Egypt, the Israelites accuse Moses of bringing them into the wilderness to starve (Exod 16:3). In other words, they see Moses as exercising the power of life or death over them. Their situation is also like that of Joseph's brothers in that, while there is no food elsewhere, there is food in Egypt: "When we sat by the flesh pots, and when we did eat bread to the full" (Exod 16:3). The deity causes food (manna) to be rained down upon the ground to relieve the Israelites' hunger. Its distribution proves to be remarkably exact and fair. As measured by the technical quantity, the omer, each family receives according to its needs, nothing more, nothing less (Exod 16:18). The narrator places much emphasis on this aspect of the deity's action. He, probably the Priestly redactor, even gives the technical information that an omer is the tenth part of an ephah (Exod 16:36). Unlike Joseph's underhandedness while providing his family with grain in their time of need, the deity's dealings with the Israelite families at their time of need are open and honest.

Joseph doubtless views his deception as a means to a just end in his dispute with his brothers. God's provision of the manna presents a contrasting situation; there is no deceptive practice here designed to bring about the resolution of a dispute.[12] Nonetheless, the two narratives overlap substantially in their aims. The deity's eminently fair action is intended to lead to a furtherance of Israel's commitment to law-abiding ways. God's action is in this regard comparable to Joseph's in its intent. The purpose of providing food to the Israelites is not just to relieve their hunger but to inculcate the habit of Sabbath observance. This is why two omers of manna, not one as on the previous five days, are provided on the sixth day (Exod 16:5, 22–30). Even then, despite instructions to the contrary, some Israelites try to gather food on the seventh day. The focus on proper conduct is manifest.

The thrust of the narrative about the manna is not, at least not explicitly, to have the Israelites imitate in their future dealings among themselves the example of the deity in the matter of fairness in providing full and just measures of grain. Rather, the curious episode of the deity's procedure is like Joseph's curious if deceitful one. It is an intervention in the lives of hungry Israelites who are to be taught a lesson.

The manna story provides, then, an example of how a narrator of a later episode in the history of the nation looks back at an unacceptable feature in a tradition about the founding members of the nation. His aim is to counter this feature by presenting a story that sets out proper ethical conduct. The narrator's use of the earlier history is thus decidedly similar to that of the biblical lawgivers, who zero in on problematic conduct in this same history and set out rules designed to correct any comparable problem that might arise in the later history of the nation.

THE INSTITUTION OF THE ISRAELITE JUDICATURE (EXODUS 18)

We can see just how detailed and thorough this process of revision on the part of the biblical recorders of history is by noting how Joseph's deception is under review in the write-up of another episode in the later history of the nation. Joseph's replacement of money in his brothers' sacks can, from another angle, be characterized as a gift with a twist.[13] When the brothers speak to Joseph's steward about the matter, the steward tells them, "Your God, and the God of your father, hath given you treasure in your sacks; I had your money" (Gen 43:23). The statement is patently false. He does not have their money; they do gain from the transaction, but the gain is of a decidedly dubious kind.

Joseph's purpose, as already noted, is to convict his brothers of their original wrongdoing against him. Indeed, the presence of the money in their sacks is to remind them of the profit (beṣa'; Gen 37:26) they sought when they decided to sell him into slavery. On that occasion the brothers' attempt was frustrated because they did not actually sell Joseph and acquire money for him. It was Midianite traders who came along and sold Joseph. In a manner consistent with so many subtleties of the story,[14] the money the brothers originally tried to obtain by selling Joseph comes to them when they receive the grain plus money from him. The development with the sacks of grain, we are to understand, relates back to the brothers' initial treatment of Joseph.

Evidence that later developments echo earlier ones is also seen in what happens on a comparable occasion. When Joseph, in disguise, insists that one of the brothers remain behind in Egypt as punishment for the made-up charge that they are spies, the brothers' bad conscience about their original treatment of Joseph is triggered. Joseph's order immediately reminds them of their original offense against him (Gen 42:21). The reason the brothers had sought money for him in the first place was because they could not tolerate the idea that they were to bow to him as sheaves of grain ("stookies" in the personified, negative sense in Old Scots) bowing down to a sheaf set apart. But just after they receive the sacks of grain a second time, with their money again inside them, the brothers pay homage to Joseph just as his dream about the sheaves had predicted they would (Gen 44:14).

Joseph's status at the time when he torments his brothers is that of vizier of Egypt. It is a position of leadership recognized by both the native Egyptians and his visiting brothers. Moses too in his role as a leader is intent on justice. To this end—under God's direction (Exod 18:23)—he appoints rulers or magistrates to administer it. One of the requirements in the exercise of their judicial function is that they hate (ill-gotten) gain (beṣaʿ; Exod 18:21). We might perhaps have expected the term soḥad, "bribe."

The particular God-given requirement that ill-gotten gain is to be eschewed in any judicial inquiry stands in sharp contrast to the deception that Joseph's steward associates with God when the brothers find money in their sacks. Plainly, Joseph's use of money is intended to influence his case against his brothers. His malevolent return of their money forces them to defend themselves against the charge that they have stolen it (Gen 44:8). Their defense in turn leads to Judah's telling the disguised Joseph about their original offense against him (Gen 44:14–34). The term beṣaʿ, "ill-gotten gain or profit," occurs in the Pentateuch only in Exodus 18:21 and in Genesis 37:26, when Judah has his brothers—with the important exception of Reuben, whose intention is to restore Joseph to his father—agree with his judgment that they should sell Joseph rather than slay him.[15] Their earlier attempt to acquire money to be rid of their dispute with Joseph comes back to haunt them in a quite concrete way when Joseph reopens the dispute.

There is, in fact, a larger, substantive link between the etiological account of how a formal judicial system had its origin in ancient Israel (Exodus 18) and the Joseph narrative. The story of Joseph is itself an account of the first dispute ever in the history of the sons of Jacob/ Israel, the very first generation of Israelites. In that this dispute constitutes such an important development, its account, I am suggesting, would have demanded scrutiny of the issues it raises. Scholars who think that the Joseph story had no impact on other biblical literature have not been puzzled by the ethical problems that it poses, and consequently have never wondered whether these problems might not be addressed elsewhere. After all, to cite but one familiar example, Jacob's cheating Esau out of his birthright meets with a precise response when he in turn is cheated by his father-in-law, Laban, in the matter of his daughters' marriages to Jacob (Genesis 25, 27, 29).[16]

The dispute between Joseph and his brothers begins when Joseph brings a negative report about them to Jacob (Gen 37:2). There is no indication of the rightness or wrongness of Joseph's report. The dispute escalates, goes through all sorts of twists and turns, and does not end until the brothers resolve their difficulties with the vizier of Egypt— who turns out to be Joseph himself. In fact, the resolution of the original dispute is far from satisfactory. Only in an indirect and subtle manner does the reconciliation between Joseph and his brothers bring in its wake attention to the issues that first divided them. Their making up their differences, moreover, comes about in circumstances far removed from those surrounding the original dispute.

If a critical eye is cast on the dispute in Genesis 37, it is clear that the paterfamilias, Jacob, favors Joseph over his brothers. There is, consequently, a serious obstacle in the way of any resort to some higher human authority, to the *iudicium domesticum*, for example, to resolve the dispute between Joseph and the other sons. I am suggesting that for those who exercised their "historical" imagination about the beginnings of Israelite nationhood and who reflected on the unsatisfactory resolution of the dispute between Joseph and his brothers, the question would be: How did the resolution of disputes among future sons of Israel come to be provided for? The answer they set out, I claim, is Moses' institution of "able men [*'anšē-ḥayil*], such as fear God [*yir'ē' 'elohim*], men of truth [*'emet*], hating unjust gain [*beṣa'*]," to be rulers (*śarim*) of thousands, of hundreds, of fifties, of tens, and to be judges (Exod 18:21).

It is noteworthy that so much of the language used to define the criteria for these officials (*śarim*) is found in the Joseph story. When the brothers eventually settle in Egypt, Pharaoh inquires of Joseph whether there are among them "able men" (*'anšē-ḥayil*) who "could be rulers [*śarim*] over my cattle" (Gen 47:6). The rulership in this instance, because of the brothers' situation in Egypt and their occupation at the time, consists in holding a domestic position in the court of Pharaoh. In keeping with the later situation in the time of Moses, when the Israelites attain independence from foreign dominance, there is need for the abler among them to become rulers over men, and not just over herds of animals. The contrast between the situation in Egypt and the one reflecting Israelite political autonomy may then account for the overlap in language we are observing. It is also worth pointing out that in both instances, two foreigners, Pharaoh and Jethro, are the ones who initiate the organizational arrangements for the Israelites.[17]

In addition to this example of shared language between the Joseph and Moses stories there are two others, and, most pertinent, they concern the resolution of disputes. The examples are found in a comparison between Moses' institution for the resolution of disputes and Joseph's sham resolution of the dispute about spying between the brothers and himself. When the disguised Joseph falsely accuses them of being spies, they respond by telling him who they are, where they come from, and the names of their present and past family members. Joseph expresses a desire to test their claim that they are not spies by asking whether "there be any truth [*'emet*] in you" (Gen 42:16). When he goes on to suggest to them a procedure by which they might resolve this particular dispute, he avows his fear of God (*'et-ha'elohim 'ani yare'*; Gen 42:18). It is a notable fact that the qualities sought for in the rule about judicial officials—fear of God, truthfulness, and the quite specific one of hating unjust gain—are the very ones that Joseph per-

verts in trying to convict his brothers. In this light it is little wonder
that Moses upholds these particular qualities as important for those
who are to administer justice.

I submit that one aspect of the explicit concern with justice in the
narratives about the manna in the wilderness and Moses' task of ap-
pointing judges is that the biblical writer perceived a need to respond
to the unsatisfactory way that justice had been dispensed among the
first sons of Israel. Just as the kind of history writing we are observing
points to a good deal of reflection on the part of the writer(s), so the religious dimension—namely, the pronounced role of the deity—in the
two narratives in Exodus 16 and 18 is a manifest indication of reflective activity. Especially of the story of the manna in Exodus 16, we
have to ask what could possibly have prompted a writer to have the
deity play the role of distributing food so precisely that there is confor-
mity to a universal law of giving full and exact weights and measures
(Deut 25:13–16; Prov 11:1, 16:11, 20:23)? The answer, I suggest, is that
the preceding history, Joseph's, tells of events and developments in
which this kind of problem arose. It was consequently deemed important to indicate how the nation should have before it a perfect example, that of the deity himself, in the matter of using correct weights
and measures.

For anyone reflecting on the problem, as presumably the biblical
writers did, there is much else in the stories about Joseph and Moses
that points to the need to introduce a proper means of resolving disputes. There is Joseph's unjust imprisonment for an action he is not
guilty of, attempted rape. Joseph in turn jails his brothers for an offense they never committed (Gen 42:17), just as he forces one of them,
Simeon (Gen 42:24), to remain in Egypt as he, Joseph, had been forced
to remain there. Moses, like Joseph, sets himself up as judge over his
fellow Hebrews when two of them are engaged in a brawl, and his
judgment sharply raises the issue that there is no effective legal machinery to deal with disputes (Exod 2:13, 14).

T. E. Fretheim has observed a similar interrelationship between narratives with regard to certain traditions in the Book of Exodus.[18] He
notes that the devastating effects of the plagues in Egypt have their
counterparts in the aftermath of the Exodus, but that this time there is

a good outcome.[19] For example, as a result of the first plague in Egypt, the water is undrinkable (Exod 7:24). In Exodus 15:23 the Israelites are in a similar situation, but the bitter water is made sweet and the wilderness itself is filled with springs of water.[20] In Exodus 9:18, 23 God rains (*mṭr*) hail upon Egypt, and it destroys the fields of food. In Exodus 16:4 there is the opposite development. God rains (*mṭr*) bread from heaven to feed the hungry Israelites. From one perspective, these sophisticated repetitions of theme are but one characteristic of the Pentateuch. Two further examples are how the firstborn loses out in succeeding generations, and the occurrence of famine first in Joseph's Egypt, then in the Egypt of the time of the Exodus, and latterly in the wilderness after the departure from Egypt.

The process in question, however, instances in which a topic in biblical history is taken up in another part of the history, is, as I have attempted to demonstrate, precisely paralleled in the presentation of biblical law itself. As I have argued elsewhere,[21] the Deuteronomic lawgiver's consideration of Joseph's deceptive transaction with the grain and the counterexample, the deity providing manna in the wilderness, similarly inspired the setting down of a law about false weights and measures (Deut 25:13–16). The two incidents together appear to underlie the rule's particular formulation.

The lawgiver reflects on the ethical aspect of Joseph's ploy and consequently sets down the initial negative statement: "Thou shalt not have in thy bag divers weights, a great and a small. Thou shalt not have in thine house divers measures, a great and a small." The proverbial concern about shortchanging someone in weights and measures is set down as the likeliest parallel in ordinary life to Joseph's extraordinary action. In turn, the deity's example in the wilderness prompts the subsequent positive formulation: "Thou shalt have a perfect and just weight, a perfect and just measure shalt thou have: that thy days may be lengthened in the land which Yahweh thy God giveth thee." Moses promulgates this law to the Israelites in the wilderness (Deut 1:1, 27:2). The implication is that during his time there he had occasion to address the problem. The lawgiver characterizes the resort to underhanded practices as an "abomination to Yahweh," a phrase he probably employs because Yahweh's activity in the wilderness (Exodus

16) is a negative reaction to Joseph's practice when trading in commodities (Gen 42:25, 44:1).

There is one especially persuasive indication that we should link the Deuteronomic law on false weights and measures to the narrative in Exodus 16 about the exact provision of manna. There is a manifest connection between the law in Deuteronomy 25:17–19, about the extermination of the Amalekites—the law that immediately follows, most haphazardly it might appear, the law on weights and measures—and the narrative about the Amalekites' dastardly attack on the thirsty Israelites in Exodus 17. The account about the Amalekites in Exodus 17 follows the story about the distribution of the manna in Exodus 16.

There is nothing surprising about a process whereby certain rules undergo change in light of biblical history. The plainest example is the incorporation of the events of the Exodus into the institution of the Passover. It is agreed on all hands that what was originally an agricultural festival has been transformed into a historical commemoration. Just so, an ageless rule about weights and measures has been grounded in experiences associated with the beginnings of the Israelite nation. Re-creations of a nation's legal traditions are, in fact, common.[22]

The literary process I have been commenting on can be put into a broader historical perspective. Considered together, the legal and narrative portions of the Pentateuch reveal the existence of a sophisticated, highly developed form of scribal art at some period in Israelite antiquity. This scribal activity is probably the Israelite equivalent of what Meir Malul describes for the ancient Near Eastern legal corpora, a "literary tradition" rather than a "practical legal tradition."[23] The biblical scribes may well have been acquainted with the Near Eastern legal tradition, one that was known well into the first millennium B.C.,[24] in a manner comparable to their knowledge of Babylonian mathematics (which Dwight Young so convincingly demonstrates).[25] On this assumption, in order to set out a distinctive body of Israelite rules, the biblical scribes scrutinized the problems and disputes that they found in their own national traditions about the patriarchs, about Moses, about the Judges, and about the kings.

Equally sophisticated is the attention interpreters around the beginning of the Christian era gave to the laws and narratives in the Bible. Josephus, Philo, and the author of the Letter of Aristeas, while approaching the Pentateuch—or rather the Torah—from a milieu in which the Hellenistic rhetorical schools had considerable influence,[26] were in fact accurately focusing on one of its most salient features, the quite definite links between the narrative portions and the precepts. When we turn to the Tannaitic period of Rabbinic activity (from about 50 B.C.E. to about 200 C.E.), we should analyze Midrash Halakhah and Midrash Haggadhah, Rabbinic law and the exegesis of biblical narrative, in light of certain historical developments that have little or no continuity with any biblical precedent. We should nonetheless recognize a typological parallel between the Tannaites' work on the relationship between law and narrative in their interpretation of the Torah and the activity of the original compilers of the Pentateuch.[27]

NOTES

Introduction

1 In current legal scholarship, Walter Weyrauch shows how modern rules are themselves more likely to be the product of responses to contemporary mythical stories circulating about the nature of society than responses to the reality of what is actually going on in society. He cites readily recognizable examples from American criminal law (crimes of violence prompt tough crime legislation, but criminality, as distinct from rates of incarceration, is generally in line with Australia and England) in "Oral Legal Traditions of Gypsies and Some American Equivalents," *AJCL* 45 (forthcoming). Compare his "Law as Mask—Legal Ritual and Relevance," *CLR* 66 (1978): 699–726.

2 See the seminal work of J. G. A. Pocock, *The Ancient Constitution and the Feudal Law: A Study of English Historical Thought in the Seventeenth Century* (Cambridge, Eng., 1957).

3 Alan Watson's *The Spirit of Roman Law* (Athens, Ga., 1995), in this series, takes issue with this view as it applies to Roman law.

4 On the procedure of the ancient historians, see Pocock, *The Ancient Constitution*, 3, 6. For an attempt to relate biblical historiography to Mesopotamian and Greek historiography, see John Van Seters, *In Search of History: Historiography in the Ancient World and the Origins of Biblical History* (New Haven, 1983).

5 I shall largely refrain from pursuing the question to what extent the lawgivers and the redactors of these traditions overlap in their use of national records. There are indications that they proceed in tandem. See chapters 8 and 9.

6 See Menachem Haran, "Behind the Scenes of History: Determining the Date of the Priestly Source," *JBL* 100 (1981): 321–33; and Jacob Milgrom, *Leviticus 1–16*, AB 3 (New York, 1991), 26, 28. Milgrom asserts on the basis of such links between the rules and the historical narratives: "What can unquestionably be accepted . . . is that H [Leviticus 17–26] arose from the socio-economic crisis . . . in the 8th century" (28). Montaigne's remark is apt: "Nothing is so firmly believed as what we least know" (*Of Divine Ordinances*, bk. 1, ch. 31).

7 See my forthcoming *Law, Legend, and Incest in the Bible: Leviticus 18–20* (Ithaca, 1997), ch. 7.

8 On the invention or reinvention of a nation's legal system in particular, see, for ancient Athens, David Cohen, "Greek Law: Problems and Methods," *ZSS* 106 (1989): 101; for Scotland, Hector L. MacQueen, "*Regiam Majestatem,* Scots Law and National Identity," *Scottish Historical Review* 74 (1995): 1–20; for seventeenth-century England, Pocock, *The Ancient Constitution;* also, on more general aspects, see *The Invention of Tradition,* ed. Eric Hobsbawm and Terence Ranger (Cambridge, Eng., 1983).

9 For the thesis that the laws of the Book of the Covenant are also a Deuteronomic product, see C. M. Carmichael, *The Origins of Biblical Law* (Ithaca, 1992).

10 See my detailed analysis in *Origins of Biblical Law,* 79–97.

11 For an incomplete analysis of the rule, see C. M. Carmichael, *Law and Narrative in the Bible* (Ithaca, 1985), 81–83.

12 I agree with David Daube about the relationship between social rules and the story of the Exodus when he states, "We have before us, then, a development in three stages. There were social laws more primitive than, though similar to, those extant in the Pentateuch. These determined the whole way in which the exodus was thought of and described. And the narratives of the exodus in turn influenced, on the one hand, the further history of the social laws and, on the other, the direction which the ideas about God's intervention on behalf of his people or man in general were to take" (*The New Testament and Rabbinic Judaism* [London, 1956], 269–70).

13 For a prime example of this approach, see Sara Japhet, "The Relationship between the Legal Corpora in the Pentateuch in Light of Manumission Laws," *Scripta Hierosolymitana* 31 (1986): 63–89. Japhet begins her article with the following statement: "One of the abiding achievements of biblical research is the general recognition of several legal corpora in the Pentateuch, each composition an independent unit and deriving from a particular historical and social background." Yet her acute sense of history never leads her to ask why the biblical record has Moses give one rule about the manumission of slaves at the time of the wilderness wandering and another, similar rule still in the wilderness but just before entry into the land of Canaan. Out of respect for the biblical narrator one would want to ask whether the differences between the rules are in any way related to the different matters engaging Moses' attention at these two periods.

14 The famous puzzle about the meaning of the statement in Deuteronomy 15:18 that the slave has been worth double the hire of a hired servant is

soluble if the model is Laban's dealings with Jacob. Laban asks Jacob what his wages (hire) are to be (Gen 29:15). They agree on Jacob's receiving Rachel for seven years' service. At the end of the seven years Jacob is given Leah instead, someone he neither wished nor asked for. He then has to serve another seven years for Rachel. In effect, Jacob is a slave for the first seven years and a hired servant for the second seven. To Laban, then, Jacob's period as a slave is worth twice the cost of a hired servant because if he had treated him properly—that is, as a hired servant—and not brought Leah into account, he would have had to pay Jacob twice what he paid him. It is surprising that the lawgiver points out what might be readily assumed; namely, that it is to an owner's advantage to use a slave instead of a hired servant. The reason is that the lawgiver takes stock of Laban's exploitation of Jacob and his unwillingness to let Jacob leave his service. Rules often come into being not from some situation in which there is a genuine problem between two parties, but because one party has triumphed over another by a deception and the situation requires that the true reckoning be spelled out.

15 In a recent essay on the slave rules in the Covenant Code (Exod 21:2–11), "The Anthropology of Slavery in the Covenant Code," in *Theory and Method in Biblical and Cuneiform Law*, ed. B. M. Levinson, *JSOT* suppl. 181 (Sheffield, 1994), V. H. Matthews begins by saying, "Since legal systems or individual laws are never created in a social vacuum, one of the major questions to be raised about the law is its original intent within the community that formulated it" (119). By "social vacuum" he means, in regard to the slave laws, for example, the reality of slave life in ancient Israel. There would have been such a reality, but the assumption that the biblical laws reflect it directly is wrong. Alan Watson points out how frequently laws do not directly reflect the society in which they operate in *Legal Transplants: An Approach to Comparative Law*, 2d ed. (Athens, Ga., 1993); and "The Importance of 'Nutshells,'" *AJCL* 42 (1994): 1, 2, especially 20–23; on slave law, see Watson, *Slave Law in the Americas* (Athens, Ga., 1989). Matthews begins his concluding remarks, "Slavery as an institution in ancient Israel, unlike that in ancient Greece and Rome, probably did not account for a large percentage of the labor force" (134). But Matthews produces no data whatever to support such a judgment.

16 Jacob Milgrom is throwing stones from a glass house when he describes other scholars' historical reconstructions as "unadulterated speculation" or as "dead wrong" (*Leviticus 1–16*, 628, 952).

17 An example is his treatment of the rule about the irregular sexual union with the bondwoman in Leviticus 19:20–22. See R. Westbrook, *Studies*

in *Biblical and Cuneiform Law, Cahiers de la Revue Biblique* 26 (Paris, 1988), 101–9; also see Westbrook, "Adultery in Ancient Near Eastern Law," *RB* 97 (1990): 564–69; and Westbrook, "Slave and Master in Ancient Near Eastern Law," *Chicago-Kent Law Review* 70 (1995): 1669.

18 See W. F. Albright, *Archaeology and the Religion of Israel* (Baltimore, 1953), 113; also J. M. Myers, *Judges*, IB 2 (Nashville, 1953), 752; N. M. Sarna, *Genesis*, JPSC (Philadelphia, 1989), 233.

19 Note again how the narrative about Jacob and Esau is written up with later developments in focus; namely, those involving the relationship between the two later nations, Israel (Jacob) and Edom (Esau).

20 See Geoffrey P. Miller's "Contracts of Genesis," *JLS* 22 (1993): 15–45; and "The Legal-Economic Approach to Biblical Interpretation," *JITE* 150 (1994): 755–62. For Miller's discussion of the Adam and Eve, Cain and Abel material, see "Ritual and Regulation: A Legal-Economic Interpretation of Selected Biblical Texts," *JLS* 22 (1993): 477–501.

Chapter 1. Narrative Inspired Law

This chapter is an expanded version of Calum Carmichael's contribution to a joint lecture, *The Return of the Divorcee*, by him and Professor David Daube, that appeared as an occasional paper of the Oxford Centre for Postgraduate Hebrew Studies (1993). The foreword to that publication, by David Patterson, emeritus president of the Oxford Centre, records a historic first in the study of Jewish law in Oxford, and is reprinted below.

The agreement of the Governors of the Oxford Centre for Postgraduate Hebrew Studies in 1987 to establish a Fellowship in Jewish Law constituted a milestone in the Centre's history. To mark the occasion Professor David Daube and his erstwhile student Professor Calum Carmichael were invited to give the Inaugural Lecture. How appropriate that the joint appearance of a great teacher and an outstanding pupil should convey to the assembled audience of academics, which included many law dons from both Oxford and Cambridge, lawyers, and other interested members of the Oxford community, the educational significance of such a Fellowship. How appropriate too that Professor A. M. Honoré, Professor Daube's successor in the Regius Chair of Civil Law at the University of Oxford, presided on the occasion at Yarnton Manor on June 10, 1987. Some time has passed since that occasion. I have come to the end of my tenure as President of the Oxford Centre, and to my delight, at a dinner on the occasion of my retirement on October 29, 1992, the Lord Chief Justice of England, Lord Taylor of Gosforth, announced that the Jewish Law Fellowship had been named after me. Nothing could give me greater satisfaction than my association over many decades with the legal scholarship represented by Professors Daube and Carmichael.

1 R. Yaron, "The Restoration of Marriage," *JJS* 17 (1966): 1–11. S. R. Driver's remarks anticipate Yaron's solution; see Driver, *Deuteronomy*, ICC (Edinburgh, 1902), 272: "It [the provision] would also be of value in a different direction by checking, on the part of a woman desirous of returning to her former home, the temptation to intrigue against her second husband."

2 E. P. Thompson reports one such instance in England in 1829, when the first husband harassed the new couple, in *Customs in Common, Studies in Traditional Popular Culture* (New York, 1993), 449.

3 I recall a conversation on the (former) BBC *Third Program* between C. Day Lewis and Robert Frost in which Frost said, "The three most important things are science, religion—and gossip." He then went on to discuss how the imaginative quality that goes into gossip is the same as that found in, for example, the writing of history. For a more searching inquiry, see R. G. Collingwood, *The Idea of History* (London, 1956).

4 See C. M. Carmichael, *The Story of Creation: Its Origin and Its Interpretation in Philo and the Fourth Gospel* (Ithaca, 1996).

5 Sodom and Gomorrah, for example, will be judged (Matt 11:22).

6 On the related topic of legislation designed to protect people's unwillingness to be generous, see David Daube, *Roman Law, Linguistic, Philosophical, Social, and Philosophical Aspects* (Edinburgh, 1969), 117–30.

7 Compare the privilege of eating with a king but guarding oneself against indulgence (Prov 23:1, 2).

· 8 For an illustration of the Rabbinic principle, see Mekhilta on Exodus 15:9.

9 Kinship ties play a dominant role in a succession of laws at this point in Deuteronomy. See C. M. Carmichael, *Law and Narrative in the Bible* (Ithaca, 1985).

10 Unlike the position in the comparable story in Genesis 12. The difference raises important questions about possible relationships between one Genesis narrative and another.

11 In line with later Jewish law, until about the early third century C.E., so long as the man's intent was to make the woman his wife and she

consented, intercourse alone would have been sufficient to establish Sarah's status as Abimelech's wife. See David Daube, *Collected Works: Talmudic Law*, ed. C. M. Carmichael (Berkeley, 1992), 1:157.

12 Yet, curiously, that is just the position in the nonstory of Isaac and Rebekah at Abimelech's court in Genesis 26.

13 The topic has a long history. E. P. Thompson writes, "The sale or exchange of a wife, for sexual or domestic services, appears to have taken place, on occasion, in most places and at most times. It may be only an aberrant transaction, with or without a pretended contractual basis—it is recorded sometimes today" (*Customs in Common*, 408). In our joint Oxford lecture (*The Return of the Divorcee* [Oxford Centre for Postgraduate Hebrew Studies, 1993], 5, 6, see note 1 above), David Daube refers to the example in Roman antiquity of Cato's release of his wife to his wealthy friend Hortensius, who subsequently died. After his death she returned to Cato considerably enriched from her second marriage. See Plutarch, *Lives*, Cato the Younger, LCL (London, 1919), 25.2–5; Susan Treggiari, *Roman Marriage* (Oxford, 1991), 145, 470.

14 In general, prior to the introduction of the bill of divorce, a husband divorced his wife simply by expelling her. See Z. W. Falk, *Hebrew Law in Biblical Times* (Jerusalem, 1964), 154.

15 In the Book of Esther, Queen Vashti's refusal to expose herself to a (drunken) male audience is cause for her dismissal from the matrimonial home. Unlike Abraham, King Ahasuerus need not have feared the loss of his wife to another male. Indeed, his impregnable position is the very opposite of Abraham's predicament.

16 See Jonathan Magonet, "The Themes of Genesis 2–3," in *A Walk in the Garden, JSOT* suppl. 136, ed. Paul Morris and Deborah Sawyer (Sheffield, 1992), 42–44.

17 Compare the modern formulation, "Dirt is matter out of place."

18 Different is the ritual of wife selling in eighteenth- and nineteenth-century England, a procedure for the poor who had no access to the legal machinery of divorce. Divorce involved an act of Parliament and was obtainable only by the rich and influential. See Ronald Paulson, *Popular and Polite Art in the Age of Hogarth and Fielding* (Notre Dame, Ind., 1979), 15; and E. P. Thompson's major study, *Customs in Common*, 404–66.

19 Jezebel uses witnesses in the proper way in order to throw a cloak of legality over her criminal move to be rid of Naboth (1 Kings 21:10). For other examples of conduct that appears to be in order but is in fact crooked, see David Daube's discussion of purists and pragmatists in later Talmudic law

and New Testament literature, "Neglected Nuances of Exposition in Luke–Acts," *Principat* 25 (1985): 2329–56.

20 See Treggiari, *Roman Marriage*, 288–90.

21 The biblical lawgiver's attitude is similar to the Roman legislator's: "A [husband] is seen as having made a profit out of his wife's adultery if he has accepted anything in return for her committing adultery" (*D.* 48.5.30[29]). John Calvin's view of the prohibition in Deuteronomy 24:1–4 is that "by prostituting his wife, he [the husband] would be, as far as in him lay, acting like a procurer." Compare Philo, *De Specialibus Legibus* 3.30, 31. Calvin's view comes from his reading of Matthew 5:31 and 19:9. Jesus recognizes no divorce. Consequently, a man who divorces his wife is indeed encouraging her to prostitute herself. See Calvin, *Commentaries on the Last Four Books of Moses arranged in the form of a Harmony*, trans. C. W. Bingham (Grand Rapids, 1950), 3:94; also G. P. Hugenberger, *Marriage as Covenant, SVT* 52 (1994): 76–78.

22 In a different context, Philo comments on such a link when he discusses the earth's curse upon Cain, "For if inanimate and terrestrial nature opposes and revolts against wrongdoing . . ." (*Quaestiones et Solutiones in Genesin* 1.71).

23 It should be clear that I cannot go along with the reading of this law as depicting the historical realities of ancient Hebrew society. Here is a typical treatment of how such a law is understood: "In pre-prophetic times all that a man had to do if his wife 'found no favor in his eyes' was to write her a bill of divorcement and send her out of his house. He might not, however, remarry her" (see entry: "Marriages, Law of," *Encyclopedia Americana*, 1965 ed. 18:315).

24 For a parallel in a twentieth-century Greek sheep-herding community to a man's leaving his place of business for a number of months in order to establish his wife's pregnancy, see J. K. Campbell, *Honour, Family, and Patronage* (Oxford, 1964), 12.

25 On the association with childbearing of language about giving pleasure to a wife, see C. M. Carmichael, "Marriage and the Samaritan Woman," *NTS* 26 (1980): 333–35. Amusingly, the authors of the article cited in note 23 above translate—as does the JPS version—"Shall cheer up his wife."

Chapter 2. Laws of Leviticus 19

1 "Das sozialethische Grundgezetz der Jahvereligion" (Johannes Hempel, *Gott und Mensch im Alten Testament*, BWANT 38 [Stuttgart: 1926] 18 n. 1).

2 Arie Noordtzij, *Leviticus*, BSC (Grand Rapids, 1982), 189.

3 See Jacob Milgrom, *Leviticus 1–16*, AB 3 (New York, 1991), 26.

4 B. A. Levine, *Leviticus*, JPSC (Philadelphia, 1989), 257. Compare also J. E. Hartley, *Leviticus*, WBC (Dallas, 1992), 308; Jonathan Magonet, "The Structure and Meaning of Leviticus 19," *HAR* 7 (1983): 151; and Gordon Wenham, *Leviticus*, NICOT (Grand Rapids, 1979), 264.

5 For various attempts to delineate such sources, see H. G. Reventlow, *Das Heiligkeitsgesetz formgeschichtlich Untersucht*, WMANT 6 (Neukirchen, 1961), 65–78; Rudolph Kilian, *Literarkritische und formgeschichtliche Untersuchung des Heiligkeitgesetzes*, BBB 19 (Bonn, 1963), 57–65; Christian Feucht, *Untersuchungen zum Heiligkeitgesetz* (Berlin, 1964), 37–42; Alfred Cholewinski, *Heiligkeitgesetz und Deuteronomium: Eine vergleichende Studie*, AnBib 64 (Rome, 1976), 44–54.

6 The thesis I develop received serious and positive discussion at the turn of the century, as reported in S. R. Driver's masterful commentary, *Deuteronomy*, ICC, 3d ed. (Edinburgh, 1902), 213: "Unless, indeed, the other alternative be adopted, and the author of Dt. 17:14–20 [law of the king be supposed to have been influenced, as he wrote, by his recollections of the narrative of Sam. (so Budde, *Richter und Samuel*, p. 183 f.; Cornill, *Einl.* par. 17.4). As the nucleus of 1 S. 8; 10:17–27a 12 appears to be pre-Deuteronomic (L.O.T. *l.c.*), the latter alternative is not the least probable one."

7 For the laws of the Book of the Covenant (Exod 21:1–23:19) as the product of the Deuteronomist, see C. M. Carmichael, *The Origins of Biblical Law* (Ithaca, 1992).

8 For example, God's judgment on Onan's failure to meet his levirate obligation to his dead brother in Genesis 38 has its legal equivalent in the rule about the levirate in Deuteronomy 25:5–10. See C. M. Carmichael, *Law and Narrative in the Bible* (Ithaca, 1985), 295–97.

9 God's opposition to Sarah's going from her husband, Abraham, to another man and back to Abraham in Genesis 20 becomes a rule against the renovation of a marriage when the legal machinery of divorce has been used for the first husband's gain; see chapter 1.

10 See Meir Malul, *The Comparative Method in Ancient Near Eastern and Biblical Legal Studies*, AOAT 227 (Neukirchen-Vluyn, 1990), 105–7 n. 13.

11 Compare how the prophet Nathan presents King David with a made-up case for judgment about the theft of a ewe lamb (2 Sam 12:1–6), and the woman of Tekoah with one about a widow threatened with the loss of her one remaining son because, this son having killed his brother, other family members seek vengeance for the killing (2 Sam 14:4–7). David's

adultery with Bathsheba and Absalom's exile from his father, David, because he had his brother Amnon slain inspire the two hypothetical constructions. See chapter 8.

12 Martin Noth, *The Deuteronomistic History, JSOT* suppl. 15 (Sheffield, 1981).

13 Noth claims that "the document of practical significance [for the Deuteronomistic history] was the Deuteronomic law" (*Deuteronomistic History*, 92), yet in his attempts to understand the history he cites only seven Deuteronomic laws in his index of sources.

14 Noth, *Deuteronomistic History*, 140.

15 On the major points of contact between the write-up of Amaziah's history and the history of Jacob/Israel at the time of the Shechem incident, see Carmichael, *Law and Narrative*, 270–76.

16 Bernard Levinson, "Calum M. Carmichael's Approach to the Laws of Deuteronomy," *HTR* 83 (1990): 239. See my fuller response, "Laws of Leviticus 19," *HTR* 87 (1994): 239–44. On the esoteric character of all legal systems—for example, contemporary American law—see Walter Weyrauch, "Taboo and Magic in Law," *SLR* 25 (1973): 797–800.

17 When William Johnstone, in "The Decalogue and the Redaction of the Sinai Pericope in Exodus," *ZAW* 100 (1988): 373, states, regarding biblical legal material, that it is the nature of law codes to change over time, he openly states a common assumption. S. E. Loewenstamm, in "Exodus xxi 22–25," *VT* 27 (1977): 355, points out, however, that we have not the slightest evidence for the mechanisms or processes by which these supposed additions to the law codes were made. The biggest problem is the endless speculation about what historical event or movement brought about a supposed change in a law. Unfortunately, no evidence is available for such historical reconstruction. However much one may desire to locate a history of ancient Israel, the gulf between the biblical sources and the reality of the past is too great to be bridged. See Philip Davies's critique of attempts at such reconstruction, *In Search of "Ancient Israel,"* *JSOT* suppl. 148 (Sheffield, 1992).

18 Levinson, "Carmichael's Approach," 255.

19 For the reasons why this rule follows the rule about bestiality and the problem of Canaanite idolatrous influence (Lev 18:23–30), see my forthcoming *Law, Legend, and Incest in the Bible: Leviticus 18–20* (Ithaca, 1997), ch. 3.

20 Arie Noordtzij (*Leviticus*, 193) says that the mother is cited first because in a polygamous society children have a more intimate attachment to

their mother than to their father. That attachment, however, is true regardless of the society's structure. It is no accident that we refer to our "mother tongue."

21 Moshe Weinfeld, *Deuteronomy 1–11*, AB 5 (New York, 1991), 250–53.

22 Weinfeld, *Deuteronomy 1–11*, 310.

23 See chapter 5.

24 Weinfeld, *Deuteronomy 1–11*, 251.

25 Compare how Sennacherib was likened to a god in heaven to whom the sun, moon, and stars are subservient (Ahikar 6:16 in both the Syriac and Armenian versions). See R. H. Charles, *The Apocrypha and Pseudepigrapha of the Old Testament* (Oxford, 1913), 2:759–60. Nabonidus was greeted by the moon, a star, and Jupiter (*ANET*, 310); further, Pericles was compared to Zeus (Plutarch, *Pericles* 8.3). See D. B. Redford, *A Study of the Biblical Story of Joseph*, SVT (Leiden, 1970), 204.

26 The expression *'elilim 'ilemim* (dumb idols) occurs in Habakkuk 2:18.

27 B. J. Schwartz suggests that the unexpected selection of the term *shiphah* in Leviticus 19:20a and not *'amah* for "slave-girl" is a wordplay reflecting the fact that she is not *ḥpsh* (free); see "The Slave-Girl Pericope," *Scripta Hierosolymitana* 31 (1986): 244.

28 Gerhard von Rad, in *Genesis*, 3d ed. (London, 1972), 351, 352, is at pains to stress that Joseph's dreams in no way signify a religious dimension. They are, he implies, just the vivid imaginings of a young boy. One wonders why he feels the need to emphasize the lack of religious, mythological overtones. The issue that von Rad attempts to deny is precisely the one that lies behind the Priestly lawgiver's concern. I am not claiming that the Priestly lawgiver read the dreams as idolatrous in character, but that in light of his knowledge of Israel's religious history, the dreams raised the issue of idolatry.

29 See Jacob Milgrom's discussion of the comparable rule in Leviticus 7:11–21, in *Leviticus 1–16*, 413.

30 The harvesting of sheaves in the dream explains why in the rule an injunction about the harvest precedes the injunction about the gleaning of grapes (Lev 19:9–10).

31 Joseph is sold for twenty shekels of silver. In Leviticus 27:5 this is the valuation placed on a minor above five years old in order to buy him back after he has been vowed to the sanctuary. Dedication of a person to the sanctuary is the religious equivalent of the secular institution of slavery.

32 The term used for the grain that Joseph put in storage is *piqqadon*, "deposit" (Gen 41:36). Its only other occurrence is in Leviticus 5:21 (ET 6:2, cheating in regard to a neighbor's deposit).

33 See Carmichael, *Law and Narrative*, 278–88. Gerhard von Rad states (*Genesis*, 352), without giving any reason: "One ought not to see in it [the vision of the sheaves] a reference to Joseph's later policy of storage." Daphne du Maurier's *Rebecca* is an example of a later literary work that opens with a dream that points to the story's ending.

34 Weinfeld, *Deuteronomy 1–11*, 33.

35 There is a switch from the use of the second-person plural (You) to the second-person singular (Thou) in the presentation of these rules, perhaps because the lawgiver is going back and forth between a judgment on individuals in Genesis to a judgment that is intended for all the people of Israel.

36 On theft as the leitmotif of the story of Jacob's relationship with Laban, see Ktziah Spanier, "Rachel's Theft of the Teraphim: Her Struggle for Family Primacy," *VT* 42 (1992): 404–12.

37 Deception by exploiting problems of sight is a factor in Jacob's fraud against his father, Laban's fraud against Jacob on his wedding night, and Rachel's concealment of Laban's household gods, the protectors of the family home. It is possible that the narrator intends Rachel's action as a mirroring retribution for her father's denial of her to Jacob on the night of their wedding; by substituting Leah for Rachel, Laban was denying Rachel the protection of a new home.

38 See David Daube's analysis, *Studies in Biblical Law* (Cambridge, Eng., 1947), 190–200; and the very similar analysis by Robert Alter, *The Art of Biblical Narrative* (New York; 1981), 42–46.

39 See S. R. Driver, *The Book of Exodus*, CBSC (Cambridge, Eng., 1911), 217.

40 This incident prompted the rules against treating a parent with contempt (the verb is *qalal*) in Exodus 21:17 (and Lev 20:9). See Carmichael, *Origins of Biblical Law*, 112, 113. Robert Alter identifies the link between the two episodes as the deceptive use of garments (*Art of Biblical Narrative*, 181).

41 Both the Joseph tradition (relevant to the rule about unrighteousness in judgment) and the tradition about Isaac's blessing of Esau or Jacob (relevant to the preceding rules about swearing falsely and misleading the blind) contain a report about the doings of others. The Genesis narrator may have intended to link the two reports. Just as Jacob offends by wrongly acting on his mother's report about a father's love for a son (Esau), so Jacob in turn runs into trouble with his sons because he fails to act on Joseph's report about them, his failure also being motivated by love for his son (Joseph).

42 It is not accurate to translate *dal* as "poor" and *gadol* as "rich," as B. A. Levine claims that the context requires (*Leviticus*, 129). *dal* is usually

paired with *'ašir,* "rich" (Exod 30:15; Prov 10:15, 22:16, 28:11); *it* does have the meaning "poor," but in light of the narrative background, "weak, lowly" is more accurate.

43 See Carmichael, *Origins of Biblical Law,* 187–89.

44 Claus Westermann claims in *Genesis 37–50. A Commentary* (Minneapolis, 1986), 36, that from one angle, "Joseph's action in the context of vv. 1–2 together with vv. 3ff. is to be understood as an act of tale-bearing by which he wanted to make himself important."

45 The Targum Onkelos on Leviticus 19:16 reads the sentence in the sense of conspiring against someone: "Do not rise up against the life of your comrade."

46 In the *Testament of the Twelve Patriarchs* (probably originally from the second century B.C.E.), Joseph's brother Gad explicitly relates the rule found in Leviticus 19:17 to the relationship between Joseph and his brothers (*Testament of Gad* 6:1–5). For an important discussion, see James L. Kugel, "On Hidden Hatred and Open Reproach: Early Exegesis of Leviticus 19:17," *HTR* 80 (1987): 49–61. At the very least, it is interesting that this early wisdom composition links the law to the Joseph narrative. Whether or not the author of *Testament of Gad* was familiar with the process of legal and ethical formulation that I am describing, and his work consequently represents a continuation of it, is a question that has to remain open.

47 Levine (*Leviticus,* 130), noting the use of the term *naṭar,* "to keep, guard, retain," paraphrases: "One ought not to keep alive the memory of another's offense against him." The Babylonian *Counsels of Wisdom,* ANET, 426, contains the advice, "Unto your opponent do no evil; Your evildoer recompense with good; Unto your enemy let justice [be done]."

48 See Takamitsu Muraoka's decisive arguments in favor of the translation of *lere'aka kamoka* as "[thy neighbor] who is like thyself"; that is, "[thy neighbor] who is like thyself, an Israelite," in "A Syntactic Problem in Lev. xix. 18b," *JSS* 23 (1978): 291–97.

49 There is increasing recognition of the importance of this fact. See, for example, G. C. Chirichigno, "The Narrative Structure of Exod 19–24," *Bib* 68 (1987): 457–79.

Chapter 3. Laws as Miniature Narratives

1 C. M. Carmichael, "Forbidden Mixtures," *VT* 32 (1982): 394–415. Carl Steuernagel, in *Deuteronomium und Josua,* HAT (Göttingen; 1900), 1:81,

82, suggests that the rules in Deuteuronomy 22:9–11 had to do at some early stage with sexual and religious matters, possibly to do with nature cults. Compare G. J. Botterweck: "These various kinds of hybridization could point back to different spheres of activity and areas of worship of various deities" (entry, *"behemah,"* TDOT, 2:12).

2 The tendency has been to give priority to P, but the arguments are less than convincing. For example, A. D. H. Mayes states on the basis of the use of a single word, the verb meaning "to sow," that Leviticus 19:19 in relation to Deuteronomy 22:9 "is undoubtedly original, as being more suitable to the verb 'to sow'" (*Deuteronomy,* NCBC [Grand Rapids, 1981], 308). "To sow" is indeed the appropriate term in Deuteronomy 22:9 because the vineyard is figurative for human reproduction, and a man sows seed in a woman (e.g., Lev 12:2; Num 5:28; and Sir 26:20; cp. Sir 25:8a with its reference to Deut 22:10 about plowing with an ox and an ass). Michael Fishbane reasons as follows. Originally, the rules in Leviticus 19:19 had a rhythmical and formulaic character. The word *shatnez* disrupts the rhythm, so it must be an addition by legal draftsmen whose task it was to qualify and clarify the rule in question for different times in the history of ancient Israel. Solely on his subjective sense of the use of rhythm in a language from a very distant past does he built up a complicated history of development for an original "legal model" that first receives explication in P, and later, further explication in D; see Fishbane, *Biblical Interpretation in Ancient Israel* (Oxford, 1985), 58–62.

3 C. F. Keil and F. Delitzsch seem to be aware of the problem when they claim that the mules frequently mentioned in the Old Testament were imported from abroad; see *Leviticus,* BCOT 2 (Grand Rapids, 1951), 422. The implication is that the rule in Leviticus 19:19 was duly observed within Israel.

4 "If it [the rule in Leviticus 19:19] means that two fibers may not be used in a single garment, it goes counter to the specifications for the holy garments, since the girdle calls for wool and linen, and the robe, breastpiece, and ephod call for wool, linen, and gold" ("Cloth," IDB, 1:654). See also "Dress and Ornamentation," ABD, 2:232–38.

5 R. K. Harrison, *Leviticus,* TOTC (Downers Grove, Ill., 1980), 200. Compare Mayes, *Deuteronomy,* 308, which states that the rule in Deuteronomy 22:9 about the mixed seed in the vineyard "may have a utilitarian reason in the inappropriate and wasteful use of crops and land." Michael Fishbane claims that we are dealing not with "theoretical ritual considerations," but with an "entirely practical agronomic concern that over-

cultivation of a circumscribed area eventually results in the premature exhaustion of arable soil." Different legal draftsmen, modifying the rules to meet changing social-historical circumstances, told the farmers about the modifications, "possibly prior to the planting and breeding season" (see Fishbane, *Biblical Interpretation*, 58–62).

6 R. L. Harris, *Leviticus*, EPC 2 (Grand Rapids, 1990), 606.

7 Arie Noordtzij, *Leviticus*, BSC (Grand Rapids, 1982), 200.

8 See, for example, Gordon J. Wenham, *Leviticus*, NICOT (Grand Rapids, 1979), 269; "Mixing of kinds has to be prevented, because the order of the world must not be endangered" (C. Houtman, "Another Look at Forbidden Mixtures," *VT* 34 [1984], 227).

9 J. R. Porter, *Leviticus*, CBC (Cambridge, Eng., 1976), 157.

10 Martin Noth, *Leviticus*, OTL (Philadelphia, 1977), 142.

11 Fishbane, *Biblical Interpretation*, 59, 60. G. J. Botterweck does not interpret in terms of species: "The law against hybridization in Lev 19:19, according to which a cow (*behemah*) was not allowed to copulate with a breed of cattle different from its own" (entry: "*behemah*," *TDOT*, 2:12).

12 Wenham, *Leviticus*, 269.

13 Rebekah and Isaac had been concerned about the possibility of Jacob's marriage to a Canaanite woman because his brother, Esau, married Canaanite wives (Gen 27:46–28:1). Isaac took means to ensure that Jacob would not make such a union.

14 The ox in Genesis 49:6 is a figure for Jacob/Israel's fighting strength, which is weakened by the vengeful action of Simeon and Levi against the Hivites for Shechem's misconduct with Dinah. See C. M. Carmichael, *Law and Narrative in the Bible* (Ithaca, 1985), 195, 196. For further evidence that bulls, oxen, and the like were symbols of fighting strength, see J. G. Janzen, "The Character of the Calf and Its Cult in Exodus 32," *CBQ* 52 (1990): 597–607.

For the celebrated legal adage about a child's legitimacy, "Whoso bulleth the cow, the calf is yours" (first cited in 1406 as, "For who that bulleth my Cow, the calf is mine"), see John Barton, "Nullity of Marriage and Illegitimacy in the England of the Middle Ages," *Legal History Studies*, ed. D. Jenkins (Cardiff, 1975): 40.

15 See Carmichael, *Law and Narrative in the Bible*, 185–203.

16 Scholars acknowledge P's hand in the Joseph story. See Artur Weiser, *The Old Testament: Its Formation and Development* (New York, 1961), 136. Gerhard von Rad, in *Genesis*, 3d ed. (London, 1972), 343, refers to "unimportant sections from the Priestly source." One might ask: unimportant from whose point of view?

17 See, however, R. H. Helmholz's discussion of the role of the Bible in the formation of canon law: "The Bible in the Service of the Canon Law," *Chicago-Kent Law Review* 70 (1995): 1557–81.

18 See chapter 2 on Leviticus 19:18.

19 On the complex nature of the Priestly insertion in Genesis 46, especially the notice about Joseph's sons, see Claus Westermann, *Genesis 37–50* (Minneapolis, 1986), 160. He states (156) the common view about the Priestly insertion: "The patriarchal stories as a whole and the exodus story as a whole were both at hand to the transmitter." Gerhard von Rad states, "Our list has to be thought of as the work of very late and theoretical erudition. It is the product of erudite occupation with ancient traditions and belongs, therefore, to a theological, Priestly literature" (*Genesis*, 398). Von Rad's description of such literary activity well describes, I contend, the work of the compilers of the laws.

20 I presume R. L. Harris (*Leviticus*, 606), has in mind the Egyptian development regarding the brothers' work with Pharaoh's cattle when he interprets the rule as an attempt to preserve a superior breed of "cattle" that the Israelites brought from Egypt. In the Joseph story the term for "cattle" is *miqneh*, probably to indicate that these are the cattle they acquired (*qanah*) in Canaan (Gen 46:6). Genesis 47:18 refers to *miqneh habehemah*, "herds of cattle," that the Egyptians give Joseph in exchange for food. In the rule the term is *behemah*, "cattle," and it is commonly used throughout Leviticus. The term is a collective and includes both large and small domestic animals, especially those the brothers possess (Gen 46:32, 34).

21 Several ancient writers (e.g., Juvenal, *Saturnalia* 15; Plutarch, *Isis and Osiris*, 379–81; Cicero, *De natura deorum* 3.15.59; Lucian, *The Parliament of the Gods*, 10, 11) mention how the Egyptians deified and worshipped all sorts of beasts and consequently bred them with great care. I doubt, however, if these Egyptian practices are relevant to P's stance. For their relevance in the later history of Judaism, see David Daube, "The Finale of Horace's Satire 1.4," *Index* (International Survey of Roman Law) 22 (1994): 375–77.

22 Westermann, *Genesis 37–50*, 168.

23 The use of the vineyard for Judah's role in adding to the stock of Jacob comes from Jacob's comments in Genesis 49:8–12 about Judah's attempts to attend to his family line. Jacob employs a metaphor about tying asses to the vine. The reference is to the fatal outcome that befalls Judah's half-Canaanite, half-Israelite sons because of their unions with Tamar; see Carmichael, "Forbidden Mixtures," 398–403. Judah almost loses all his

sons in his dealings with Tamar, and the peculiar sanction in the Deuteronomic rule about how the produce of the vineyard might become forfeit reflects the story. There is no comparable threat of death to Joseph's sons in the story about them, and there is consequently no sanction in the Priestly rule about the field.

24 So M. H. Pope, also, "The plowing and cultivation of a field is a natural figure for sexual intercourse" (*Song of Songs*, AB [New York, 1977], 323). For the biblical and ancient Near Eastern evidence, see 323–28, 644.

25 N. H. Sarna draws attention to this feature in *Genesis*, JPSC (Philadelphia, 1989), 314.

26 The intent of the rule about mixed seed has echoes in later literature. In Sirach 26:20 the young man who is the recipient of Ben Sira's counsel is urged to "single out from all the land [among the Jews] a goodly field [literally, a portion of good soil, that is, a good wife] and . . . sow the seed [beget a family]." See P. W. Skehan and A. A. Di Lella, *The Wisdom of Ben Sira*, AB (New York, 1987), 351. Somewhat similar to the sentiment expressed by Ben Sira is Tobit 4:12, 13: "Choose your wife from the seed [race] of your ancestors. Do not take a foreign wife who is not of your father's tribe. . . . Remember, my son, that Noah, Abraham, Isaac and Jacob, our ancestors, back to the earliest days, all chose wives from their kindred" (NEB). Note that Joseph is not cited. Interestingly, some texts in Tobit are related both to the legal material in Leviticus 19 and to the Joseph story (e.g., Tob 4:14 to Lev 19:13; and Tob 3:10 and 6:15 to Gen 42:38 and 44:29, 31). The concern about mixed seed in Tobit 4:12, 13 may reveal an awareness of Leviticus 19:19. The Apocryphal *Josephus and Aseneth* shows how sensitive later interpreters were to Joseph's marriage to an Egyptian woman. See D. Cook's introduction to his translation in *The Apocryphal Old Testament*, ed. H. F. D. Sparks (Oxford, 1984), 468–70.

27 On this sexual sense of *labaš*, "to put on a garment," see Carmichael, *Law and Narrative*, 198–201; cp. G. A. Hugenberger, *Marriage as a Covenant*, SVT 52 (1994): 74–76. There are many interesting texts about linen and the prostitute's trade: see Joshua 2:6; Isaiah 1:18; Jeremiah 4:30; Hosea 2:7 (5); Proverbs 7:16; Judith 16:8; Revelation 18:16.

28 Gerhard von Rad comments, in regard to Joseph's getting an Egyptian name, "By it [the name] Joseph was drawn completely into the Egyptian court circle, and this did not happen, furthermore, without Joseph's being placed within the protective sphere of an Egyptian deity." He expresses surprise at the development and contrasts Daniel's situation (Dan 1:7, 8); see *Genesis*, 378.

29 According to Herodotus (*Histories* 2.37), the Egyptian priests wore such linen garb.

30 In the summary of his overview of Israelite dress, Douglas R. Edwards states, "What you wore conveyed who you were and the nature of your relationship to those around you. The biblical writers adeptly tapped the symbolic power of ancient dress to convey social, theological, or political messages" ("Dress and Ornamentation," ABD, 2:238). D. K. Edelman points out how the narrator of the story of King Saul uses clothing as a marker of ethnic or national identity in *King Saul in the Historiography of Judah*, JSOT suppl. 121 (Sheffield, 1991), 297.

31 G. G. V. Stonehouse, *Zephaniah and Nahum*, WC (London, 1929), 36. "Double allegiance is the root evil here"; so C. L. Taylor, noting particularly Zephaniah 1:5, in *Zephaniah*, IB 6 (Nashville, 1956), 1015, 1016. On the tragedy of Esther: "delivering her nation at the price of her place in it," see David Daube, *Esther* (Oxford, 1995), 57.

32 From Robert Herrick's "Delight in Disorder." Like *shatnez*, the term *clothes* is personified.

33 Compare the Koranic statement that wives are "raiment for you and ye are raiment for them" (Q.2:187).

34 Michael Fishbane wrongly claims that "the now obscure term *shatnez* was introduced" to indicate the precise constitution of a mixed garment (*Biblical Interpretation*, 58). It has to be stressed that the Hebrew formulation of the sentence with its use of the term *shatnez* is crucial in imparting the meaning intended. The *shatnez* in conjunction with the Israelite dress *is* the garment of two kinds.

35 Jacob Milgrom's conventional understanding of *shatnez* produces confusing results. He takes for granted that the term refers to a mixture of wool—not mentioned in Leviticus 19:19—and linen, and interprets Leviticus 19:19 to mean that an ordinary Israelite must not wear such a mixture. An Israelite priest, on the other hand, must wear a garment that combines wool and linen (a combination that Milgrom, with no textual base, designates *shatnez*). A few lines later he interprets the rule (Num 15:37–41) requiring an ordinary Israelite to attach fringes (*tsitsit*) to his garment as a requirement to wear wool and linen. In his commentary, *Leviticus 1–16*, AB 3 (New York, 1991), 548, 549, there is no awareness of the contradiction. In his "Of Hems and Tassels," *BAR* 9 (1983): 65, Milgrom argues that "in a small way" an ordinary Israelite wears a priestly garment: "Every Israelite wears his priestly clothing, the *tsitsit*." The Israelite, then, is both a priest and a nonpriest. Even if there was some merit in this position, the clash with the prohibition of *shatnez*, as under-

stood by Milgrom, remains. Actually, his reading of the tassels rule in Numbers 15:37–41 would support my contention that there was nothing untoward about an Israelite's wearing a combination of wool and linen so long as it did not denote a dual identity. Moreover, if Milgrom gave up his reading of the *shatnez* rule, his position would be more intelligible.

36 The term *šeš*, "fine linen," used of Joseph's Egyptian garb is an Egyptian loanword, but its frequency in the Old Testament suggests that it had become part of standard Hebrew vocabulary.

37 The proverb "Don't look a gift-horse in the mouth" is an example of a prohibition that seemingly goes against sensible procedure; in fact, one should always look at the horse's mouth to judge its health. The introduction of the word *gift* is what indicates that in this particular situation one should not do what one ordinarily does.

Chapter 4. Incest in the Bible

1 James B. Twitchell, *Forbidden Partners: The Incest Taboo in Modern Culture* (New York, 1987), 26–32.

2 Discussed by David Daube in *Ancient Jewish Law: Three Inaugural Lectures* (Leiden, 1981), 14–18.

3 Even more so than the headline in the *London Times* in July 1984: "Man's wish to marry his ex–mother-in-law to be considered by Parliament." See Sybil Wolfram, *In-Laws and Outlaws. Kinship and Marriage in England* (New York, 1987), 42, and her discussion of the increasing tendency to permit marriage between affines.

4 Eusebius, *Ecclesiastical History* 5.1.14; Tacitus, *Histories* 5:5; Athenagoras, *Plea for the Christians* 31.1. See David Daube, *Ancient Jewish Law*, 15.

5 On the religious value placed on mother-son, father-daughter, and brother-sister unions in Zoroastrian practice, see R. N. Frye, "Zoroastrian Incest," in *Orientalia J. Tucci Memoriae dedicata*, ed. G. Gnoli and L. Lanciotti (Rome, 1985), 452.

6 If a Gentile and his children become Jews, in strict law a debt owing to the Gentile need not, on his death, be paid to his children (*mishnah Shebiith* 10:9). The reason is that the convert and his children all count as newly born, and consequently they are no longer related.

7 For illuminating remarks about scholars' avoidance of the topic of new birth in regard to the Jewish law of conversion, see David Daube, *Appeasement or Resistance, and Other Essays on New Testament Judaism* (Berkeley, 1987), 64.

8 2 Samuel 21:20 (=1 Chron 20:6) tells of a Philistine warrior who had six fingers on each hand and six toes on each foot. Jacob's breeding experiment indicates that the ancients were aware of the effects of inbreeding in animal husbandry (Gen 30:25–43), but exactly what they knew is impossible to judge.

9 One has to be careful not to generalize for every society. Among the Manchus, group marriage existed in that younger brothers had the right of physical access to the wives of elder brothers. See R. D. Jamieson, *Three Lectures on Chinese Folklore* (Peiping, 1932), 75.

10 In regard to the incest laws, the titles of studies reveal this bias; for example, S. F. Bigger, "The Family Laws of Leviticus 18 in Their Setting," *JBL* 98 (1979): 196; in his recent commentary, *Leviticus,* WBC 4 (Dallas, 1992), 280, J. E. Hartley has the heading "Laws Governing the Extended Family"; Baruch A. Levine has an excursus, "Family Structures in Biblical Israel," in his commentary, *Leviticus,* JPSC (Philadelphia, 1989), 253–55.

11 On this characteristic aspect of ancient law codes in particular, and also of language—there are no words, for example, for those who do not murder; and until 1892, with the introduction of the word *heterosexual* (to indicate a negative feature: "a morbid sexual passion for one of the opposite sex," *Merriam-Webster's New International Dictionary*), for those who are sexually active only with partners of the opposite sex—see David Daube, "The Self-Understood in Legal History," *JR* 85 (1973): 126–34; Daube, *Ancient Jewish Law,* 123–29; Daube, "The Contrariness of Speech and Polytheism," *Festschrift John Noonan, JLR* 11 (1995): 1601–5.

12 In the Hittite laws (189) both a son (with a mother; cp. CH 157) and a father (with a daughter; cp. HL 189, a father with a son) are targeted (*ANET,* 196).

13 Consider the impressionistic reporting of a Mrs. Christian Annersley, "magistrate and Chairman of the Bench," in an East Anglian village in the twentieth century:

> There was more incest in the past and it was always fathers and daughters, never brothers and sisters. It happened when mother had too many children, or when mother was ill, or when mother was dead. And very often it didn't matter a bit. The daughter usually proved to be very fond of the father and there would be no sign of upset in the family. No, I think it was quite an understood thing that a daughter would take on the father when the mother was ill or dead. It would always happen in a "basic" family, of course. Then somebody would give them away. Or it would come out when the daughter became pregnant. You would then come up against a strange

form of innocence. Not ignorance, innocence. You would hear all about it from police notebooks, pages and pages and pages, and you'd wonder why the man didn't look like a monster. Then you'd realize that what he'd done and what we were saying he had done seemed to be two quite different things. We had strayed into the dark, into the deep—the hidden ways of the village." (From Ronald Blythe, *Akenfield, Portrait of an English Village* [New York, 1969], 244)

14 A. Tosato thinks that intercourse with a foreign woman is at issue in the Molech rule , so intent is he to introduce some homogeneity into the list of rules in Leviticus 18:18–23. His view underlines the problem rather than solving it; see "The Law of Leviticus 18:18: A Reexamination," *CBQ* 46 (1984): 206.

15 See my discussion in *Law, Legend, and Incest in the Bible: Leviticus 18–20* (Ithaca, 1997), ch. 2.

16 See *Marriage, IDB* suppl. (Nashville, 1976), 574; also Levine, *Leviticus*, 253.

17 See his contribution, "Law," in *Old Testament Form Criticism*, ed. J. H. Hayes (San Antonio, 1974), 128. All lists of rules about incest have something of this character. The philosopher John Locke expresses the matter as follows: "To know whether his idea of adultery or incest be right will a man seek it anywhere among things existing? Or is it true because anyone has been witness to such an action? No; but it suffices here that men have put together such a collection into one complex idea that makes the archetype and specific idea, whether ever any such action were committed in *rerum natura* or no" ("Names of Mixed Modes and Relations," in *An Essay Concerning Human Understanding*, ed. A. C. Fraser [Oxford, 1894], 2:44).

18 The account is confusing. Ham is the offender, but his son, Canaan, is cited in Noah's condemnation. It is as if there is a reversal of actions. Ham, who is explicitly cited as the father of Canaan, offends against his father, Noah, and Noah in turn acts against Ham's son, Canaan. The lawgiver concentrates on Ham's offense.

19 It is safe to assume that sexuality is involved, that Ham is not looking at his father's left ear or right toe, but at his genitals. In light of Canaan's punishment—he loses his status as a member of Noah's line and becomes a slave to his brothers—the offense seems to be disrespect of a progenitor's status. Noah's drunkenness is not considered relevant to the matter.

20 For those who think the incident between Ham and Noah involved a homosexual act, see Anthony Phillips, "Uncovering the Father's Skirt,"

VT 30 (1980): 39, 40. They speculate—wrongly, I think—that because the act was so abhorrent the biblical author did not spell it out. My view is that a lawgiver found the narrative *suggestive* of the topic of sexual encroachment on a father. If a homosexual act had taken place I doubt if the lawgiver would have bothered to set down a prohibition about it, because its condemnation would have been clear from the tradition. See the comments of S. D. Kunin in *The Logic of Incest. A Structuralist Analysis of Hebrew Mythology* (Sheffield, 1995), 173–75.

21 To cite but one example, the rule in Deuteronomy 12:18: "Thou, and thy son, and thy daughter, and thy manservant, and thy maidservant . . ."; the first "thou" includes the man's wife.

22 Karl Elliger (who first introduced me to the study of biblical law) feels compelled to introduce it. It had, he believes, inadvertently dropped out; see "Das Gesetz Leviticus 18," *ZAW* 67 (1955): 2.

23 Recent translations—for example, RSV and JPS—interpret the rule as solely about intercourse with a mother. They choose to read not the literal, "The nakedness of thy father and the nakedness of thy mother shalt thou not uncover," but instead place on the connecting particle *waw* (and) the weight of a circumstantial clause: "The nakedness of thy father which is [=*waw explicative*] the nakedness of thy mother." While it is a possible, if a rather free, translation, it is an awkward one that badly overloads the sentence, as interpreters who accept the translation point out; for example, Bigger, "The Family Laws of Leviticus 18 in Their Setting," 196. Usually the lawgiver is more explicit when he makes the point that uncovering the nakedness of one person uncovers a related person's nakedness. For example, in the immediately following rule in Leviticus 18:8, we have: "The nakedness of thy father's wife shalt thou not uncover: it is thy father's nakedness." In Leviticus 18:14 ("Thou shalt not uncover the nakedness of thy father's brother, thou shalt not approach to his wife"), uncovering an uncle's nakedness does indeed mean intercourse, not with him but with his wife. There is no connecting particle *waw* between the two parts of the rule. Anthony Phillips also opposes the transferred meaning: "It is much more natural to understand Lev xviii 7a in its present form as prohibiting sexual relations with either of one's parents" ("Uncovering the Father's Skirt," 39, 40).

24 A major reason why intercourse with a father's wife is thought of as uncovering the father's nakedness has to do with the near universal use of clothing to indicate the marital relation. As well illustrated in Deuteronomy 22:30 ("A man shall not take his father's wife, nor shall he uncover

his father's skirt"), a husband and wife, for both protective and sexual purposes, cover each other as if each is a garment. The Koranic statement that wives are "raiment for you and ye are raiment for them" (Q.2:187) well describes the biblical position also. See my discussion in *Law and Narrative in the Bible* (Ithaca, 1985), 198.

25 See note 5, chapter 2.

26 On the role of hypothetical constructions in legal culture ancient and modern, see, for ancient Near Eastern codes, F. R. Kraus, "Ein zentrales Problem des altmesopotamischen Rechts: Was ist der Codex Hammurabi," *Geneva* 8 (1960): 283–96; for Roman law, H. F. Jolowitz, *Historical Introduction to Roman Law* (Cambridge, Eng., 1952), 93, 95. For contemporary America, there is the role of the Restatements of the Law by the American Law Institute. Judges typically treat its formulations with respect, and some even regard them as the "law." See R. S. Summers, "The General Duty of Good Faith—Its Recognition and Conceptualization," *Cornell Law Review* 67 (1982): 810–40.

27 The lawgiver must have been all the more impelled to address the issue of brother–half-sister marriage because a similar incident occurs in the generation after Abraham. To protect himself from the men of Gerar, Isaac falsely claims that the woman (Rebekah) to whom he is married is his sister (Gen 26:6–11).

28 August Dillmann, *Die Genesis* (Leipzig, 1892), 227.

29 If S. A. Naber's emendation of "sister" into "niece" is correct, Plutarch cites a prohibition in Roman law for marriage with a niece (but not, I repeat, between a man and his grandniece). See F. C. Babbitt, *Plutarch's Moralia*, LCL 4 (Cambridge, Mass., 1936), 16 n. 2.

30 So David Daube, "The Self-Understood in Legal History," 126–34. It is a factor for a sister. Thus in Leviticus 18:11, the reason given for prohibiting a relationship between a man and his father's daughter by a wife other than the man's own mother is that "she is thy sister." It follows that there is a bar to a relationship with a full sister.

31 CH 154 has the prohibition: "If a seignior has had intercourse with his daughter, they shall make that seignior leave the city."

32 Well represented by Frank Crüsemann, *Die Tora: Theologie und Sozialgeschichte des altestamentlichen Gesetzes* (Munich, 1992).

33 Hartley, *Leviticus*, WBC, 287.

34 Recall how Lot's daughters' intercourse with him prompted the lawgiver to set down a rule prohibiting a son's intercourse with a mother.

35 The rule speaks of uncovering the nakedness of the woman and her daughter, but of taking (to wife, *laqah*) the granddaughter. Tamar would not have

lain with her father-in-law if he had done his duty by her and arranged for Shelah's fulfillment of the levirate marriage. It would then have been appropriate to have spoken of Shelah's taking Tamar (to wife) for this purpose. As just indicated, for the lawgiver, "granddaughter" is equivalent to Shelah in Judah's family.

Interpreters have been puzzled by the use of the term *ša'ra,* "relative," and typically read it as "they are her kin." The problem with this reading is that it states the obvious and we have to wonder why the lawgiver felt it necessary to use the term. The Septuagint is probably more accurate: "they are your kin." The law's background may again prove illuminating. The reference to kinship may reflect the fact that Judah is Tamar's father-in-law.

36 See Martha T. Roth for the position in Babylonia and Assyria of the first millennium B.C.E.: "Age at Marriage: Ancient Babylonia and Assyria," *Comparative Studies in Society and History* 29 (1987): 715–47. Her tentative conclusion is that "a bride will be in her middle or late teens . . . and a mother in her early to mid forties" (747).

37 C. F. Keil and F. Delitzsch translate the verb *ṣarar,* usually translated "to make a rival wife" or "to vex," in its other, doubtless related sense of "to pack together"; that is, in a bond of marriage. This translation brings out the fact that Laban forces Jacob into a marital bond with both of his daughters; see *Leviticus,* BCOT 2 (Edinburgh, 1869), 416. *'alehah,* "upon her," in the sense of beside the other sister as a wife, occurs also in Genesis 28:9 (Esau's acquiring other wives) and Genesis 31:50 (Jacob's acquiring wives in addition to Leah and Rachel). S. D. Kunin states that the rule is about incest on the ground that a man's marrying one sister automatically creates a kin relationship with the other (*The Logic of Incest,* 265 n. 2). If this were the case, however, there would have been no need to bring up the issue of rivalry.

38 I do not accept the view of A. Tosatu that this rule has been properly interpreted by the Dead Sea community ("The Law of Leviticus 18:18: A Reexamination," *CBQ* 46 [1984], 199–214). CD 4:20–21 paraphrases the rule as a prohibition of bigamy, not as prohibiting marriage to two sisters while each is alive. I agree with Tosatu that we should not introduce the notion of incest into this rule—a major part of his argument—but his interpretation that the rule is a general prohibition of bigamy still does not follow. He finds himself in considerable difficulty when he argues against the usual view that the rule is about two sisters. Thus he comments (212), "One cannot forget that Jacob-Israel had at the same time two sisters as wives. . . . It is hard to believe that such personages were made into

breakers of the Law on account of incest, with the counterproductive consequence for these 'sons of Israel' of portraying themselves as a people irremediably unclean (just the opposite of the holiness sought!)." Not incest, to be sure, but on other grounds the lawgiver condemns a marriage comparable to Jacob's marriage. One wonders what Tosatu would have to say about Abraham's marriage to Sarah in light of the Levitical prohibition against that incestuous union, and also about Moses' rule in Leviticus 18:12, 13 legislating against the union his parents contracted.

39 Harry Hoffner points out how sparse, for example, is the evidence for bestiality and homosexuality (prohibited in Lev 18:22, 23, 20:13, 15, 16) in Syro-Palestine and Mesopotamia; see "Incest, Sodomy, and Bestiality in the Ancient Near East," in *Orient and Occident, AOAT* 22 (Neukirchen-Vluyn, 1973), 82.

40 Cited by Frye, "Zoroastrian Incest," 448.

41 In his *Logic of Incest*, 92, 266, Kunin argues that a mythological—but, he stresses, only a mythological—analysis of the Genesis narratives suggests that in some of the instances of incest there is positive assessment in order to resolve some of the fundamental issues that the redactors of the material confronted.

42 Philonic, New Testament, and Talmudic ethical judgments sometimes take into account the influence of harmful milieu. For example, the reference in Genesis 6:9 that Noah was "just and perfect in his generation" has occasioned much debate as to whether he possessed absolute virtue or whether he stood out only among his contemporaries (Philo, *De Abrahamo* 7.36–40; *Genesis Rabba* on 6:9). See David Daube, "Neglected Nuances of Exposition in Luke–Acts," *Principat* 25 (1985): 2329–56.

43 Tosatu forgets this fact, hence his difficulty when he states, "It is hard to believe that such personages [the patriarchs] were made into breakers of the Law" ("Law of Leviticus 18:18," 212).

44 On brother-sister marriage in Roman Egypt in the first three centuries of the Christian era, see Keith Hopkins, "Brother-Sister Marriage in Roman Egypt," *Comparative Studies in Society and History* 22 (1980): 303–54.

45 Without realizing just how important is the connection, commentators have long drawn attention to the notices about the iniquity of these cultures in Genesis (13:13, 18:20, 21, 19:1–29, 20:11) and the similar ones in Leviticus (18:24–28, 20:22–24). See Dillmann, *Die Genesis*, 251; also M. A. Fishbane, *Biblical Interpretation in Ancient Israel* (Oxford, 1985), 420, which states that while Abraham, on divine authority, would inherit the land defiled by the Amorites (Gen 15:7, 16), Abraham's descendants

would forfeit it if they defiled it with those sins decried by Ezekiel. Fishbane then cites Ezekiel 33:25, 26 and Leviticus 18:20, 26–30.

46 Compare how later, when the Jews lived under the Romans, Edom was a code word for Rome. See G. F. Moore, *Judaism in the First Centuries of the Christian Era* (Cambridge, 1966), 2:115, 116.

Chapter 5. The Decalogue

1 *De Decalogo* 18–19; *De Specialibus Legibus* 1.1.1. For Philo, the contents of the Decalogue constituted the principles of all law (*kephalaia nomōn*). They summarized the special provisions (*en merei diatagmata*) that were given through Moses. A modern version of this view is G. Braulik's *Die deuteronomischen Gesetze und der Dekalog. Studien zum Aufbau von Deuteronomium 12–16*, SBS 145 (Stuttgart, 1991).

2 See, for example, J. J. Stamm and M. E. Andrew, *The Ten Commandments in Recent Research*, SBT 2 (Naperville, 1967), 18–20; Eduard Nielsen, *The Ten Commandments in New Perspective*, SBT 7 (Naperville, 1968), 81, 82. A staple view since Hugo Gressmann's *Mose und seine Zeit: Ein Kommentar zu den Mose Sagen*, FRLANT 18 (Göttingen, 1913) is that the poetic items in the Pentateuch are very ancient and predate the prose sections.

3 See *The New Encyclopaedia Britannica, Macropaedia* (Chicago, 1990), 23:94, under "The Art of Literature, Poetry," by H. Nemerov.

4 See David Daube, "Polytheism and the Contrariness of Speech," *Festschrift John Noonan, JLR* 11 (1995): 1601–5. Professor Daube excluded his discussion about poetry and prose from this article. The quotations are from an unpublished longer version of it.

5 For what follows, see R. H. Helmholz, "The Bible in the Service of the Canon Law," *Chicago-Kent Law Review* 70 (1995): 1557–81.

6 On the different issue of whether legislators should give reasons for their laws, see Plato, *Laws* 4.718–24.

7 On this sense of *'al panay*, "upon the face of," in a hostile sense, see C. M. Carmichael, *The Origins of Biblical Law* (Ithaca, 1992), 30 n. 12; cp. Moshe Weinfeld, *Deuteronomy 1–11*, AB (New York, 1991), 276–77.

8 On the switch between the singular and the plural in this part of the Decalogue as a reflection of their use in references to the golden calf in Exodus 32, see C. M. Carmichael, *Law and Narrative in the Bible* (Ithaca, 1985), 320.

9 The prophet Hosea's comment about the calf's construction is, "The workman made it: therefore it is not God" (Hos 8:6); the Psalmist's, "They

made a calf in Horeb, and worshipped the molten image. Thus they changed their glory into the similitude of an ox that eateth grass" (Ps 106: 19, 20).

10 It is telling evidence that the original compiler of the Decalogue is the Deuteronomist. I agree with R. H. Pfeiffer that it is impossible to separate some original form of the Decalogue from the Deuteronomic language in its makeup; see Pfeiffer, *Introduction to the Old Testament* (New York, 1941), 229–32.

11 Well recognized by interpreters. For example, M. Aberbach and L. Smolar detect at least thirteen links between the story of the calf and the story of the installation of the calves by King Jeroboam at the sanctuaries in Bethel and Dan in 1 Kings 12:20–33; see their "Aaron, Jeroboam, and the Golden Calves," *JBL* 86 (1967): 129–40.

12 So Weinfeld, *Deuteronomy 1–11*, 296.

13 The Levites commited the same apostasy as the people they slaughtered. From an objective point of view, they, like Aaron, deserve to die, so why do they receive unequal treatment? This narrative is an etiological one designed to explain an existing fact in the narrator's time; the Levites enjoyed a special role among their people, and it had to be accounted for.

14 Moshe Weinfeld thinks (*Deuteronomy 1–11*, 371) that Deuteronomy 7:9, about Yahweh showing "to a thousand generations" mercy to those loyal to him and who keep his commandments, is but a variation of the word "thousands" in the Decalogue. Apart from overlooking the glaring difference in language, he fails to realize that the expression in Deuteronomy 7:9 represents a typical phenomenon in law and other matters; namely, there is a move from the particular to the general. For example, Deuteronomy 22:1–3 goes from specific lost objects to "every lost thing"; and the rule about coveting in the Decalogue lists particular objects of envy and then states, "Nor any thing that is thy neighbour's." Deuteronomy 7:9 is indeed similar to the commandment in the Decalogue. The latter takes up from the particular incident about the Levites' action, and Deuteronomy 7:9 in turn, as the context so well brings out, generalizes in reflecting on Yahweh's treatment of Israel in Egypt.

15 One reason to believe that the actions of the Israelites preceded the Decalogue is that it is implausible that, having encountered the commands of the Decalogue in such overwhelmingly impressive circumstances, the people and Aaron should proceed almost immediately to break God's commands.

16 Neal Ascherson describes how in the Black Sea region one finds to this day descendants of Greeks who inhabited the Crimea back in Hellenic

times, who regard themselves as every bit as Greek as the inhabitants of Athens, with whom they can barely communicate; see Ascherson, *Black Sea* (London, 1995).

17 Saint Augustine, *City of God* (New York, 1958), 350.

18 Anthropologists' attempt to introduce incest into the Genesis myth fails to appreciate that when the biblical narrator constructed his history he was perfectly aware that a biographical storyline was but a useful medium to probe his interests. S. F. Moore's assertion that "any myth [she cites the Genesis myth] about the creation of man which postulates a single first family is bound to give rise to some incestuous riddles" is a problem for her, not for the biblical narrator; see Moore, "Descent and Symbolic Filiation," in *Myth and Cosmos*, ed. John Middleton (New York, 1967), 65.

19 On the profound effect this view of marriage had on English thought, see Sybil Wolfram, *In-Laws and Outlaws: Kinship and Marriage in England* (New York, 1987), 16–18. She points out how in many non-Western societies a marriage creates an alliance between two groups of blood relations. In English thought, however, husband and wife are not relatives but occupy the position of being "one flesh." Wolfram thinks this view is probably unique to the Western world and contributed, before it began to be eroded in the nineteenth century, to the following legal facts: "Husband and wife had the same surname. Their property was held in common. Neither could give evidence at law against the other, nor could they form a conspiracy. They had the same domicile whether living together or not. They enjoyed the same rank and status. Sexual intercourse was supposed to be confined to husband and wife. The union was to all intents and purposes for life" (18).

20 The Rabbis read the narrative this way, *babylonian Sanhedrin* 58a.

21 The role of ultimate causation comes into the narrative in the form of "the woman whom thou [Yahweh] gavest to be with me" (Gen 3:12); it is Yahweh, then, who is ultimately responsible for the offense coming about. Compare the item about idolatry in the Decalogue, in which Yahweh causes the iniquity of the fathers to be visited upon the sons. The sense is that God, being ultimately responsible for everything that takes place in the world, "causes" the sons to commit the same sins as their fathers.

22 A contrary view is that of Johannes Pedersen in "Die Auffassung vom Alten Testament," *ZAW* 49 (1931); 177: "Die Gesetze sind in Erzählungen einverleibt, zu welchen sie in keinem inneren Verhältnis stehen [The laws are embodied in narratives with which they have no inner relation]."

23 Thus, as B. S. Childs points out, the promise to Moses in Exodus 32:10 picks up the identical words of the previous promise to Abraham (Gen 12:2); see *Exodus*, OTL (Philadelphia, 1974), 567.

24 Compare the pattern among the patriarchs: Abraham passes his sister off as his wife (Gen 12:10–20, 20); Isaac does likewise (Gen 26:6–11); Jacob has a problem with his wives, Leah and Rachel (Gen 29:31–30:21); and Joseph has to cope with Potiphar's wife (Genesis 39).

25 Raymond Westbrook argues that the Deuteronomic provision about the runaway slave (Deut 23:16, 17) reflects a concern on the part of the Israelites to oppose international treaties of the time, which contained extradition clauses for the return of runaway slaves; see Westbrook, "Slave and Master in Ancient Near Eastern Law," *Chicago-Kent Law Review* 70 (1995): 1673. Unfortunately, the evidence for reading the Deuteronomic law in light of international politics of the time is lacking.

26 My view of the laws and narratives of the Bible is the opposite of that of Yehezkel Kaufmann in *The Religion of Israel* (New York, 1972), 166: "There is an essential difference between the redactors' treatment of the narratives and that of the legal portions of the Torah. What criticism analyzes into originally separate narrative sources has been blended by the redactors into a fairly integrated whole that only the critical eye can resolve. The laws, however, have not been so blended."

27 See Carmichael, *Law and Narrative*, 97–101.

28 See C. M. Carmichael, *Women, Law, and the Genesis Traditions* (Edinburgh, 1979), 78–93.

29 See chapter 9 for this feature in some Pentateuchal material. On the pervasive role of imitation and emulation in ancient literature in general, see T. L. Brodie, *The Quest for the Origin of John's Gospel* (Oxford, 1993), 34–47. For Esther, see David Daube, *Esther* (Oxford Centre for Postgraduate Hebrew Studies, 1995), 3, 8–12, 17.

30 Further examples may be Sarah with Abimelech (Genesis 20), the aim being to acknowledge an adulterer's bona fide error as to the married status of the woman; the adoption of Ephraim and Manasseh by the dying Jacob (Genesis 48), the aim being to recognize the legitimacy of two Josephite tribes; Ananias and Sapphira (Acts 5:1–11), the aim being to denounce the damnability of claiming membership of a saintly band while in secret breach of its ideals. See Daube, *Esther*, 7.

31 Weinfeld, *Deuteronomy 1–11*, 242.

32 Weinfeld, *Deuteronomy 1–11*, 253–55.

33 Weinfeld, *Deuteronomy 1–11*, 246. There is major confusion about the scope of many other biblical rules in addition to the rule about false wit-

ness. Dale Patrick would have each rule in the Decalogue "as governing a maximum range of actions. The prohibitions were, from the outset, abstractions intended to apply to a host of different actions" (*Old Testament Law* [Atlanta, 1985], 41). But in no sense are they abstractions, a view central to Patrick's understanding of biblical law. The confusion here is the failure to appreciate how law develops over time. It took hundreds of years for so-called principles to emerge in Jewish legal culture. Only in the Mishnah and the Talmud do we begin to see this development come to fruition with accompanying terminology; for example, terms such as *'abh* (father), *toladha* (descendant), *guph* (body), *kelal* (the universal), and *perat* (individual). For more on this development, see David Daube, *The New Testament and Rabbinic Judaism* (London, 1956), 59.

34 On the origin of the prohibition against suicide in later Christianity and Judaism, see David Daube, "The Linguistics of Suicide," *Philosophy and Public Affairs* 1 (1972): 387–437; and Daube, "Judas," *RJ* 13 (1994): 317–19.

Chapter 6. An Eye for an Eye, and a Tooth for a Tooth: The History of a Formula

1 See my analysis in *The Origins of Biblical Law* (Ithaca, 1992), 119–29, in which I argue that the rules in the Book of the Covenant (Exod 21:2–23:19) are all Deuteronomic formulations. For the difference in prepositions in the formulas in Exodus and Deuteronomy, see my *Biblical Laws of Talion* (Oxford Centre for Postgraduate Hebrew Studies, 1986), 33, 34.

2 Recently, for example, Stuart West, "The *Lex Talionis* in the Torah," *JBQ* 21 (1993): 183–88.

3 Gerhard von Rad, in *Deuteronomy*, OTL (Philadelphia, 1966), 129, writes: "This ancient and weighty legal maxim occupies merely a modest position here, being cited as part of a sermon-like addendum." Nothing could be further from the truth, I shall argue; neither its ancient character, nor its modest nature, nor its being an addendum. In that Near Eastern sources lack such a formula, there is no support for the ancient character of the formula there.

4 N. H. Sarna states, "It [the talion formula] is a rhetorical formulation in concrete terms of an abstract principle—the law of equivalence. On the operational level this is possible only in respect of the death penalty" (*Exploring Exodus* [New York, 1986], 186). Apart from the problem of the existence of an "abstract principle" at such an early stage in Israelite culture, Sarna's statement obscures the question one wants answered, namely, what accounts for the language of the formula?

5 See Peter Linebaugh, "The Tyburn Riot Against the Surgeons," in *Albion's Fatal Tree. Crime and Society in Eighteenth-Century England*, ed. Douglas Hay (New York, 1975), 76–78. I am indebted to Alan Watson for drawing my attention to this essay. For the use of the cadavers of criminals (since the time of Galen) for anatomical purposes, especially in sixteenth-century Italy, see Samuel Y. Edgerton, *Pictures and Punishment: Art and Criminal Prosecution during the Florentine Renaissance* (Ithaca, 1985), 157–64, 213–19. John Diamond of Hastings Law School reminded me of the ignominious treatment of a suicide; for example, the law might require the suicide to be deprived of religious rites and buried, with a stake driven through the heart, at a crossroads. Lucia Diamond, librarian at the Robbins Collections, School of Law, University of California, Berkeley, drew my attention to R. S. Guernsey, *Suicide: History of the Penal Laws Relating to It in Their Legal, Social, Moral, and Religious Aspects, in Ancient and Modern Times* (New York, 1883), 17, 21.

6 The expression of C. F. Keil and F. Delitzsch in *Commentar über das Alte Testament* 2d ed. (Leipzig, 1870), 2:510, in regard to the law about the hanged man (Deut 21:22, 23).

7 Roger Cooper tells how during his time in Iran's Evin Prison, he learned one day that his sentence was to be death plus ten years. He asked which came first and was told he would serve ten years and then be hanged. "Please don't make it the other way round," he requested. See Cooper, *Death Plus Ten Years* (London, 1993), 208. Until 1830 the Common Law hanged traitors and then beheaded them. On the mutilation of a traitor in medieval England, see A. S. Diamond, *Primitive Law, Past and Present* (London, 1971), 103.

8 Compare how King David's cruelty to the Ammonites "disappeared" just when the rationalists of the European Enlightenment subjected Christianity to severe criticism. As a reaction, eighteenth-century commentators defended David (and their religion) by watering down or explaining away his cruelty. See John Sawyer, "David's Treatment of the Ammonites (2 Samuel 12:31). A Study in the History of Interpretation," *Proceedings of the Glasgow University Oriental Society* 26 (1978): 96–105.

9 J. A. Thompson, *Deuteronomy* (London, 1974), 218. David Daube points out that limitless vengeance usually acted as a curb on blood feuds; see *Appeasement or Resistance, and Other Essays on New Testament Judaism* (Berkeley, 1987), 19.

10 My colleague at Cornell, Walter LaFeber, draws attention to the historian Charles Tilly's estimation that in the eighteenth century 50 people per

million in the population died in wars; in the nineteenth century it was
60 per million; and in the twentieth century it has been 460 persons per
million; see LaFeber, "The End of the Cold War: The Global Context,"
Bookpress (October 1992): 2.

11 As David Daube points out in a more recent contribution to the subject,
"The Contrariness of Speech and Polytheism," *Festschrift John Noonan*,
JLR 11 (1995): 1601–5, it is Philo, believer in one god, who first spoke of
the polytheism of the Greeks. The Greeks themselves, believers in many
gods, never used the term. The Old Testament contains no word for
"health" or "healthy." By contrast, from the earliest sources there is a
word for "sick" (*ḥalah*). Even the word *health* (from "to heal") in English
comes from the focus on the end of a period of sickness. Only recently has
the word *wellness* (from the seventeenth century) become common—
because, I suspect, in contemporary American culture certain classes recognize that they can anticipate long periods without significant illness.

12 As A. D. H. Mayes rightly states, "Except for the doubtful case of Isa
59:13, there is no example of *sarah* having the general sense of 'wrongdoing,' whereas it is used of apostasy in Dt. 13:6; Isa. 1:5; 31:6; Jer. 28:16;
29:32. Apostasy was a capital crime." See Mayes, *Deuteronomy*, NCBC
(Grand Rapids, 1981), 290.

13 S. R. Driver states, "Elsewhere the term (*sarah*) is used of defection from
God in a religious sense (on 13.6); but here it appears from the context to
be used more generally" (*Deuteronomy*, ICC [Edinburgh, 1902], 235). The
RSV translates *sarah* as "wrongdoing"; the AV has "that which is wrong";
the NEB has "false evidence"; and the JPS, "perverted witness."

14 CH 3 and 4 indicate that in Near Eastern antiquity talion could cover
false testimony about offenses other than capital ones. It is not possible to
say if this view also prevailed in biblical legal circles.

15 Why alleged offenses that involved only mutilation came under consideration is a question critics do not raise.

16 The Deuteronomic lawgiver has a keen interest in the instigator of an
offense, as indicated, for example, in his rules in Deuteronomy 13. Interpreters (e.g., Mayes, *Deuteronomy*, 289) get caught up in the apparent
contradiction between the single witness of Deuteronomy 19:16 and the
two or three witnesses of the preceding verse (15) who are required in any
legal procedure. These interpreters postulate different historical layers—
needless to say, badly pasted together—in the Deuteronomic presentation
of the overall law. It is Jezebel's fundamental role as the one who instigates the others to witness against Naboth that accounts for the reference

to a "witness of violence" in verse 16. In the comparable story of Susannah (21) two witnesses collude in their false witness without any instigator like Jezebel being involved.

17 See R. H. Charles, *The Apocrypha and Pseudepigrapha of the Old Testament* (Oxford, 1913), 651.

18 This ideal notion comes to expression in the trial of Susannah (45) in the role of the divinely inspired Daniel.

19 On the position in Rome in preclassical, classical, and postclassical periods, see J. M. Kelly, *Roman Litigation* (Oxford, 1966).

20 See A. Graeme Auld, *I and II Kings* (Philadelphia, 1986), 142–43, on Israel's claim to the town of Ramoth-Gilead, which lay in Israel's natural border territory.

21 Compare how Judith, in dealing with the Assyrian general Holofernes, has God respond to her request: "Turn my word and deceit to wound and bruise" (Jth 11:19).

22 A number of commentators refer to Micaiah's mocking tone; e. g., J. A. Montgomery, *The Book of Kings*, ICC (New York, 1951), 338.

23 They function much like the Greek philosopher Theophrastus's characters—for example, Wilful Disreputableness; see *Characters of Theophrastus*, LCL, ed. J. M. Edmonds (Cambridge, Mass., 1946), 52–57.

24 The term used, *letummo*, "innocently, in his simplicity," may well draw attention to the contrasting character of the deviants who moved against Naboth. The innocence of the archer's action accomplishes by heaven's direction what the witnesses accomplished against Naboth by their inwardly crooked disposition. An arrow is sometimes a figure for the actions and deceptions of the wicked against the innocent (e. g., Ps 11:2, 64:4, 91:5; Prov 26:18, 19; Jer 9:8). Note in particular Proverbs 25:18: "A man who bears false witness against his neighbor is like . . . a sharp arrow."

25 See the comments of P. D. Miscall about the complex way in which prophecies come to fulfillment in "Elijah, Ahab and Jehu: A Prophecy Fulfilled," *Prooftexts* 9 (1989): 75, 81.

26 S. J. DeVries, *1 Kings*, WBC 12 (Waco, 1985), 269.

27 One of the most interesting examples of law influencing religion is the fourth-century Pelagian heresy. The use of *gratia* in the negative sense of "favor, favoritism" often secured salvation in legal cases. The recognition of such corruption in earthly justice influenced the religious view of Pelagius, that grace (*gratia*) was not necessary for salvation because God judged people strictly according to their merits. See J. N. L. Myres, "Pelagius and the End of Roman Rule in Britain," *JRS* 50 (1960): 21–36.

28 See the comments of David Daube in "Fraud on Law for Fraud on Law," *Oxford Journal of Legal Studies* 1 (1981): 52, 53.

29 The divergence between the two episodes is only partly accounted for by the likely fact that this aspect of Ahab's death was part of the historical record available to the narrator. See the comments of Miscall, "Elijah, Ahab, and Jehu," 74, 75; and my comments below.

30 See C. M. Carmichael, *Women, Law, and the Genesis Traditions* (Edinburgh, 1979), 63, 64.

31 That the harlots represent a category recalls how the two unnamed thugs represent a category, namely, lawlessness.

32 Compare how the sight of Amasa's body on the ground prompted the law about the blemish to the land caused by a slain man (Deut 21:1–9), and how the ceremony of expiation in a very precise way serves to recall the offense; see C. M. Carmichael, *Law and Narrative in the Bible* (Ithaca, 1985), 136–39; also chapter 7.

33 On the ferocious nature of biblical dogs, see David Daube, "Gideon's Few," *JJS* 7 (1956): 155–61.

34 Recall too how God has many prophets bear witness to Ahab about success on the battlefield.

35 Montgomery, *I Kings,* ICC, 403.

36 P. D. Miscall, who is alert to the subtleties of the narrative, misses this link and instead asks, "Is this [Jehu's eating and drinking] what Jezebel and the elders did after Naboth's death?" ("Elijah, Ahab and Jehu," 80).

37 In one Greek version (the LXX) of the story of Susannah (62a) there is a description of the actual death of the offending false witnesses *and* the aftermath: "So when they had gagged them, they led them out and hurled them into a chasm; then the angel of the Lord cast fire in the midst of them." This looks like intensified death, the casting down on a rock being the Pharisaic reformed mode of stoning a person for a capital offense (*mishnah Sanhedrin* 7:3), and the fire the appropriate penalty for the offenders' misplaced sexual passion. 2 Maccabees 5:10 furnishes an example in which what happens to a person after his death mirrors what he did to people after their deaths: "He [Jason] who had cast out many to lie unburied had no one to mourn for him; he had no funeral of any sort and no place in the tomb of his ancestors." On the concept of *niwwul,* "disgrace," as it applies to corpses, see David Daube, *The New Testament and Rabbinic Judaism* (London, 1956), 301–24.

38 A. S. Diamond's assessment is typical: "The talion is irrelevantly inserted in vv. 17–22" (*Primitive Law, Past and Present,* 150).

39 For the thesis that the Priestly writer proceeds in identical fashion to the Deuteronomist and has knowledge of the Deuteronomic laws, see chapter 2.

40 See Carmichael, *Law and Narrative,* 97–101.

41 This same issue is the subject of the Deuteronomic rule (Deut 19:14) just before the rule about false testimony.

42 On the many links between the two stories, see M. Aberbach and L. Smolar, "Aaron, Jeroboam, and the Golden Calves," *JBL* 86 (1967): 129–40.

43 The narratives about the blasphemer in Leviticus 24:10–23 and about Naboth's death in 1 Kings 21 have at least ten features in common: (1) the topic of blasphemy is central, (2) there is the offense of cursing God, (3) the offense of murder comes up, (4) there is an offense involving property (a man's animal and a man's vineyard), (5) there is a judicial inquiry, (6) stoning is the punishment, (7) the stoning takes place outside the camp (outside the city), (8) all the people are involved in punishing the offender, (9) the real offender is an alien (an Egyptian and a Sidonian), and (10) there is divine consultation (with Moses, with Elijah).

44 Martin Noth, in *Leviticus,* OTL (Philadelphia, 1977), 179, thinks that the case in question—a foreigner is living among the Israelites—is an attempt to deal with comparable cases during and after the exile. He too, then, reads this account in Leviticus 24 as largely an invention to support a later stance.

45 Baruch A. Levine so argues in *Leviticus,* JPSC (Philadelphia, 1989), 166.

46 See Carmichael, *Origins of Biblical Law,* 175, 176.

47 Both Martin Noth and David Daube attempt to explain the puzzle away: the former by declaring that "life for life" can only refer back to the homicide (*Leviticus,* 180); the latter by having "life for life" apply to both the homicide and the bovicide (*Studies in Biblical Law* [Cambridge, Eng., 1947], 111, 112). A further indication that the Priestly lawgiver divorces himself from the Deuteronomic position is the curious repetition of the two rules about homicide and bovicide in Leviticus 24:21: "He who kills a beast shall make it good; and he who kills a man shall be put to death." The life for a life has been omitted—perhaps some indication of a reaction against its original use in the Deuteronomic law.

48 Compare Leviticus 21:19, where the term *sheber,* "fracture," is used for physical blemishes that render a priest unfit to serve.

49 For details, see Carmichael, *Origins of Biblical Law,* 114–16.

50 Mary Douglas, *Purity and Danger* (London, 1966), 51, 52.

51 See, for example, *tosephta Niddah* 6:4; and *yerushalmi Yebamoth* 1:2d.

52 Lyle Eslinger, "The Case of the Immodest Lady Wrestler," *VT* 31 (1981): 269–81.

53 See H. L. Strack and Paul Billerbeck, *Kommentar zum Neuen Testament aus Talmud und Midrasch* (Munich, 1922), 1:340, 341.

54 "The Sadducees are rather savage even among themselves" (Josephus, *Jewish War* 2.8.14.166).

55 David Daube thinks that his view is simply out of touch with the main position, and that it may have been influenced by Roman law. The *Twelve Tables* contain a regulation somewhat comparable to the one he put forward. However, as Daube points out, the Roman regulation was out of date by Josephus's time (*New Testament*, 256).

56 Daube's latest discussion is in *Appeasement or Resistance, and Other Essays in New Testament Judaism* (Berkeley, 1987), 19–23.

57 In Russian, the term *insult* still has a physical sense, as in "an insult to the brain" (that is, a stroke). In Constantine FitzGibbon's *Life of Dylan Thomas* (Boston, 1965), 345–46, the author tells how the autopsy on Dylan Thomas recorded that the cause of his death was "insult to the brain," a phrase "equally meaningless in British and American parlance." The author's implication is that the doctor in attendance had made a tasteless attempt to relate the poet's death to his alcoholic life. What the author did not know was that the doctor in question was, according to the late Ephim Fogel of Cornell's Department of English, a recent Russian immigrant to New York.

58 The two phrases, "an eye for an eye" and "a tooth for a tooth," constitute the only language that is common to Matthew, Exodus, Leviticus, and Deuteronomy.

59 See Daube, *New Testament*, 259–65.

60 On the rule's origin, see my *Law and Narrative in the Bible*, 297–99.

Chapter 7. Life/Death

1 R. A. Carlson argues that the distinction between the blessing and the curse that is laid out in some detail in Deuteronomy 28 underlies the presentation of the history of David; see *David the Chosen King* (Stockholm, 1964).

2 David Daube, "The Scales of Justice," *JR* 63 (1951): 109.

3 Maimonides, *The Guide for the Perplexed* (New York, 1910), pt. 3, ch. 48. See also Hans Kosmala, "The So-Called Ritual Decalogue," *ASTI* 1 (1962):

50–56; J. C. Rylaarsdam, *Exodus*, IB 1 (Nashville, 1952), 1013–14; Umberto Cassuto, *Exodus* (Jerusalem, 1967), 305.

4 Ch. Virolleaud's "La naissance des dieux gracieux et beaux," *Syria* 14 (1933): 132–33, 140, is the first text published with a translation. Compare G. R. Driver, *Canaanite Myths and Legends* (Edinburgh, 1956), 121.

5 T. H. Gaster, *Myth, Legend, and Custom in the Old Testament* (New York, 1969), 389 n. 2a.

6 Gaster, *Myth, Legend, and Custom,* 253.

7 Philo's view may owe something to Heraclitus's theory about opposites. See H. A. Wolfson, *Philo, Foundations of Religious Philosophy in Judaism, Christianity, and Islam* (Cambridge, Mass., 1947), 1:332–47. Jacob Milgrom adopts my solution to the kid law and accepts my claim that Philo is the one interpreter who grasps the lawgiver's concern. See Milgrom, *Leviticus*, AB 3 (New York, 1991), 740–41. I originally published my views in "On Separating Life and Death: An Explanation of Some Biblical Laws," *HTR* 69 (1976): 1–7.

8 The historian of medicine Walter Pagel, in "The Vindication of 'Rubbish,'" *Middlesex Hospital Journal* 15 (1945): 42–45, shows how crucial this view about the blood was to Harvey's working out its pattern of flow from the right heart through the pulmonary artery and the lungs into the left heart. According to Servetus in his religious tract "Restitution of Christianity" (1553), the blood is the seat of the soul.

9 S. R. Driver, *Deuteronomy*, ICC, 3d ed. (Edinburgh, 1902), 165.

10 G. E. Wright, *Deuteronomy*, IB 2 (Nashville, 1953), 42.

11 S. R. Driver, *Deuteronomy*, 156.

12 See N. H. Snaith, *Leviticus and Numbers*, NCBC (London, 1967), 86.

13 For the details, see C. M. Carmichael, *Law and Narrative in the Bible* (Ithaca, 1985), 135–55, 159.

14 "Eine Verschärfung der Todesstrafe"—so C. F. Keil and F. Delitzsch, *Commentar über das Alte Testament* 2d ed. (Leipzig: 1870), 2:507. See chapter 6.

15 The NEB reads *'br* (mated) for *'bd* (worked). See L. H. Brockington, *The Hebrew Text of the Old Testament* (Oxford, 1973), 26; cp. BDB, 718, 1125. If *'br* (mated) is read, the observation is equally valid. Both the land and the virgin heifer represent potential fertility—both are unplowed.

16 Because they cannot imagine ground that is eminently cultivable but never used, some scholars take the opposite view and understand the ground to be wasteland: rough, sterile wilderness. See R. Patai, "The Egla

Arufa or the Expiation of the Polluted Land," *JQR* 30 (1939): 66–67;
Alexander Rofé, "The Breaking of the Heifer's Neck" (in Hebrew), *Tarbiz*
31 (1961): 140–41; Gerhard von Rad, *Deuteronomy*, OTL (Philadelphia,
1966), 136. H. McKeating puzzles over this cultivable land beside the
stream in "The Development of the Law on Homicide in Ancient Israel,"
VT 25 (1975): 63. He thinks there is some contradiction and posits a clash
of conflicting ideas from different periods. But he too fails to read the rule
in the wider context of its overall presentation. This and all the other laws
are for the time when Israel enters the new land. There will then be land
that the Israelites have yet to cultivate. It is irrelevant that the previous
Canaanite inhabitants will have used it in their time, a point also misunderstood by Z. Zevit, who changes "neither plowed nor sown" to "may
not be tilled or sown" ("The Egla Ritual of Deuteronomy 21:1–9," *JBL*
[1976]: 387 n. 54). The land's special sanctity comes from the notion that it
is God's gift to Israel.

17 Keil and Delitzsch, *Commentar*, 507.

18 S. R. Driver, *Deuteronomy*, 241–42; Anthony Phillips, *Deuteronomy*,
CBC (Cambridge, Eng., 1973), 138; Patai, "The Egla Arufa," 63. Compare
Carl Steuernagel, *Das Deuteronomium* (Göttingen, 1923), 128.

19 They furnish an example of what Alan Watson warns about in *The Spirit
of Roman Law* (Athens, Ga., 1995), 34: "Modern readers . . . view it
[Roman law] through the prism of their own exposure to other systems.
Often what seems strange to us is so only because we have come to know
something else, somewhere else."

20 See A. S. Diamond, *Primitive Law, Past and Present* (London, 1971), 96.

21 For a similar view, see Patai, "The Egla Arufa," 66–67.

22 S. R. Driver, *Deuteronomy*, 242; Patai, "The Egla Arufa," 66; Rofé, "Heifer's Neck," 141. Von Rad stresses that there is no shedding of blood
(*Deuteronomy*, 136); so too does McKeating, in "Homicide," 63. Z. Zevit
thinks that an earlier, pre-Deuteronomic stage of the ritual involved
slaughter and sacrifice—that is, bloodshed; see "Egla Ritual," 383–84. In
many cultures, the mode of executing murderers avoids bloodshed; see
Diamond, *Primitive Law*, 397.

23 R. Patai ("The Egla Arufa," 66, 67) is forced to read these words as referring to the heifer's blood. The argument becomes tortuous to the point
where he claims that the unknown murderer is also responsible for the
heifer's death.

24 Such a combination has its parallel in other cultures. Compare how
among the Greek Sarakatsani the departure of the bride from her parental

home occasions laments on the part of her family; see J. K. Campbell, *Honour, Family and Patronage* (Oxford, 1964), 59–61, 132.

25 S. R. Driver, *Deuteronomy*, 245. Although he refers to her actions as "a symbolical expression of the fact that her forsaken condition is at an end," he thinks they are based on mourning customs. Von Rad (*Deuteronomy*, 137) understands them as mourning customs, and not a symbolic removal of foreign impurity. Anthony Phillips (*Deuteronomy*, 140) is less sure that her actions are mourning; they may instead indicate renunciation of her country of origin. He is rightly disturbed by the problem that if they *are* mourning rites, there is a conflict with the rule in Deuteronomy 14:1 that prohibits such actions to the body. There is, as I shall shortly point out, a most interesting reason for this conflict.

26 See E. F. de Ward, "Mourning Customs in 1, 2 Samuel," *JJS* 23 (1972): 8–10.

27 See E. W. Lane, *An Arabic-English Lexicon* (London, 1863–93), 2409. Hindus shave themselves and cut their nails after a death; see H. Oldenberg, *Religion des Veda* (Berlin, 1894), 427.

28 The term *'innah* often has the technical meaning of taking a woman without the correct formalities; see David Daube, *The Exodus Pattern in the Bible* (London, 1963), 65, 66.

29 Compare the punishment in England, where a person has his effigy burnt and the funeral service read over him; see E. P. Thompson, *Customs in Common, Studies in Traditional Popular Culture* (New York, 1993), 480. Humor also furnishes an illustration. A folktale found apparently only in Yorkshire that expresses the tight and frugal mode of living in that region of England has it that the wife of a dying man asked him if there was anything he would like before he died. He replied, "I would love a piece of that boiled ham there, lass." She in turn replied, "Oh, but you can't have that, that's for the mourners!" On King David's odd conduct in regard to his child by Bathsheba, see chapter 8.

30 S. R. Driver, *Deuteronomy*, 156.

31 Von Rad notes the discrepancy but is at a loss to explain it (*Deuteronomy*, 137). The physical marks differ somewhat from those in the mourning law of Deuteronomy 14:21. She is not a Canaanite woman—the law of Deuteronomy 20:16–18 enjoins the slaughter of all Canaanites—and since the mourning customs in Deuteronomy 14:21 were both Israelite and Canaanite ones, her ethnic background may account for the different mourning actions in her case.

32 For the Rabbis' view, see note 13, chapter 8.

33 This concern is the primary motivation for the sequence of the four apparently unrelated rules in Deuteronomy 22:1–8, the rules that follow the five under consideration. See C. M. Carmichael, "A Time for War and a Time for Peace," in *Studies in Jewish Legal History*, ed. B. S. Jackson (London, 1974), 50–56.

34 Greek law required that an estate had "to be passed on, not thrown back." See J. W. Jones, *The Law and Legal Theory of the Greeks* (Oxford, 1956), 193. The rule of intestate succession denied the claims of any ascendant of the deceased. A father (from his son), a mother, or a grandfather could not claim as heir. CH 168 indicates how a father's right to disinherit a son in Babylonia was limited. In CH 169 a father may disinherit a son who has committed two grave wrongs.

35 Unless one is like the philosopher Thales, who said that there is no difference between life and death. "Why, then," he was asked, "don't you die?" "Because," said Thales, "it makes no difference" (Diogenes Laertius, *Lives of Eminent Philosophers*, Thales, LCL [London, 1925], 1.36).

36 Elisha asks to inherit a double portion of Elijah's spirit at a time when the latter is approaching his death (2 Kings 2:9–12). The analogy is with the relationship of a firstborn to his father, which justifies a double share of the father's possessions. In light of the above observation that a firstborn son's claim to represent his father's life force in a unique way should not need to come into reckoning at the father's death, what is remarkable is that Elijah in fact does not experience death.

37 Like Jacob with Leah, he has not divorced the hated wife; see Carmichael, *Law and Narrative*, 142–45.

38 Jesus' family tries to control him because of his conduct (Mark 3:21), and his opponents charge that he is a glutton and a winebibber who associates with unworthy types (Matt 11:19; Luke 7:34). David Daube argues that in line with Jewish law of the time Jesus is "characterized as the stubborn and rebellious son of the code whose crime consists in a general, calculated, incorrigible defiance of those in authority, the feasting and drinking being only its most visible mark" (*Appeasement or Resistance, and Other Essays in New Testament Judaism* [Berkeley, 1987], 25). One Rabbinic authority, Abbahu, declares that only if the son consorted exclusively with dissolute types could the legislator's severity apply. This is the point of the charge that Jesus is not only a glutton and a winebibber, but that he consorts with publicans and sinners as well.

39 See David Daube, *Collected Works: Talmudic Law*, ed. C. M. Carmichael (Berkeley, 1992), 1:1–13. For a philosophical critique of actions that are

basically wrong but are nonetheless required by the law, see Hans Kelsen, *General Theory of Law and State* (Cambridge, Mass., 1945), 21.

40 Scholars claim that a final process of redaction explains the lack of coherence of subject matter in the order of the rules, and hence it is not possible to see the hand of a single lawgiver at work. Alexander Rofé posits no less than five different stages of redaction; see *Introduction to Deuteronomy* (in Hebrew) (Jerusalem, 1975), 1:159–77.

41 Keith Hopkins, "Brother-Sister Marriage in Roman Egypt," *Comparative Studies in Society and History* 22 (1980): 350–51.

42 He was echoing David Daube's comment, "Death, like justice, must not only be done but be seen to be done," in "Transplantation: Acceptability of Procedures and the Required Legal Sanctions," in *Ciba Symposium on Ethics in Medical Progress*, ed. G. E. W. Wolstenholme and M. O'Connor (London, 1966), 188–201.

43 Humor often focuses on precisely this contrast. One form of humor involves the deliberate attempt to turn matters upside down in order to exorcise fear about the precariousness of human existence. Such humor comes into its own in life-threatening situations. For example, a man goes to his doctor with pains in his chest and is told, "It is all in your mind." He comes back the next day with similar pains, and the doctor again tells him that it is all in his mind. The visits recur over a range of time, and the doctor gives the man the same response each time. The visits stop, some weeks go by, and the doctor meets the man's wife in the street. "How is your husband?" he asks. To which she replies, "He thinks he's dead." He is dead, but it is the blurring of the distinction between life and death that makes the joke work. Very similar is the legendary story about Stalin's last illness. Among his many purges was one of a group of doctors in Moscow, some of whom escaped death. When Stalin had his final stroke, he was rushed to a hospital in Moscow. The doctors in attendance sent a telegram to the doctors who had escaped the purge: "Prime Minister at death's door. Come at once and pull him through!" There is again the same ambiguity as to whether they were meant to save him or kill him. The distinction between life and death is deliberately blurred.

Humor all over the world expresses such ambiguity about life and death because the ambiguity does indeed have a basis in the real world. I recall seeing a graffiti in Melbourne, Australia: "Life is a terminal disease—sexually transmitted." I also recall chalked on a wall in strife-ridden Belfast the words: "Is there a life before death?" What gives the special point to such a statement is not just the horrors of the civilian strife and killings but the religious nature of the conflict. In this sectarian war, both sides—the Catholics and the Protestants—affirm as a nonnegotiable belief that there is a life after death. By ironically posing the question "Is there a life before death?" and implicitly subjecting it to the kind of doubt associated with the religious claim that there is a life after death, the witticism is a telling commentary on the discomfort of living in that city. The merging of the two opposites, life and death, bewilders and frightens because it too readily recalls the reality of the situation. The funeral service from the Book of Common Prayer includes the words "In the midst of life we are in death."

Chapter 8. Law in the Narratives: Retribution

1 See C. M. Carmichael, *Women, Law, and the Genesis Traditions* (Edinburgh, 1979), 57–65.

2 Cain protests that his punishment is really a double one. His expulsion from the ground he tills results in his becoming a wanderer on the earth, and thus he is in danger of being murdered himself. God agrees with Cain's assessment and puts a protective mark on him to prevent his murder.

3 David Daube, "The Linguistics of Suicide," *Philosophy and Public Affairs* 1 (1972): 387–437.

4 P. R. Ackroyd, noting that no word of condemnation appears, thinks the story implies Saul's action to be heroic and courageous; see *First Book of Samuel* (Cambridge, Eng., 1971), 227–28. While this view may have prevailed during Saul's time, it is not, I shall argue, the view of the biblical author.

5 R. H. Pfeiffer reconciles the two accounts by claiming that the author had a right to assume that the reader would recognize the falsehood of the Amalekite's version of Saul's death; see *Introduction to the Old Testament* (New York, 1941), 350–51. D. K. Edelman tries to support the view that the Amalekite is lying by appealing to the use of language in the text; see *King Saul and the Historiography of Judah, JSOT* suppl. 121 (Sheffield, 1991), 299–303. Edelman takes over Peter Ackroyd's suggestion that David's question to the Amalekite about Saul's death, "How do you know?" (2 Sam 1:5), is designed to make the man convict himself of an offense. Even weaker is the suggestion, taken over from Adele Berlin, that the use of two *hinneh* (behold) clauses in the Amalekite's

description of the battle is reminiscent of dream reports—therefore the man's story is a concoction, like a dream.

6 This is an instance where the formulation of a law and the shaping of a narrative go hand in hand.

7 There is possibly also a link between the detail that when the Amalekite servant first approaches Saul on the battlefield he comes from behind Saul (2 Sam 1:7), and the fact that Samuel orders the total slaughter of the Amalekites because their original fault against the Israelites, which invited so harsh a judgment, was that they attacked them from behind when they were weak from thirst. On this aspect of the Amalekites' conduct and why they were judged so harshly, see C. M. Carmichael, *Law and Narrative in the Bible* (Ithaca, 1985), 305.

8 MacBeth, oppressed by Banquo's ghost, declares, "The times have been, that, when the brains were out, the man would die. And there an end; but now they rise again" (act 3, scene 4, ll. 77–79). In parts of Greece, laments over the dead aroused fear because they were viewed as songs of magic that opened up perilous channels of communication between the living and the dead. See A. Caravali-Claves, "Bridge between Worlds: The Greek Women's Laments as Communicative Event," *JAF* 93 (1980): 130.

9 Recall how the slaughter of the heifer at the special place in the land is a dramatic, fundamentally wrong but necessary enactment of the murder in the countryside.

10 Contrast the view of Edelman in *King Saul*, 286: "I am not convinced that modern readers will ever be able to know for certain how the writer intended his ancient audience to view Saul's act of suicide."

11 On the tentativeness of the results obtained by literary criticism in assigning priority to one or another of the accounts, see G. W. Anderson, *A Critical Introduction to the Old Testament* (London, 1959), 73.

12 This section is an extended version of a lecture given at the Institute of Advanced Legal Studies, London, on December 7, 1992, sponsored by the Oxford Centre for Postgraduate Hebrew Studies and the Institute of Advanced Legal Studies.

13 I am skeptical that this rule has to do with some notion that sexual activity interferes with military prowess in the sense that it saps male energy. More likely is the aim to hold out to the warriors the prospect of acquiring women as part of the spoils of war: "to every man a damsel or two" (Sisera's mother referring to the division of the booty; Judg 5:30; cp. Jdt 4:12). The Rabbis were alert to the way in which sexual appetite goads the warrior when they claimed that the rule about the captive

woman in Deuteronomy 21:10–14, who, they argued, might well be married, was a concession to human weakness, the deliberate giving in to a wrong. To forbid such appropriations, they thought, would lead to uncontrolled licentiousness on the part of the warriors (*Siphre* on Deut 21:10–14; *babylonian Kiddushin* 21b-22a). See David Daube, *Collected Works: Talmudic Law*, ed. C. M. Carmichael (Berkeley, 1992), 1:7.

14 See Exodus 4:25; Deuteronomy 28:57 (a woman's); 2 Kings 18:27 = Isaiah 36:12, 7:20; Jeremiah 2:25; and Ezekiel 16:25 (a woman's). German advice to the bridegroom is "Man muss nicht die Füsse in fremde Schuhe stecken [Do not stick your feet in others' shoes]."

15 For an excellent analysis of the literary aspects and sound arguments for the view that the material is first and foremost storytelling, not historical reporting, see D. M. Gunn, *The Story of King David: Genre and Interpretation* (Sheffield, 1978).

16 See R. A. Carlson, *David, the Chosen King* (Stockholm, 1964).

17 See David Daube, "Biblical Landmarks in the Struggle for Women's Rights," *JR* 90 (1978): 177–97.

18 For the position in Babylonia, see W. F. Leemans, "King Hammurapi as Judge," in *Symbolae Iuridicae et Historicae Martino David dedicatae*, ed. J. A. Ankum, R. Feenstra, and W. F. Leemans (Leiden, 1968), 2:107–29.

19 A. A. Anderson rightly upholds a meaning that brings the culprit under a sentence of death in *2 Samuel*, WBC 11 (Dallas, 1989), 162. He cites Jonathan's reply to Saul after the latter speaks of David as *ben maweth:* "Why should he be put to death?" (1 Sam 20:31, 32; cp. 1 Sam 26:16).

20 Interestingly, that law was originally focused on a shepherd's economic status. See C. M. Carmichael, *The Origins of Biblical Law* (Ithaca, 1992), 187–89.

21 I make no judgment as to whether or not Nathan actually did confront David with the case about the poor man's lamb. I incline to think that its historicity is in doubt and that the development was built into the overall story to account for David's avoidance of earthly penalties at the time. The narrator introduces the notion that David repents of his misdeeds in order to come to terms with such lack of earthly punishment. While we can readily surmise that David's adultery was known in courtly circles—for example, among the servants who brought Bathsheba to him—it is not very believable that Nathan could go to him and present such a simple case of theft. Note Gunn's comments about parables and their narrative settings in *The Story of King David*, 41, 42.

22 Uriel Simon, however, thinks the statement about how the lamb eats of its owner's morsel, drinks from his cup, and lies in his bosom recalls Uriah's words about eating, drinking, and lying with his wife; see Simon, "The Poor Man's Ewe-Lamb: An Example of a Juridical Parable," *Bib* 48 (1967): 229.

23 Uriel Simon is an exception; see "The Poor Man's Ewe-Lamb," 226.

24 Note too the link between a journey and sexual desire when David directs Uriah to go to his home "and wash his feet"—that is, his sexual feet—once his other feet have arrived at their destination.

25 Ecclesiastes 6:9 speaks of the "wandering [*halakh*] of desire." Compare Job 9:26, Proverbs 13:12, and Jeremiah 3:19. In the Adam and Eve story the serpent signifies the human trait of curiosity or intellect.

26 Contrary to Anderson, 2 *Samuel*, 163.

27 "Punishment of a ruler by taking away or damaging his free subjects" (David Daube, *Studies in Biblical Law* [Cambridge, Eng., 1947], 163).

28 *Washington Post* article, "Teenage Sex," March 24, 1991.

29 See my discussion in chapter 7.

30 On the legal character of "to humble," see David Daube, *The Exodus Pattern in the Bible* (London, 1963), 65, 66. That force is also involved in the humiliation of Tamar emerges in 2 Samuel 13:14.

31 There is consequently no need to resort to textual surgery that transposes texts so that David's mourning refers to the dead Amnon. For such an attempt, see P. Kyle McCarter, *II Samuel*, AB 9 (Garden City, 1984), 332.

32 When she appears before David she pretends to be mourning a son. We might recall David's strange mourning habits.

33 See S. Freud, *Psychopathology of Everyday Life* (London, 1966), 122–26.

34 On how legal reasoning always has the potential to dehumanize persons through the use of conceptual "legal masks," see John Noonan, *Persons and Masks of the Law—Cardozo, Holmes, Jefferson, and Wythe as Makers of the Masks* (New York, 1976).

35 See Carmichael, *Law and Narrative*, 150–55.

Chapter 9. Law in the Narratives: Dispute Resolution

1 David Daube, *He That Cometh* (London, 1966), 1. Historic because, in rearguing a view put forward some forty years earlier by Robert Eisler, he established decisively the link between the *aphikoman* of the Passover Seder and the origin of the Eucharist. For a recent critique, see D. B. Carmichael, "David Daube on the Eucharist and the Passover Service," *JSNT* 42 (1991): 45–67.

2 John Van Seters, in *The Life of Moses. The Yahwist as Historian in Exodus-Numbers* (Louisville, 1994), 16, 17, draws attention to the striking resemblance between the accounts about Joseph's death (Gen 50:26; Exod 1:6–8) and Joshua's death (Judg 2:8–10). I would suggest that a similar mode of recording the history of Moses' successor applies. Van Seters is not alert to any of the links between Joseph and Moses.

3 The phenomenon of an outsider standing out in this way is commonplace at all times and places; for example, Napoleon and Hitler. See David Daube's assessment of the phenomenon in *Sons and Strangers* (Boston, 1984), 1.

4 For a masterly presentation of the role of imitation in the ancient world at all levels of literary activity, see Thomas L. Brodie, *The Quest for the Origin of John's Gospel* (Oxford, 1993), 38–47.

5 J. J. Sheehan, *German History 1770–1866* (Oxford, 1989), 386–87.

6 D. B. Redford, *A Study of the Biblical Story of Joseph* (Leiden, 1970), 249–50.

7 M. Niehoff, "The Figure of Joseph in the Targums," *JJS* 39 (1988): 234–50. She has not noted the important article by M. Gan, who lays out the extent of the influence of the Joseph story on the Book of Esther in "Megillath 'ester be'aspaqlariyath qoroth yoseph bemiṣrayim" (The Book of Esther in the light of the story of Joseph in Egypt) *Tarbiz* 31 (1961): 144–49, English summary I, II.

8 J. L. Kugel, *In Potiphar's House* (San Francisco, 1990), 13, 14, 22.

9 On just how extensive is the criticism of Joseph's ways, see my discussion of the rules in Exodus 23:6–9 in *The Origins of Biblical Law* (Ithaca, 1992), 193–203. These rules are formulated precisely in response to Joseph's questionable conduct with his brothers.

10 On the theme of life and death in the Joseph narrative, see W. Brueggermann, "Life and Death in Tenth Century Israel," *JAAR* 40 (1972): 96–109.

11 Remarkably, it happens again (Gen 44:1). The reason why this repetition does not stretch one's credulity is because the second time it happens they have been drinking (Gen 43:34).

12 Contrast God's putting a lying spirit into one of his prophets in order to bring about the death of Ahab. See chapter 6.

13 On the later Rabbinic and early Christian focus on the issue of conduct that is outwardly meritorious but internally flawed, see D. Daube, "Neglected Nuances of Exposition in Luke–Acts," *Principat* 25 (1985): 2329–45.

14 On the tightly knit nature of the Joseph story, see C. M. Carmichael, *Law and Narrative in the Bible* (Ithaca, 1985), 282–88; and G. Rendsberg,

"Redactional Structuring in the Joseph Story: Genesis 37–50," *Bucknell Review* 33 (1990): 215–32.

15 While the tendency in later Rabbinic sources is to exonerate Judah, some (*Genesis Rabba* 85, *Exodus Rabba* 42) view his action negatively, as the biblical narrator and the *Testament of Judah* (possibly second century B.C.E.) certainly did.

16 See note 41, chapter 2.

17 If this parallel is accurate, it throws light on the well-recognized problem as to why it is the Midianite Jethro who initiates Israel's judicial administration. See B. S. Childs, *The Book of Exodus*, OTL (Philadelphia, 1974), 331.

18 T. E. Fretheim, "The Plagues as Ecological Signs of Historical Disaster," *JBL* 110 (1991): 385–96.

19 The pattern of narration that Fretheim draws attention to is comparable to what S. Bertman uncovers in his analysis of the story of Ruth: "Elements of content, either analogous or contrasting, stand over against each other in the structure of the story and appear thereby to counterbalance one another" ("Symmetrical Design in the Book of Ruth," *JBL* 84 [1965]: 165).

20 For the importance in the history of medicine of the curative process exhibited in this story, see David Daube, "Example and Precept: From Sirach to R. Ishmael," in *Collected Works: Talmudic Law*, ed. C. M. Carmichael (Berkeley, 1992), 1:205–11.

21 Carmichael, *Law and Narrative*, 299–305.

22 See note 8, Introduction.

23 Meir Malul, *The Comparative Method in Ancient Near Eastern and Biblical Legal Studies*, AOAT 227 (Neukirchen-Vluyn, 1990): 129.

24 See Meir Malul, *Comparative Method*, 105–7 n. 13.

25 Dwight Young, "On the Application of Numbers from Babylonian Mathematics to Biblical Life Spans and Epochs," *ZAW* 100 (1988): 331–61; Young, "A Mathematical Approach to Certain Dynastic Spans in the Sumerian King List," *JNES* 47 (1988): 123–29; Young, "The Influence of Babylonian Algebra on Longevity among the Antediluvians," *ZAW* 102 (1990): 321–35.

26 See David Daube, *The New Testament and Rabbinic Judaism* (London, 1956), 86–89; Daube, "Rabbinic Methods of Interpretation and Hellenistic Rhetoric"; and Daube, "Alexandrian Methods of Interpretation and the Rabbis," in *Talmudic Law*, 1:333–76.

27 Sometimes, in fact, the Rabbinic authorities proceed in a way that is quite close to the procedure I have outlined for biblical law. For example, in

giving the opinion that a husband should take another wife if the couple is childless after ten years of marriage, they find a suggestion (*zekher*) for this position in the account of Abraham's taking Hagar (Genesis 16; *tosephta Yebamoth* 8:4). See my forthcoming *The Spirit of Talmudic Law* (Athens, Ga., 1997), in this series, for a description of the salient features of Rabbinic law.

INDEX OF SOURCES

References are to the numbering in the English versions.

BIBLICAL SOURCES

OTHER JEWISH WRITINGS

OTHER SOURCES

SUBJECT INDEX

The Spirit of the Laws

Alan Watson, General Editor

R. H. Helmholz, *The Spirit of Classical Canon Law*
Geoffrey MacCormack, *The Spirit of Traditional Chinese Law*
Alan Watson, *The Spirit of Roman Law*